EMANCIPATION
IN
LATE MEDIEVAL
FLORENCE

EMANCIPATION IN LATE MEDIEVAL FLORENCE

THOMAS KUEHN

RUTGERS UNIVERSITY PRESS

NEW BRUNSWICK

NEW JERSEY

Library of Congress Cataloging in Publication Data

Kuehn, Thomas, 1950–
Emancipation in late medieval Florence.

Revision of thesis—University of Chicago.
Bibliography: p.   Includes index.
1. Parent and child (Law)—Italy—Florence.
2. Children—Legal status, laws, etc.—Italy—Florence.
I. Title.
LAW   346.455101'7   81–19876
ISBN 0–8135–0924–6   344.5510617   AACR2

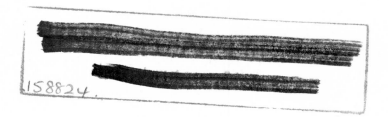

For Linda

Contents

Tables

Preface

This study contributes to both the legal and social history of late medieval and Renaissance Italy by focusing on a single institution, emancipation, and on a single city-state, Florence. Too often, social and legal historians labor in blissful ignorance of each other's work or with only a nodding acquaintance with what the other is up to. Equally, historians of the various Italian city-states have sometimes not looked beyond the boundaries of their particular area to investigate comparable events or ideas elsewhere. While I cannot claim to offer a comparative study of emancipation, I do hope that this work provides some idea of the fruitful dialogue that may exist between social and legal history and that it also helps to expand comparative research into late medieval Italian history.

For stylistic reasons, I have employed the Latin term *emancipatus* (or the plural *emancipati*; occasionally also the feminine forms *emancipata* and *emancipatae*) throughout the book as a substantive in place of the cumbersome English equivalent "emancipated person" or "the emancipated one." All translations unless otherwise designated are my own. Quoted passages from unpublished sources are given in the footnotes to allow the reader to check the translations.

Any scholarly book rests on a foundation of the accumulated wisdom of many others. This is especially so in a first book in which one's debts are numerous if not always obvious. My intellectual debts to many and more learned scholars in a variety of fields are acknowledged in the footnotes and bibliography.

Julius Kirshner of the University of Chicago first suggested emancipation to me as a dissertation topic. His generous aid and penetrating criticism have helped shape this book in both its earlier stage as a thesis and in its very different final form. What strengths this work may have are due in great part to his expertise, energy, and unflagging enthusiasm for the project.

Anthony Molho of Brown University first introduced me to the riches of the Florentine archives. His patient advice in helping me locate and decipher documents was supplemented by that of Gino Corti, to whom I—like many who work in the Florentine archives—am deeply grateful. Detailed and careful readings of the manuscript by Anthony Molho and David Herlihy have saved the reader from a number of mistakes and garbled passages and have immeasurably improved the final product. Professor Herlihy has also been generous with information that has been incorporated into the analysis.

When this work was still in its first form as a dissertation, I profited from the advice and criticism of Professors Eric Cochrane and Bernard Cohn. Before the research even began to take shape, Jeff Newton and Ronald Weissman were friends whose enthusiasm and ideas, poured forth over morning coffee and lunchtime wine, sustained me in no small way as we shared the daily struggle of dealing with intractable archival materials. And years before, Philip Niles of Carleton College first instilled in me an abiding curiosity and interest in medieval history.

For advice pertaining to the study of medieval civil law, I must thank Professor Domenico Maffei. Professor Paolo Grossi graciously allowed me to use the legal historical materials in his study at the University of Florence. I am also grateful to the archivists and librarians at the following institutions: Archivio di Stato and Biblioteca Nazionale, Florence; Harvard University Center for Renaissance Studies, Villa I Tatti; Regenstein Library and the Law Library, University of Chicago; Newberry Library, Chicago; The Institute of Medieval Canon Law, Berkeley; and the Reed College Library.

Financial support for research in 1975/76 came from the Division of Social Sciences and the Division of Humanities of the University of Chicago and from the Renaissance Society of America. A summer fellowship from the National Endowment for the Humanities allowed me to return to Florence in the summer of 1978 to check references and gather new material.

Finally, while I must thank my parents for their many gestures of support, my greatest debt of gratitude is to my wife, Linda Berri. This book simply would not have been completed, perhaps not even begun, without her. Readers should know that her careful reading of the penultimate version has spared them a number of verbal infelicities and opacities. By rights, this book can be dedicated to no one else.

EMANCIPATION
IN
LATE MEDIEVAL
FLORENCE

Introduction

Originally a Roman legal term, emancipation referred to freeing a son or daughter from paternal control (*patria potestas*). The term later entered the vernacular languages of Western Europe and in the course of its diffusion, underwent a semantic transformation, which was especially marked in the last two centuries. According to the *Oxford English Dictionary*, emancipation currently means to set free from control, and much the same meaning adheres to the word in French and Italian. The modern definition retains no trace of the word's original meaning in Latin and Roman law; only the formal meaning of emancipation (that is, liberation) remains. Thus stripped of its substantive meaning, emancipation is now used in a variety of contexts: We refer to the emancipation of American Negro slaves (and in the same context, to the Emancipation Proclamation of 1863), to the emancipation of serfs, to the emancipation of Jews, and to the emancipation of women.

Generally, only among historians, especially historians of law, does an awareness of the primal meaning of emancipation exist.[1] Within the law itself, emancipation has all but disappeared, and where it remains, it is a rarely used and little-known legal mechanism.[2] In the Middle Ages, on the other hand, in areas under the influence of Roman law, such as southern France and the communes of northern and central Italy, emancipation was a viable legal institution. While it seems that the linguistic transformation of the term emancipation began in the Middle Ages, the legal meaning of the term (freedom from paternal control) continued to be important[3] and began to give way only in the eighteenth century. According to the legal historian Manlio Bellomo, the disappearance of this meaning coincided with the structural transformation from the medieval to the modern family.[4] In the late seventeenth century, the first criticisms were advanced against the legal concept of paternal power that dictated that only the father was to possess full legal rights and that, therefore, all others, including grown children, were subject to legal control and tutelage. Emancipa-

1

tion as liberating children from such an extensive and perpetual paternal power and bestowing legal rights upon them was clearly tied to this ideology then coming under attack.

The most noted eighteenth-century critic of the traditional, familial legal ideology was Cesare Beccaria (1738–1794). Writing in 1764, Beccaria argued for a society made up of the union of individuals and not of the union of families. The latter type of society, based on a monarchical order where all family members were subject to the family head, was antithetical to Beccaria's vision of liberty and of the "republican spirit" that should pervade both public and domestic places. The family, claimed Beccaria, demanded continual sacrifice for its common good, which was, in his eyes, "an empty idol" and often not "the good of anyone who [was] part of it" (that is, the family). The free state, on the other hand, encouraged pursuit of one's own happiness within defined limits. [5]

Among his other arguments against the eighteenth-century family, Beccaria touched upon the "irrationality" of the position of children. As he put it, "in the republic [composed] of families, children remain under the power of the family's head for as long as he lives and are forced solely by law to endure a dependent existence until his death."[6] Children were thus unable to participate actively either in society or in the family, and they were deprived of experiences that would serve them and their society in later life. Likewise, the Torinese Francesco Dalmazzo Vasco (1732–1794) asserted that the paternal power contained in the law was not natural but merely a legal construct.[7] From this position, criticism could be launched against the excesses of paternal power. The arguments of Alfonso Longo (1738–1804) against the "irrational" extension of paternal power by means of testamentary entail were based on such a distinction between natural and legal.[8]

The arguments of the critics eventually carried the field. Legal reforms enacted in Tuscany and Lombardy in the late eighteenth century placed a temporal limit on paternal power by establishing an emancipatory age of majority at 21; the Italian national legal code later did the same. Emancipation, as a result, survived only in a very attenuated form since one could emancipate a child between the ages of eighteen and twenty-one only.[9] The revision of Italian family law in 1975 reduced the age of majority to eighteen and, thereby, put an end to emancipation.[10]

The *patria potestas* that Beccaria denounced was one of the central legal and cultural symbols of the medieval Italian family and emancipation, the means by which the *patria potestas* could be terminated before the death of the father, was an important concept. This study analyzes the structure and workings of the institution of emancipation in late medieval Florence to determine its meaning and role in the life of the family. Florence is an excellent area for this research because the wealth of surviving documentation makes such a study feasible and because the history of Florence and of Florentine families has attracted so much scholarly attention.

Very little historical research has been devoted to emancipation by either historians of law or historians of society; of the two, legal historians have provided the most of what little there is.[ ] Historians of classical and postclassical Roman law have fashioned an outline of the early normative structure of emancipation.[11] Historians of later civil law have been content merely to outline the necessary modifications as they trace the effects of Lombard law, canon law, Aristotelian philosophy, and Renaissance humanism on the development and elaboration of civil-law institutions.[12] A few detailed and specialized studies have been devoted to very limited, and even incidental, features of emancipation law.[13] Only recently has a single scholar, Bellomo, investigated emancipation law in any depth.[14] While his work offers provocative insights into the nature of emancipation and the family in the Middle Ages, Bellomo has utilized only a limited range of legal doctrinal sources. The canvas he has painted with such broad and bold strokes is subject, therefore, to emendation through expansion. Several students of Italian society have also offered initial and tentative hypotheses concerning the role of emancipation within the social milieu of the medieval and Renaissance Italian city-states. However, their work too rests on a limited documentary base drawn from notarial and familial records. Noteworthy among these studies are those of Paolo Cammarosano, Diane Hughes, and David Herlihy.[15]

What these and other studies have produced are two divergent views on the role of emancipation. One view is that emancipation was a disaster for the emancipated son or daughter because it cut him or her off from the rest of the family, which was the individual's source of material and symbolic support. The other view is that emancipation was an act of more fundamental, generational fission; an act that benefited the emancipated child by granting him or her independence and opportunities. Both of these views rest on the historian's vision of the family and on the approach taken to the evidence—legal or nonlegal. No analysis of emancipation can, therefore, avoid coming to terms with the different concepts of the family and with the methods and materials employed in their formulation.

Legal historians have exclusively utilized various doctrinal legal sources in their investigations, so that their accounts of the family are based on the norms. The family emerges as a legal unity or as a prior affective unity codified into a normative one.[16] The central normative construct in this legal unity was the *patria potestas*, which was of un-limited duration. This authority gave the *paterfamilias* (father of the family) control over his children and together with his legal power over his wife, made him the upholder of familial unity and order. Bel-lomo's extensive and painstaking research into areas of family law like dowry and filial property has added an important dimension to the legal history of the family by emphasizing the political, social, eco-nomic, and religious functions of the medieval Italian family and the role of familial substance—the patrimony—in fulfilling those func-tions. The father was able to provide for the needs of the family be-cause he controlled both its members and its property.[17] The patrimony was, therefore, at least as much a defining feature of the medieval family as was the *patria potestas*.[18]

Social historians studying the family have used documentary mate-rial generally pertaining to a single city and sometimes to only a few families. Florence has been the particular object of these labors. The major debate among social historians has not been over the relative role of the *patria potestas* versus the patrimony, however, but over the question of the essential form of the domestic unit—whether the fam-ily was, as a rule, nuclear or extended. The Burckhardtian thesis that the Renaissance marked the historical emergence of the modern form of the family, the nuclear-conjugal household, has attracted its ad-herents and received elegant formulation by Richard Goldthwaite.[19] On the other hand, there are those who argue that the family was not so small and the individual not so alone and vulnerable as Gold-thwaite and others maintain. They argue, instead, for the typicality, at least among the patriciate, of an extended family form.[20] The recent exemplary works of Francis William Kent, on the one hand, and Her-lihy and Christiane Klapisch, on the other, have transcended this debate.[21] Their patient and difficult labors in the face of masses of in-tractable archival materials have initiated a new phase in the social history of the Italian, and specifically the Florentine, family.

The many studies by Herlihy and Klapisch represent the results of a long-term research project that culminated in their landmark book, *Les toscans et leurs familles*.[22] The core of the research involved a statis-tical compilation and analysis of data pertaining to the Florentine tax census (*catasto*) of 1427. The data yielded a demographic and economic profile of the Tuscan population under Florentine rule and formed the basis for hypotheses and conclusions concerning, among other things, the family. Most importantly, in terms of the nuclear-versus-extended debate, Herlihy and Klapisch have demonstrated that various household forms coexisted in Florence and the countryside and that these forms were not irreconcilable types but the manifestation of economic, residential, and developmental factors.[23]

Kent's study is based on the preliminary findings of Herlihy and Klapisch regarding the domestic developmental cycle in Florence. By examining correspondence and other sources and utilizing anthropological notions about the relationship between a lineage and its constituent households, Kent has confirmed the sentiments of solidarity and the patterns of interaction that held together these aristocratic households and joined them to the lineage. He has taken pains to show how the ideology of the family was reflected in its structure and in the behavior of its members and how the household, whatever its form at a particular time, was the functional outcome of that ideology. As a result, Kent denies that the aristocratic family of fifteenth-century Florence was "the isolated nuclear-conjugal unit (newly seceded from a completely corporate clan) which a long line of historians has described."[24]

The works of Kent and of Herlihy and Klapisch have changed the terms to be used in analyzing the family. The question of familial structure or form has been superseded by the question of the relationship between the cultural conception of the family and social praxis. The aim of my book is to continue the discussion along these new and exciting lines by undertaking a project, the study of emancipation, that provides a new perspective on the relationship between theory and practice in the history of the Florentine family.

Among the questions to be answered is that of the relationship between the legal culture and the culture of which it was a partial and privileged expression, namely, the culture of society at large. Social historians have been loath to bloody themselves with the law because of the difficulties in its arcane and complex language. Yet, so many of the texts they use—contracts, statutes, and administrative records— are legal texts that encode economic and social realities in a web of language bearing its own significance. A disregard for legal methodological problems and for the formal meanings of the "plastic and polysemic terminology of the law" opens the way to anachronism and misinterpretation.[25] Legal historians, on the other hand, have not looked beyond the law to social realities and wider cultural concerns. They have delineated only the normative order as expressed in rules written by learned jurists, thereby overlooking those rules that were never formally promulgated and minimizing conflicts between differing norms and processes of conflict resolution.[26]

The net result of this approach has been to reify the family and to abstract it from the ebb and flow of history or to so subordinate it to

changing conditions that continuities in cultural logic remain unde-
tected or unappreciated. [27] Either the family is conceived of as a product
of external forces (demographic, economic, social, political) and the
ideology of the family viewed as an epiphenomenal superstructure
(the canonization of practices as norms), or the family is seen as the
concrete expression of the norms that supposedly governed, indeed
dictated, behavior. Accordingly, the complex and sophisticated analysis of Herlihy and Klapisch, on the one hand, notably postpones the
discussion of cultural concepts until after all structures, events, and
causative factors have been discussed, so that customs may appear to
have been purposeful, rational, and practical. For example, the practice of Florentine patrician fathers of composing *ricordi* to advise their
sons and the sons' tendency to glorify the image of the father can be
interpreted as practical responses to demographic factors. Florentines'
speculations on the family can be seen as meditations on existing structures, practices, and functions. [28] As a consequence, the bases of these
practices and functions are not always located in the culturally constituted interests of the actors. All of the factors Herlihy and Klapisch
point to, many of them brought to light for the first time as a result of
their labors, certainly did play their part in the domestic experiences
of Florentines. Herlihy and Klapisch generally display a fine sensitiv-
ity to the flexibilities and nuances in the data they analyze, and they
carefully avoid abstracting domestic structures from history or reify-
ing them into static or even organic entities. [29]

On the other hand, Kent and Bellomo have tended to fix the form
of the family in its rules and ideals, taking events as their expression
in practice in a manner that does not easily account for deviance, conflict, or failure. [30] Kent especially tries to reduce different historical facts
to a single legalistic scheme. He sees the changing forms of households
over time as an accommodation to biological rhythms in accord with
a rule of patrilineal association. Division of a household into two or
more separate households is ascribed to the pressures generated by
lack of space; conflicts (deviance from the norm) leading to the separation of households or to the severing of a familial relationship are psy-
chologized. The role of divergent interests or clashes of ideals in conflicts is ignored or minimized. Yet, the dissociation of certain branches
of a lineage from the rest may, for example, have owed as much to the
active interests of the other branches as it did to the humble circumstances and normative transgressions of the pruned member, so that
separation was a strategy as well as ostracism. Kent's valuable insights
have demonstrated to historians how a wide variety of activities and
ideas of Florentines can be comprehended within an ideology of kinship; but in forcefully denying that households were static entities

and that kinship can be reduced to domestic structures, Kent has, nonetheless, reified both households and kinship as "living things whose size and nature changed as generations passed."[31]

As Herlihy and Klapisch have demonstrated, the physical and patrimonial unity of the family was not something that could be taken for granted by Florentines; it did not exist by virtue of coresidence and blood relationships and was not free of the potentially disruptive effects of social, economic, and political developments. The biological, patrimonial, and symbolic continuity of the family could be realized only by continuous and deliberate effort. Families could and did fail.[32] And just as the dysfunctional moments of the family were located within the prevailing cultural code, the strategies conceived to deal with its failure were made possible by that very same cultural logic and its ambiguities or inconsistencies.[33]

Families and individuals as actors in the historical drama were caught up in situations where they had to perceive and define their interests and adapt strategies to achieve them. Emancipation was one such strategy or element that could be used to gain valued resources because it involved real or symbolic contact between the family and the rest of society. Emancipation was employed well or badly in order to achieve goals like the preservation of the patrimony—expressed in terms of family members, property, and honor. The emancipatory practices of Florentines did not and could not rigidly conform to models; they were adjusted to the exigencies that called for reinterpretation, reordering, or recombination of norms and values. Statistically, these practices may tend to conform to types, but they are neither completely and systematically explicable by reference to rules alone, nor are they the result of external factors unmediated by values and expectations.[34]

As mentioned, there are basically two viewpoints on the nature of emancipation. That these positions do not result from a direct and detailed examination of emancipation itself is due, in part, to the fact that the approaches taken to the history of the family have thus far excluded an all but schematic account of emancipation. Emancipation has, instead, been inserted into the framework provided by historical views of the family. As a conferral of rights, for example, emancipation has been linked to maturity and life-cycle events by Herlihy and Klapisch; as an immediate response to threats to the patrimony, it has been linked to financial distress by Cammarosano. In almost every instance, historians have vigorously denied that emancipation produced any real or thorough changes in relations between fathers and sons;[35] yet, undeniably, the legal relationship inherent in the *patria potestas* was terminated. If, in real terms, emancipation did not greatly change a father-son relationship, we must then seek the reasons why it did not do so and the effects it did have. The study of emancipation offers an opportunity to investigate the family in terms of culture and social praxis by utilizing the different concerns and sources of legal and social history. But the fact that emancipation affected the *patria potestas* and ensuing patrimonial rights necessitates its study.

Just as the vision of the family and the value of its activities helped to formulate strategies for Florentines, so, too, the vision of the historical process here espoused determines the strategy of this book. The study of emancipation begins by delineating the norms, legal and extralegal, that established the range of functional possibilities generated by emancipation. As a legal institution, emancipation cannot be understood apart from the law; and, equally, as an aspect of the law affecting the relations between fathers and offspring, it cannot be comprehended apart from the values placed on domestic relations. This study proceeds, therefore, by examining first the universal norms of medieval civil law and then the local legal norms of Florence, which, taken together, constitute the legal framework for Florentine emancipatory practices. This framework emerges from studying the glosses, commentaries, treatises, and opinions of the leading jurists of Italy and the statutes and ordinances of Florence.

The cultural context of emancipation in Florence can be reconstructed with difficulty from the letters, diaries, *ricordi*, and other writings of Florentines and here my debt to my predecessors in the history of the Florentine family is apparent and considerable. An attempt must also be made at this point to locate in the structure and ideology of the family those elements that were potentially disruptive, conducive to competition or controversy, and might be affected by a careful use of emancipation.

Once having established the normative framework, it is then possible to discuss emancipatory practices in Florence in the fourth chapter. The well-preserved registries of emancipations and the rich notarial archives provide the means of examining a number of events where we can see how the Florentines responded through emancipation to developments in the world around them.

Finally, there is the task of analyzing conflicts that arose at the level of norms. The roles and meanings laid out by the law were open to interpretation, which meant that the existent flexibilities and ambiguities could be exploited. Practice, therefore, created problems for the culture, especially the legal culture, by generating conflicts that exposed inconsistencies. In their legal opinions (*consilia*), which were their creative responses to these inconsistencies, the Florentine lawyers acted as ordained experts imposing meaning where it was contested or not readily apparent. By skillfully using techniques of argument and manufacturing ingenious fictions, the lawyers were able to mask their necessary innovations and to bring practice back within the normative order, which, in their eyes, was the essence of society.

What emerges as a result of their activities is an appreciation of how emancipation as a single option available to families, and not the most important option by any means, was, nonetheless, multifunctional and polysemic. It was creatively adapted by Florentines to meet the ever-changing needs of their families, which were not in themselves fixed entities but, rather, dynamic and versatile processes possessing both coherence and contradiction.

CHAPTER ONE

Emancipation in the *Ius Civile*

Emancipation was an institution peculiar to Roman law that arose logically and historically from the singular character of the Roman legal concept of paternal power (*patria potestas*).[1] *Patria potestas* was terminated only by the death of the father (*pater*) unless an act of emancipation or adoption brought it to an end beforehand. As long as the father remained alive, his children remained legally dependent; they did not acquire full legal rights simply by attaining a certain age.

The incursion of the Lombards into Italy in the sixth century and their political dominance of much of the Italian peninsula introduced a different legal conception of paternal authority to rival that of the Roman law. The Lombard equivalent of the *patria potestas*, the *mundium*, was far more limited in scope and duration.[2] The Lombards themselves realized that the Roman conception of paternal power differed from their own and that emancipation, therefore, had no place in their legal system.[3] They adopted the term *emancipatio* from Roman law to designate the personal and patrimonial separation of a son from his father. This Germanic form of emancipation (*emancipatio saxonica*, as it was termed by medieval jurists) was an act of physical separation; it was not at all the emancipation of Roman law but simply clothed a de facto state of separation in borrowed legal terminology.[4]

By the time of the revival of Roman law in the eleventh and twelfth centuries, a variety of acts and factual states had been equated with emancipation, and they were to be honored throughout the Middle Ages in the statutes of cities and in commentaries by jurists. These forms of emancipation included separate residence, the son's open practice of the merchant's profession (even if still residing with his father), the baptism of a child whose parents remained infidels, reception of holy orders or profession of the religious vocation in a monastery or convent, and the loss by the father of his civil rights for whatever reason (for example, exile or excommunication).[5] None of these examples was a true emancipation in terms of classical Roman law because no judicial act was undertaken that specifically and solely freed the child from the *patria potestas* to which he or she was subject; such cases were called tacit emancipations (*tacitae emancipationes*).

By the eleventh century, the distinctive Lombard and Roman forms of the family had developed into a single legal type, the medieval family, that incorporated aspects of the Roman familial model, including the *patria potestas*.[6] This sociocultural change in the form of the family, coupled with the revival of Roman law at the University of Bologna, revived the fortunes of emancipation as an active and integral element in legal and social life.

Types of Emancipation

In medieval as well as in classical Roman law, the *patria potestas* was perpetual, lasting as long as the father lived and covering all legitimate descendants of the male line. Thus, a grandfather (*avus*) who remained *paterfamilias* to his sons was also *paterfamilias* to his grandsons, the children of his sons; and the *paterfamilias* retained his *patria potestas* over them, no matter what their age.[7] As the *Glossa ordinaria* (Accursius, d. 1260) succinctly put it, "even a sexagenarian . . . is under the power [of his father]."[8]

For medieval Roman law, therefore, as for classical Roman law, emancipation was one way, outside of the father's death, to dissolve the *patria potestas*. "Emancipation is the release of a child from the power of his parent or from filiation with the authority of a judge."[9] This definition by Placentinus (d. 1192) was echoed in substantially the same form by other medieval jurists.[10] To all medieval civilians without exception emancipation meant the liberation of the child from the *patria potestas* and the consequent creation of a new, fully capable legal person.[11]

After defining emancipation, Placentinus distinguished between two types of emancipation—*spontanea* (free and voluntary) and *coacta* (forced);[12] his distinction will serve as a framework for analyzing different types of emancipation and emancipation procedures. Under the heading of *spontanea* comes what must, in the first place, be considered the usual form of emancipation, a form based on the *lex Cum inspeximus* of Justinian (C. 8.48[49].6). This law abrogated as superstitions the old Roman practices of pretending to sell the child to a third party and of giving the child a slap on the cheek and a simple declaration before a competent judge or magistrate was introduced in their place.[13] As Placentinus put it, the law required that both *pater* and *filius* (or *filia*) agree to the emancipation and appear before a judge to declare their voluntary consent.[14]

The father and child were to act out a legal ritual before the judge, the content of which is briefly described by Salatiele (. . . 1237–1280) and Guglielmus Durantis (d. 1295). The former states that having arrived before the judge, the father would say to him, "Lord, I want to emancipate my son"; and the son would say, "Lord, I want to be emancipated." To this, the judge would reply, "And I lend my authority to this emancipation."[15] Durantis then furnishes an example of the ceremonial speech with which the father emancipated his son:

> I, A., by means of this emancipation, my will and yours being in agreement, in the presence of this ordinary judge and by his authority, dismiss you, B., my son, from my hand and power, so that henceforth, being *tui iuris* [possessed of full legal rights and responsibilities] and a *paterfamilias*, you should have license to write a will, do business, give gifts confirmed by death, and also enter into legal contracts, and do what a *paterfamilias* can by law.[16]

In all probability, the father held his son by the hand while reciting this formula, and then let go at the appropriate moment.[17]

Placentinus' statements and the emancipation ritual itself indicate two factors necessary for a valid emancipation—the declaration of consent and intent by both father and child and their appearance before a competent legal official. There was no disagreement among the jurists over the necessity for expressions of consent by father and child,[18] nor was there any doubt about the need for the presence of a judge or magistrate and for the observance of the proper legal solemnities.[19] Bartolus of Sassoferrato (d. 1357) did tender the opinion that neither the judge nor local legislation on emancipation was the agent in an emancipation but that it was the father who emancipated his child, albeit by means of the formalities established by law and by the authority of the presiding legal official.[20] However, his designation of the father as the agent in no way abrogated the general principle, as enunciated by Angelus de Ubaldis (1328–1407) that "simple paternal consent is not sufficient for liberating a child from *patria potestas* unless the solemnities of the law should take place."[21]

Requiring a competent official to preside over an emancipation and observing the prescribed legal forms amounted to declaring the public nature of the emancipatory act. If the act itself were public, however, the reasons for it were not. It was sufficient for the parties to express their consent; they were not required to give any reasons for the emancipation, and the presiding official could not demand a statement of cause from them.[22]

It was one thing for the jurists to demand the presence of a competent legal official at emancipations but quite another to determine who was competent in this matter. This problem was further complicated by the fact that competence was determined in the latter case ultimately by statute and custom in each locality; therefore the issue could not be fully resolved within the confines of civil law alone.

The noted jurist Azo (d. ca. 1230) acknowledged the place of custom (*consuetudo*) in matters of voluntary jurisdiction, which included emancipation.[23] The *Glossa ordinaria* later attempted to establish the limits of custom in this matter by stating that an emancipation was valid if done before a magistrate "to whom municipal custom alone had given jurisdiction in emancipations." Quite simply, the *Glossa ordinaria* held that custom defined the boundaries of voluntary jurisdiction.[24] Odofredus (d. 1265) likewise concluded that custom could make magistrates competent in emancipations.[25] Guglielmus Durantis, however, made no mention of custom and opined that only a duly appointed *iudex ordinarius* [judge with ordinary jurisdiction] was competent.[26]

Cino da Pistoia (d. 1336/7) dwelt at length on jurisdiction and privilege conferred by custom in his commentary on the *lex Si lex* (C. 8.48[49].1), where he noted that custom, law, and man were all capable of giving jurisdiction, even to political officials (*duumviri*) who were not judicial magistrates.[27] Bartolus of Sassoferrato sided with his teacher, but he made the terminological shift that placed the discussion in the context of the political realities of his time. He spoke not of the *magistratus* or the *duumvir* but of the notary and the judge and used the language of the various communal statutes rather than that of the Codex, thereby bringing legal doctrine more directly into contact with the Italian communes.[28] Angelus de Ubaldis relied on Bartolus' distinctions when he faced the question of competence in a decision (*consilium*) made while he was at Padua in 1388.[29] Angelus decided that a scribe (*tabellio*; also known as a *iudex chartularii*) was endowed with ordinary jurisdiction by the commune that had commissioned him. In the case at hand, however, the scribe did not act by authority of the commune; he was, thus, said Angelus, a simple notary who could only write out legal documents. The emancipation in question was, therefore, invalid in Angelus' opinion.

The *consilium* of Angelus shows that custom had been widely accepted as the criterion for determining competence in emancipations, but it also shows how difficult it was to pin down the meaning of custom in any one case. What was important to the lawyers and jurists was that the official involved in an emancipation be endowed with the powers of the *iudex ordinarius*. They demanded, in other words, a degree of legal authority and knowledge.

The distinction Angelus had drawn in his *consilium* was that between a judge and a simple scribe or notary. This reference to a scribe points to a third factor in emancipations—composing a written document recording the occurrence and particulars of an emancipation. The presence or possibility of such documents raised two legal questions: Should a written document be required for a valid emancipation to take place?; and should furnishing such a document in court be deemed sufficient proof that an allegedly valid emancipation had occurred? There was no question of the desirability of a written record; the question was whether it should be considered necessary either for the valid completion of an emancipation or as later evidence of its validity.

On the question of the necessity of a *scriptura* (written record) as evidence, the jurists were generally reluctant to let the burden of proof rest on documents. Azo declared that for purposes of proof "not the writing so much as the truth is usually considered."[30] So, too, the *Glossa ordinaria*, echoed later by Angelus de Ubaldis, placed its faith in the truth and not in the writing. After all, documents could be, and were, drawn up, but what was one to do if the document had merely been lost? And how was one to get around the fact that documents could be forged or could bear no resemblance to reality?[31]

This reluctance to rely on written proof did not lead, however, to an utter denial of the value of writing in emancipations. Even as he denied that proof must lie with the written word, Cino da Pistoia, for example, took the position that writing was necessary to properly complete an emancipation.[32] Bartolus, following Cino, left no doubt where he stood on the issue: "Others say, and this is by far the safest opinion, that writing should intervene from the start."[33] Baldus de Ubaldis (1327?–1400) agreed with Cino and Bartolus and even seemed to lean toward requiring proof in writing in order to avoid the simulation of emancipation.[34] The *Glossa ordinaria*, on the other hand, had shied away from requiring written proof precisely because a written document could be forged and emancipation thus simulated. Bartolomeo da Saliceto (d. 1412) likewise held to what he termed the "common" opinion that although the loss of the *scriptura* did not jeopardize the validity of the act if it could be adequately proven by other means, "writing nevertheless is necessary, and so an instrument should be made."[35]

By the fifteenth century, there was little doubt among those trained in the law that a valid act of emancipation normally required the simultaneous appearance of the *pater* and *filius* before a competent official to whom they were to voice their willingness to proceed to emancipation. The need for a written record of the particulars of an emancipation was also generally accepted.[36] Most emancipations, it was expected, would occur in the form indicated and according to specifications; there were exceptions allowed by the law, however. Placentinus' second species, the *coacta emancipatio*, was such an exception, but there were others that can properly be considered under the heading of *spontanea*.

As already noted, when speaking of the Lombard era, various circumstances were regarded as conferring emancipation. These forms of so-called tacit emancipation continued to be recognized by the glossators and commentators of Roman law. Placentinus, for example, said that according to the law, a son was emancipated if he were made a bishop or patrician;[37] the *Glossa ordinaria* and Bartolus similarly observed that the dignity of the rank of consul emancipated its holder.[38] Deportation or exile of the father also emancipated the son,[39] and Baldus affirmed that a son living apart from his father and acting as if he were emancipated was legally emancipated after ten years.[40] Baldus also stated that captivity at the hands of an enemy and consular, senatorial, and patrician rank all terminated *patria potestas*.[41] These and other exceptional forms of emancipation were often embodied in communal statutes.[42]

It is important to underline the fact that marriage was one state or circumstance that did not confer emancipation tacitly upon either sex. The son remained under his father's power in any case. The married daughter passed from the direct control of her father to that of her husband, but that did not mean that she was legally emancipated from her father (contrary to the common opinion shared by many historians). The daughter retained her father's civil origins (*origo*) and remained part of his family although married—at least with respect to the benefits (not the obligations) of citizenship. She reverted to her father's *patria potestas* at the dissolution of her marriage unless she had been emancipated.[43]

The law also allowed exceptions to the normal judicial form of emancipation. These involved the emancipation of an infant (*infans*) or a child absent from the proceedings (*absens*), both of which raised problems with respect to the form emancipation was to take. These cases were specifically dealt with by the *lex Iubemus* (C. 8.48[49].5), which raised no problems of interpretation. There was a singular unanimity among medieval jurists about the facts and procedures involved in emancipating an *infans* or *absens*, which were very similar cases.

To emancipate an *absens*, the father first had to obtain an imperial rescript (a grant of legal privilege granted by the emperor or his delegate, usually a count palatine) expressly allowing the emancipation. The father then took the rescript to a judge and received the emancipation decree. The absent child was required to go before a competent official of the place where he or she was and express consent to emancipation; the emancipation was not valid without the child's consent. Two separate judicial acts thus replaced the one act that would have been necessary if both had appeared together before a judge. The rescript was required as a safeguard for the *absens*, for (as the *Glossa ordinaria* stated) the emperor could not issue his rescript if it were to result in injury to a third party (here, the child).[44]

The legal doctrine concerning the emancipation of an *absens* provided Angelus de Ubaldis with the basis for arguing in a *consilium* that the child could be represented at his or her emancipation by a representative (*procurator*), contrary to previous opinion (mainly Azo's) on the issue.[45] The procedure for emancipating an *absens* provided legal justification for an emancipation in the absence of the child. The father could, of course, emancipate his child by means of his own *procurator* if he were absent. However, Alberico da Rosciate (d. 1360) had previously argued that a child could not be represented at his emancipation. Although he recognized that the opposite opinion was current in some circles and had some basis in the law, Alberico based his decision on the fact that "emancipation does not seem to consist of the administration of a patrimony, and therefore it does not seem that it can be performed through a *curator* or a *procurator*."[46]

The imperial rescript, a central feature in the emancipation of an *absens*, also played a crucial role in emancipating an *infans*. The difference between the two emancipations lay in the fact that the child's consent was not required. Indeed, children under seven years of age were deemed totally incapable before the law; they could not give their legal consent,[47] and the *lex Iubemus* made it clear that an *infans* could be emancipated without expressing consent.[48] Therefore, the father need only obtain the imperial rescript and appear before a judge to emancipate a child.

Emancipatio spontanea included those forms of emancipation where both father and child were willing participants (with the exception, of course, of the emancipation of an *infans*, who could not legally consent). In *emancipatio coacta*, on the contrary, one of the parties was opposed to emancipation or, at least, forced by legally defined circumstances to submit to it. Placentinus listed three situations where a father could be forced to emancipate: (1) if he were *atrocius* (for example, if he beat his child exceedingly or did not feed him); (2) if he prostituted his children; (3) if he gave a child away in adoption and the child could prove that the adoption had not been to his advantage.[49] The *Glossa ordinaria* said that a father or grandfather could be compelled to emancipate for doing great harm (*magnam iniuriam*) to his child or grandchild. Such an *iniuria* consisted of the situations cited by Placentinus plus the case where a father accepted a testamentary bequest stipulating that he emancipate his child.[50] Odofredus, Durantis, Bartolus, Paolo di Castro (d. 1441), Bartolomeo da Saliceto, and even the canonist Antonio da Budrio (1338–1408) all affirmed that normally (*regulariter*) a father could not be forced to emancipate his child; but they also held that exceptional circumstances such as those mentioned by Placentinus and the *Glossa ordinaria* did indeed justify such coercion.[51]

On the contrary point of whether a child could be constrained to accept emancipation, there was less agreement. The *Glossa ordinaria* set forth one opinion: "But it is asked whether from the same causes by which a father is compelled to emancipate, on the other hand, is a son compelled to receive emancipation against his will? The answer is no . . . because the situations are not the same."[52] Jacopo d'Arena (fl. 1253–1296), on the other hand, raised a dissenting voice, claiming that an unwilling son (*filius invitus*) could be emancipated for a good reason.[53] The prevailing viewpoint, however, seems to have been that of the *Glossa ordinaria*, later beautifully elaborated by Bartolus:

> But then it is asked whether in the same cases, if a son should treat his father badly or impose on him the necessity of sinning, whether the son may be compelled to accept emancipation, for an *invitus* is not emancipated. . . . It should be said that he cannot. And the reason why a father is forced to emancipate in the aforesaid cases is this: because the son is not being treated well while he is in his father's power. But the father is not in the son's power, and, therefore, one is not proceeding from like to like. It is a penalty for a father to [have to] emancipate because he loses the right of *patria potestas*, so he can be compelled to emancipate because of a crime. But being emancipated is not a penalty for the son, but freedom. Therefore, he is not forced to emancipation on account of his own crime because this would be convenient to him, and one should not pursue the convenience of one who deserves punishment. . . . Whence, because of his crime he does not deserve to be emancipated, rather because of his crime he should be returned to paternal control should he be emancipated.[54]

Baldus and Paolo di Castro held the same opinion.[55] Bartolomeo da Saliceto, as far as I can determine, was the only major figure to side with Jacopo d'Arena. Interestingly, he did not mention the arguments of Bartolus in setting forth his opinion.[56]

Closely related to the issues raised by *emancipatio coacta* was the problem of the ungrateful, recalcitrant emancipatus (*emancipatus ingratus*). The position of Roman law on this matter was clearly expounded in the one *lex* that dealt with the matter: Emancipation was rescinded for those children who vexed or mistreated their parents. What the medieval jurists added to this legal doctrine was an elaboration of the mechanics of the law. Azo posited that rescinding the emancipation took place by the authority of a judge.[57] The *Glossa ordinaria* asserted that emancipation could be revoked for the same reasons that permitted disinheriting a child, as enumerated in the novella *Ut cum de appellatione*.[58] The later commentators received and accepted the contributions of Azo and the *Glossa ordinaria* and merely repeated them if they took up the subject of the *ingratus* at all.

Property Rights and Transfers

When emancipating a child, the father could give some form of gift, termed the *praemium emancipationis*. In addition, the *peculium* (property legally bound to a child *in potestate* [subject to his father]) was turned over directly to the child, who could thus acquire both title and possession of *peculium* and *praemium*. The *praemium* was distinguished from other gifts by the fact that it accompanied emancipation. Because of the temporal relation between emancipation and the *praemium*, Baldus held that the two acts, legally distinct though they were, could be described in a single notarial document. He implied that the order of their written appearance was unimportant because the emancipation was presumed to have occurred first.[59]

Emancipation permitted transferring property ownership because, for purposes of the law, it made the child an *extraneus* (stranger) in relation to his father and no longer a *coniuncta persona* (a related person). According to the law, which did not allow *donationes inter vivos* (gifts during life) between people united under a single *patria potestas*, property could be given or sold only to people who were legally separate and distinct from the party relinquishing ownership. Therefore, property given to a child *in potestate* was actually and finally transferred only by emancipation or by the death of the *coniuncta persona* who had given the property.[60]

There was a great deal of debate about what type of gift the *praemium* was. Cino da Pistoia summarized the opposing viewpoints in his commentary. One school of thought asserted that the *praemium* was a gift given in response to a specific reason (*donatio ob causam*; in this case, *ob causam emancipationis*). This point of view was bent on preserving the meaning of the language used in notarial charters describing the *praemium*, which implied that the gift was the result of emancipation and even a form of compensation in return for the child's consent to be emancipated. Cino, however, concurred with those whom he called the *maiores*; their view was that the *praemium* was a simple gift (*simplex donatio*), a piece of unmotivated generosity. The overriding legal reason behind their opinion lay in the fact that simple gifts, gifts that could not be tied to a particular occasion or set of circumstances (such as marriage), were subject to the requirements of communal statutes (such as one from Pistoia that Cino cited as an example) that mandated publicizing the fact that ownership of property had changed hands. The aim of such statutes was to prevent creditors from being defrauded.[61]

Bartolus followed his master in formulating his ideas on the nature of the *praemium*.[62] Baldus was of the same opinion, for he decided that the wording of the notarial documents was an expression of affection and not a statement of legal fact.[63] But the issue was not easily resolved: A later jurist, such as Alessandro Tartagni da Imola (1424–1477), could comfortably hold the opinion that the *praemium* was a *donatio ob causam* despite the renown and authority of those who held the opposite view. Tartagni, like those against whom Cino had argued, believed that "a gift made to a son *in praemium* on emancipation is seen to have been made for a reason, namely, so that he would agree to be emancipated because an *invitus* could not have been emancipated."[64]

The other problem regarding the *praemium*—a problem perhaps more important but more easily resolved—was that of its size relative to the father's patrimony as a whole. Bartolus maintained that "a gift made by a father to an emancipated son, beyond the legitimate quantity [what he stood to inherit as his equal share], without notice, will not be valid."[65] The idea was that the other children were not to be quietly defrauded of their rightful share. Dino del Mugello (d. 1303?) in a *consilium* concerning a *praemium* similarly assumed that the *praemium* or other gift could be used as a means to cheat some of the children of their share of the estate and declared that the emancipated son was due a percentage of the inheritance and not more.[66]

The *peculium* was closely related to the *praemium*, for it, too, passed into the hands of the child at emancipation. Classical Roman law had established the *peculium* to designate the property of a child *in potestate*. Since a child *in potestate* did not have proprietary capacity, the father was considered the owner of the property, but he was not free to dispose of it. Medieval Roman law retained the concept of *peculium* and preserved the four types of *peculia*: the *profectitium* (that property acquired directly from the father), the *adventitium* (acquired from the mother or from her side of the family), the *castrense* (military pay), and the *quasi castrense* (originally, clerical wages or pay as a civil servant).[67]

The *peculium castrense* and the *peculium quasi castrense* were legal forms of property over which the father had no rights. A son was just like a father (*tanquam paterfamilias*) with respect to this property; he held full ownership (*dominium*). The *adventitium* consisted of two types —the *regulare*, to which the father had no rights of usufruct, and the *irregulare*, to which he did. The son had the least control over the *profectitium* because it was gratuitous.[68] While *in potestate*, the child could not alienate the property of a *peculium* or otherwise dispose of it in legal circumstances. Upon emancipation, the *peculium* automatically belonged to him, whether or not the father expressly conceded it to him. This principle was clearly enunciated by Jacopo d'Arena, who also thereby provided an example of the types of property that might fall into the category of *peculium profectitium* (for example, books, arms, horses).[69]

Determining the contents of the *peculium profectitium* became somewhat more difficult when it took into account any wages or profits a son may have earned in activities not covered by the *peculium castrense* and the *quasi castrense*. Ordinarily, the rule would have been that a son's lack of proprietary capacity meant that anything he gained accrued to his father. But exceptions allowed under the *castrense* and *quasi castrense* and a reluctance to see a son lose all title to the fruits of his labor led many jurists to embrace the principle that what a son gained by his own industry should remain his. If he used his father's money, then the rule was that half of the profit arose from that money and belonged to the father and the other half was the product of the son's labors and belonged to him.[70]

Just as the father was entitled to compensation for the capital he had provided, so, too, was he entitled to compensation for the loss of the *adventitium irregulare*, whose fruits he had previously enjoyed. By the thirteenth century, therefore, it was common practice for the father to retain the right to half of the usufruct on the *adventitium irregulare* following the emancipation of his child. The *Summa vindobinensis* termed this right a *pretium*, implying that it was somehow the price paid to the father by the child in return for being emancipated.[71]

Obligations and Legal Capacities

Emancipation was an enabling act that changed the legal status of the child and the legal relationship with his or her *pater* and family of origin. The child's new legal status was, potentially at least, a factor in almost all aspects of the law. The most immediate and obvious change was in the legal capacities of the emancipatus. He was henceforth a *paterfamilias* before the law, a *homo sui iuris*, fully capable jurally where before he had been incapable or had had a limited legal capacity. A female acquired all the rights of a *materfamilias*, which were not equivalent to the male's.

In terms of the law, the purpose and effect of emancipation were to endow the emancipatus with the full legal rights of the *homo sui iuris*. As a result, the lawyers resolutely declared that an emancipation was and could only be valid for all purposes. It could not be performed for a single, consequent legal action, like writing a will, only to expire upon completion of that action. As Paolo di Castro said, paraphrasing Baldus, since the *patria potestas* was indivisible, so were its effects; and, therefore, an emancipation had to be operative for all purposes.[72]

It was clear that the emancipatus enjoyed full legal rights; with regard to obligations however, the law was not nearly so unequivocal. In the case of the emancipatus, the law was faced with a legal person who was a *pater* in law but a *filius* in fact, for his father still lived. In addition, the emancipatus may have acquired property from his father that had prior legal obligations incumbent upon it. The jurists, therefore, had the task of clarifying the nature of the obligations of an emancipatus. Moreover, since obligations involve two parties, the obligations of those who had dealt with the emancipatus were also changed, and the *pater* was foremost among them.

It must be stated at the outset that not all obligations were affected by emancipation, for not all obligations were dependent on the existence of legal capacities rooted in civil law. The right to *alimenta* (food, clothing, and shelter) in medieval law, for example, was based on natural law according to the jurists and was an expression of ties of blood and affection and not legal capacities. The father was obligated by law to care for his children, regardless of their legal status as *filiifamilias* or emancipati. Only if the child were ungrateful or if, as an emancipatus, he held property or practiced a trade by which he could care for himself, did the father's obligation cease. If the emancipatus became destitute, even if he had expressly renounced seeking anything further from his father, the father was again obligated to supply him with *alimenta*. Children, in turn, and especially sons, whether emancipated or not, were similarly obligated to furnish their parents with *alimenta*; failing to do so was grounds for declaring an emancipatus ungrateful and for disinheriting the child.[73]

It is also important to note that emancipation did not always immediately confer full capacity on the emancipatus. In the case of a minor, full legal capacity came only on reaching the age of majority (25 in Roman law);[74] in the meantime, the emancipatus could act legally through a guardian (*tutor* or *curator*). Since the father was the closest relative on whom the guardianship (*tutela* or *curatela*) could devolve, the law established that the father could become the *tutor* and administrator of his emancipated child's property.[75]

As *tutor*, the father took on obligations and responsibilities that were largely paternal, in any case. Legally, however, his relation to the child's property had changed: Now he was the administrator of all the child's property, and his responsibilities were not light. A guardian could not freely alienate the property entrusted to him, although there were exceptions to this rule; in no case, however, was the *tutor* permitted to alienate property solely for opportunity or convenience. The father, like any other *tutor*, was theoretically justiciable in his person and in his property for malice or lack of diligence in managing his ward's estate.[76]

While emancipation did not change obligations involving *alimenta* and did not immediately give full legal rights to a minor, it did effect many important legal changes. Prior to emancipation, the relationship between father and child was neatly encapsulated in ideological formulas stating that a father and son were one flesh and that the voice of the father was the voice of the son. A father could not enter into a contract with his son, it was declared, because in doing so he would only be making a contract with himself.[77] As schematized in the *Glossa ordinaria*, the *patria potestas* meant that: (1) a father could sell his child *in potestate* in case of hunger; (2) he could not be summoned to court by his child; (3) the child could not act on his or her own behalf; (4) the child could not undertake a lawsuit without his or her father's permission; (5) the father gained whatever the child gained; (6) the father administered the child's *peculium adventitium*; (7) there could be no civil obligation between a father and child.[78] These legal facts were all changed by emancipation, which made of a father and child two voices and two bodies.

Among the rights gained by a child after emancipation was the freedom to choose his or her spouse and to marry without paternal consent.[79] But the father's loss of legal control over his children's marital choices was simply part of a greater loss of control, expressed by the fact that he could no longer impose duties and errands upon them.[80] The father's loss of control coincided, furthermore, with corresponding gains by the emancipatus, who could, for example, seek direct control of his wife's dowry.[81] The emancipatus also gained sole control over his earnings and profits, which had previously been part of the *peculium* under his father's administration.[82] He even gained the right to summon his father to a judicial procedure or an arbitration.[83]

Emancipation, however, did not amount solely to a lengthy list of lost rights and powers from the father's point of view; his losses were, in fact, balanced by some definite gains. Overall, therefore, emancipation could be characterized from the father's perspective as yielding certain rights in return for a degree of freedom and maneuverability. The maneuverability lay in the greater flexibility that existed in the relations between a father and an emancipated child: There could be civil obligations and contracts between them, and property, too, could be legally passed from one to the other.[84]

The freedom a father gained by emancipating a child was also due to the fact that he was released from certain obligations toward his child or on his child's behalf. If the child moved away and lived on his or her own, for example, the father was no longer responsible for the child's taxes.[85] But above all, emancipation meant that the father was not legally bound for any obligations incurred by his child.

Vis-à-vis third parties, the relations between a father and child were changed dramatically by emancipation. Here the *Glossa ordinaria* neatly contrasted the new and the old situations:

> If you contracted with a son made *sui iuris* by lending him money, you do not have the father obligated for the son, unless he should specifically obligate himself, and this in the first place. But if you lent anything to a son *in potestate*, without permission of the father, you will have the father obligated to the extent that there is something in the *peculium* or there is [something] paid in to the father's property.[86]

The general rule, as stated by Odofredus, was that "a father is not bound by a contract of an emancipatus but [he is bound to a contract] of a son in his power," and this doctrine was expounded by all medieval jurists.[87] For the father, the freedom from obligation afforded by emancipation was a distinct improvement over the situation before emancipation when he could be obligated without his knowledge or consent. After emancipation, the child became responsible for debts previously contracted. On the other hand, a son also gained a measure of freedom because he could no longer be held liable for his father's debts.[88]

The termination of liabilities for debt resulting from emancipation provided the legal opportunity to escape debt by placing property in the hands of one who was no longer legally responsible for those debts and yet a family member. Jurists and laymen alike were aware of the possibilities emancipation (as well as dowry, inheritance, and

other legal institutions and relations) presented for defrauding creditors. The communal statutes, especially those of a commercial and financial center such as Florence, dealt extensively with the problem,
as we see in the next chapter; the subject drew the attention of legal
theorists too.

The problem of fraudulent uses of emancipation became a lively
concern only in the era of the commentators, who were, in general,
very aware of practical legal problems.[89] Bartolus, speaking of the possible use of emancipation to defraud other children of their rightful
share of the inheritance, maintained that an emancipation could be
deemed fraudulent if there were doubt about its rectitude unless some
legitimate reason was subsequently provided. In general, Bartolus asserted that property alienated with intent to defraud, whether such
an alienation was real or fictitious, was subject to the claims of creditors for outstanding debts.[90] He did not, however, specifically refer to
emancipation in this context. It was Baldus who applied this principle
explicitly to emancipation. He gave an example that may well have
been common in the fourteenth century and not merely the jurist's
fantastic rendering of a legal possibility:

> Suppose that I should decide to exercise the craft of money changing by
> sending money overseas, and fearing the dangers of the sea, I emanci-
> pated my son and secretly gave him all my goods. . . . Then I began to
> engage in that trade and lost all my wealth in the sea. How can those
> who have obligated me from the business seek compensation? And it
> seems that they have no relief, because there can be no fraud in the case of
> future creditors. . . . On the contrary, it seems that because fraud gives
> rise to this contract and because it was done in bad faith, it should be re-
> scinded. Nor is it just for the son to keep the gain while the creditors feel
> the loss. . . . And I say that these things are presumed to have been
> made not only in fraud but to have been simulated, which simulation
> harms no creditors . . . but it is otherwise if the future creditors are cred-
> itors from a lucrative cause.[91]

Baldus also asserted that simulation could be alleged against any
emancipation that was used to deprive other heirs of their share of
the inheritance. To Baldus, the overriding principle was evident:

> The emancipated son should not be condemned for his father . . . and
> he can defend goods given by his father from paternal creditors . . . un-
> less the emancipation was done in fraud of the creditors, because simu-
> lated emancipation is not valid.[92]

Baldus' ideas and example were to form an integral part of the jural
doctrine on simulated or fraudulent emancipation.[93]

The problem of fraud also figured in the *consilia* of various jurists, where it was further explicated. Pietro d'Ancarano (ca. 1330–1416) dealt with a case where a young girl dying of the plague had been emancipated in order to make her will on the day before her death. He concluded that fraud had been perpetrated in this case, and he based his arguments on two facts: The act had lacked the proper judicial solemnities, and the act had occurred in close temporal proximity to the testament and death.[94] Since the weight of his argument fell, in fact, on the second point, it was really the temporal factor that both allowed and impelled him to decide that the act of emancipation had been simulated and fraudulent.

Giovanni d'Anagni (d. 1457) faced another case involving heirs defrauded by means of an emancipation and testament. He, too, based his decision on the temporal coincidence of events:

> Although on first glance it can be said that an emancipation is valid that appears to have been made in good faith . . . nevertheless, the emancipation in question can for two reasons be said to have been made in fraud and thus be invalid as far as any legal effect. First, fraud is gathered from the brevity of the period in which the emancipation and the testament took place. For from these things that were done on the same day can be presumed what was the thought and the intent regarding things done in the past.[95]

The second reason, according to d'Anagni, was simply that the act of emancipation did, indeed, defraud the other heirs and was, therefore, contrary to the civil law and applicable statutes.[96] For both Pietro d'Ancarano and Giovanni d'Anagni, not to mention Baldus, temporal coincidence was a powerful factor in determining whether an act had been performed with intent to defraud. Both lawyers recognized the possibility of using emancipation to such an end, and both fixed the legal penalty as nullity of the emancipation.

Inheritance

After emancipation, it was necessary to determine who held the *patria potestas* over subsequent generations. The law contained clear rules about how the *patria potestas* devolved when emancipation entered the picture. A grandfather had both children and grandchildren (the children of his unemancipated sons) under his *potestas*. Should he emancipate any one of them, the emancipation affected only his authority over that one. For instance, if the grandfather emancipated a son, he retained power over that son's children unless the grandfather also emancipated them individually. Those children of the emancipatus conceived after emancipation were, however, under the power of the emancipatus, their father. Those conceived or born before emancipation remained under the power of the grandfather, and they did not revert to the *potestas* of their father when the grandfather, who was their legal *paterfamilias*, died; they then became *sui iuris*. The principles of the devolution of the *patria potestas* were self-evident in the *Corpus iuris civilis* and were merely repeated by medieval jurists.[97]

The law was not nearly so unequivocal on the question of agnation (relationship calculated through males) for the purposes of inheritance. As Sir Henry Maine long ago pointed out, agnation in Roman law was based upon the *patria potestas*. Those who were subject to the same *patria potestas* were agnatically connected. By dissolving the *patria potestas*, emancipation in classical Roman law dissolved the agnatic relationship.[98] By removing agnation, emancipation also disinherited the emancipatus; however, legal reforms initiated by the Roman pretors later created the institution of *bonorum possessio*, which was based on cognation rather than agnation. This institution gave the emancipatus in particular a right to the succession along with those who had been *in potestate* at the time of the father's death. The emancipatus was compelled to figure his own property in the inheritance (*collatio*) because he had enjoyed proprietary capacity from the time of his emancipation and the property he had acquired then and since would otherwise have been the father's and thus part of the estate.[99]

In the medieval law on intestate succession, emancipation made no difference as far as the emancipatus' right to inherit was concerned. The medieval law was based on the principle that "today the difference between paternal power and emancipation is abolished" as regards succession, which was simply a logical extension of the *iura nova* (postclassical law) that medieval jurists discovered in the *Corpus*.[100] In intestate succession, the emancipatus enjoyed the right to inherit equally with other children of the deceased; in testamentary succession, he could have a will voided for passing over him in silence. Like any direct heir (*suus heres*), he had to be expressly disinherited, with a statement of cause included, in order to be left out of the inheritance.[101]

Since emancipation did not deprive the child of the right to inherit from his or her father, legal experts spent a great deal of time and effort clarifying the mechanisms of inheritance (largely by devising countless hypothetical examples of collation situations). It would be tedious and unnecessary to reproduce their examples here; it is sufficient to note that the legal experts were concerned with questions of who collated what and with whom. Property such as dowries (for men), for instance, were exempted from collation because they came from outside the family.

With regard to agnation, however, medieval lawyers were left with a problem: If emancipation had formerly meant disagnation and dis-inheritance but now did not mean disinheritance, did this imply that agnation continued as well? In other words, was the emancipatus ag-natically related (in the eyes of the law) to his father and to the male line descended from him?

The *Summa vindobinensis* assumed that agnation persisted when it laid out the order of succession. After the direct heirs and those called heirs with them or in their place (emancipati were included here), came the grandchildren, then the general class of *agnati* (defined as *filii vel filie, sorores, et patres emancipatores*), and, finally, the blood rela-tions (*cognati*; here, those related through females were considered as heirs).[102] By placing emancipati before the general class of *agnati*, the *Summa vindobinensis* appears to have considered the emancipati as ag-nates. The *Glossa ordinaria* explicitly termed the emancipati agnates, for it confirmed that agnation was preserved despite emancipation and that grandsons were agnate to the grandfather through their emanci-pated father.[103]

There was no consensus on the question of agnation, however. Cino da Pistoia noted that the various glosses disagreed and that both positions could be cogently argued. He decided that the father re-mained agnate to the emancipated son but that the son was not ag-nate to the father; therefore, a grandson conceived after emancipation was not agnate to his grandfather.[104] Bartolus revealed that some ju-rists held that a father remained agnate to an emancipated son (and had a right to succeed to the son's estate) because he did not undergo a change in emancipation; the son, however, did sustain a change through emancipation and, therefore, could not be considered agnate to his father. Bartolus decided, however, that such reasoning was faulty since it denied that an emancipatus had the right to succeed to his father's estate. The father, he maintained, retained his right to suc-ceed to the emancipatus' estate and the emancipatus to the father's; but, he agreed, agnation ceased as a result of emancipation.[105]

Baldus went somewhat further than Bartolus in delineating and maintaining a distinction between the law and its effects. Agnation, he said, was preserved in effect (since the emancipatus had the right to inherit), though not in law, or, alternatively, agnation was dissolved passively but not actively.[106] His student, Paolo di Castro, defended this distinction, declaring that biological fact was more vital than legal fact. Moreover, since even in law emancipati and their children suc-ceeded just like normal heirs, agnation did not appear to have been dissolved by virtue of emancipation.[107] Nevertheless, the general opin-ion appears to have been that legal, if not biological, agnation ended with emancipation.[108]

The decision to inherit (from the father) and thus to collate belonged to the emancipatus.[109] Should he decide to become an heir, he had to collate his property with the *sui heredes* (those *in potestate* at the time of death), not with any other *emancipati* (with the exception of *peculia profectitia*) or *extranei* who may have been heirs.[110]

The main area of legal uncertainty was over what the emancipatus was to collate. Did the collation include all he possessed at the father's death or only what he had received directly from his father? What was to be done about the *peculium castrense*, the *quasi castrense*, and the *adventitium*, which had not come from the father? With respect to what his father had given him, was a distinction to be drawn between *donationes ob causam* and *simplices donationes*?

Rogerius (twelfth century) had early argued that the emancipatus had to collate all he had received from his father and everything he possessed at his death as well as any dowry or *donatio propter nuptias*, which was a *donatio ob causam*.[111] Azo thought that all *bona profectitia*, including simple donations, were to be collated and nothing more.[112] The *Glossa ordinaria*, on the other hand, said that only *donationes ob causam* and the *peculium profectitium* were subject to collation, except in three cases: (1) to avoid inequality; (2) if the father in giving a *simplex donatio* had expressly stipulated collation; (3) if the gift had come while *in potestate*, in which case it was part of the *peculium profectitium*.[113] Azo and the *Glossa* agreed that collation should involve only what had come directly from the father (thus excluding the dowry), but they disagreed over whether a *simplex donatio* had to be collated.

Cino held that the *praemium* and all other simple gifts had to be collated along with *profectitia*. Also to be collated, naturally, was everything else the emancipatus had at the time of the father's death except the *peculia castrensia* and *adventitium* and the *aes alienum* (chiefly his wife's dowry).[114] Bartolus, Baldus, Paolo di Castro, and Alessandro Tartagni all agreed with Cino; indeed, said the latter, such was the "communis opinio."[115]

The Nature of Emancipation

What was the purpose of emancipation? What, above all, did it do? These questions go beyond matters of inheritance, validity, legal capacity, and fraud, forming part of a larger question—what was the nature of emancipation in medieval law?

In modern historiography, there are two positions on the nature of emancipation. Bellomo espoused the thesis that emancipation must have been "extraordinary," "extreme," and "occasional" to a society based, as he sees it, on familial groupings. Working mainly from statutory rubrics, he concluded that emancipation was used by the family as a remedy against a prodigal member or as a means of escaping creditors. Emancipation, in other words, accompanied critical and adverse moments in a family's existence.[116]

With regard to emancipation, Bellomo's assertions about its function rest on his conclusion (undocumented) that the *praemium* was "a conspicuous part of the familial patrimony"[117] that functioned in a manner analogous to the dowry. He interprets the legal separation of son from father as a physical and patrimonial separation (certainly involving separate residence on the part of the son), although he does believe that many aspects of the father-son relationship survived emancipation. Bellomo, however, ignores the fact that women, too, could be and were emancipated; that property need not be given to an emancipatus; and that if it were given, it need not amount to much. He also glosses over the fact that the emancipated male was not cut off from inheritance in the same seemingly absolute manner as his dowered sister.

In contrast to Bellomo's approach to emancipation, other legal historians have looked not at function but at ideology. Nino Tamassia, for example, was concerned with the *patria potestas*; his thesis is that the *patria potestas* was gradually limited in scope if not in duration. Emancipation itself was a means of severing "the strongest and most resistant of familial bonds."[118] The dissolution of the *patria potestas* brought about by emancipation was a positive act for the child. Enrico Besta similarly viewed emancipation as an advantage (*beneficium*) for the child, because it gave him or her legal capacity while not severing ties to the family or succession rights.[119] Sergio Mochi Onory, also concentrating on the legal figure of the child, emphasized the fact that emancipation created a new legal *persona* and that, therefore, it operated as a kind of freedom from a superior power.[120] All three historians conceived of *patria potestas* as onerous; therefore, emancipation appeared to them as a benefit for the emancipatus because it freed him or her from that power.

Turning from modern historiography to the medieval jurists, we quickly see that emancipation was a kind of freedom to medieval jurisprudents as well. The *Glossa ordinaria* decided that a grandson who had not been emancipated but whose father had, did not fall subject to his father's *potestas* at the death of the grandfather, because the grandson had been *quasi liberatus* by the emancipation of his father and "he who has been liberated cannot later be returned [to subjection]."[121] Bartolus, it will be remembered, said that a *pater invitus* could be forced to emancipate his son because the loss of his *potestas* over the child was a penalty for the father, but emancipation did not constitute a penalty for the child because "to be emancipated is not a penalty for a son but liberty."[122] So, too, Baldus, drawing on Cino da Pistoia, twice made apparent his adherence to the view that "emancipation is a form of freedom."[123]

Not all medieval jurists, however, agreed with the viewpoint espoused by Bartolus and Baldus. Odofredus, for instance, envisioned emancipation and disinheritance as equal forms of punishment (not, therefore, to be done without reason).[124] In equating emancipation with disinheritance, Odofredus seems to have thought of it as expulsion from the home, rather than simply as a legal proceeding. Perhaps he had in mind a contemporary statute of Bologna that considered emancipation, accompanied by the legitimate share of the estate, as punishment for a son who wasted his father's wealth.[125]

The prevailing view, however, seems to have been that emancipation was not a form of punishment for a child but an honor. Jacopo d'Arena introduced the term *honor* into the discussion of the nature of emancipation, declaring that it was an honor because the emancipatus was free to act legally.[126] Bartolus credited Jacopo with originating the idea when he, too, espoused the view that emancipation was an honor for all but adopted sons.[127] Emancipation was an honor because the child, in effect, lost nothing—neither his family ties nor his right to the succession—while his father relinquished his *patria potestas*.

In an analogous manner, Angelus de Ubaldis employed the term *liberalitas* (generosity or beneficence) to describe the nature of emancipation. Angelus emphasized the honor being bestowed on the emancipatus by concentrating on the father's incredible generosity implied in emancipation:

> Note that when a father emancipates his son he exercises liberality toward him because he makes him a *homo sui iuris*, he gives him the power of making a will and of doing other similar acts, and the son acquires not only the *adventitia* but also the *profectitia*. Because a father can give to an emancipated son, therefore, he exercises liberality. It is not required of the father that he give to his son *in praemium emancipationis*, but as it is the custom [in doing so], he adds liberality to liberality.[128]

The medieval jurists' conception of emancipation as an honor, a *beneficium* (in the feudal sense of benefice), and a *liberalitas* rested on a more fundamental conception of the nature and character of the *patria potestas*. In part, that conception rested on the distinction between *patria potestas* and the *mundium* of the Lombard law. As the commentator on Lombard law, Carlo di Tocco (fl. ca. 1200), noted, the *mundium* could be sold or given to another; in contrast, the *patria potestas* could not be alienated, and no price could be placed on it. The *patria potestas* was inestimable,[129] and so, too, was the freedom from the *patria potestas* conferred by emancipation.[130]

The *patria potestas* was much more than inestimable. In discussing the requirements for a valid emancipation, Baldus touched on another essential feature of the *patria potestas*. He stated that emancipation had to consist of a public act not only "because emancipation in itself is an inestimable gift" but also "because the *patria potestas* is sacred." And because it was sacred, the *patria potestas*, according to Baldus, could not be subject to the terms of an arbitration; in other words, an arbitrator could not order a father to emancipate his son and give him a *praemium*.[131]

Because the *potestas* was sacred, the son owed his father *pietas*. A later addition to the notarial formulary of Rolandino Passaggieri emphasized that the person of the father was always to seem "honest, sacred, and holy" to his son, even if the father did not act in accord with his *potestas*. The same source stated that the son truly owed the father a *praemium* because "he does him an honor in making him *sui iuris*." The gift of emancipation was such that "the law takes care that the emancipatus must serve the father in honor and reverence more than if he were in his power."[132]

Not only was the *patria potestas* a sacred power, making one flesh and one voice of father and child, but it was also a power that worked largely to the benefit of the father. Only very extreme acts injurious to the welfare of the child could impel a court to demand a judicial emancipation in the face of an unwilling father. The fact that the father would lose all of those powers listed in the *Glossa ordinaria* must have given the law good reason to hesitate in stripping him of his paternal authority. If the natural process of growth and aging were not sufficient to bring that "sacred" power to an end, it must have, indeed, appeared to be an awesome power. In fact, Paolo di Castro found a key to the perpetual nature of *patria potestas* in its legal meaning:

> Say that *patria potestas* was not invented for covering a child's defect in age, because, if it were, once the defect in age came to an end the *patria potestas* would cease, just as the power of a guardian ceases [when his ward comes of age]; but the contrary is true because even a sexagenarian can be in *patria potestate*. It was therefore invented in favor of the father himself, so that he may acquire things through his child and so that he can exercise it on the person of his child in favor of the father himself.[133]

There can be no more forceful statement of how the *patria potestas*, sacred and perpetual, existed in law for the benefit of its holder.

Yet there were legal limits to the father's *potestas*, as both Besta and

Tamassia have argued. The same *additio* to Passaggieri also noted that the son's duty of honor, reverence, and *pietas* to his father did not necessarily extend to obedience in tasks assigned him.[134] Bartolus declared that a father was due reverence and defense in word and deed (*verbo et opere*) but filial obligation did not necessarily extend to actual physical combat (*opponendo se*).[135] Baldus also set a limit on the son's reverential subservience to his father when he declared invalid an obligation made to a father by a son out of fear or excessive reverence for the father.[136] The son *in potestate* was not completely without legal capacities either, for, as Baldus said, a son was entitled to the profit he made by his own industry in business even if he had used his father's money.[137]

Medieval jurists' assessment of the jural character of emancipation as a kind of freedom and honor appears to jeopardize Bellomo's view of the nature of emancipation. With some exceptions, those who theorized about emancipation, who were members, moreover, of that society in which emancipation was operative did not conceive of emancipation as a low point in familial fortunes, a means of cutting off a patrimonial liability. To be sure, Bartolus did say that the emancipatus ceased to be a member of the family, but we must avoid reading into his statements more than he intended.[138] As the language of the notarial documents made abundantly clear, emancipation created a second *paterfamilias*, that was why the emancipatus was no longer a member of the family in terms of the civil law and why, according to Baldus, there were legally two families after emancipation,[139] a notion that was a legal fiction fabricated by the jurists to avoid conceptual chaos.[140] The creation of this second family did not change the son's civic rights or residence; it did not remove the "relics" of previous paternal power.[141]

On the other hand, to what extent was emancipation a form of freedom? If emancipation formally conferred freedom from paternal authority, how much substance was likely to accompany that form?

The civil law was concerned with matters of status, with dependence or independence and not with the mental or physical capacity or incapacity of the emancipatus. The law did not emphasize the ability of an individual to realize his or her newly acquired rights; only the ability to consent to emancipation mattered. Medieval law did not set an emancipatory age of majority at which a child would be considered legally mature regardless of the existence of his or her father. This feature common to modern Western law was established only in the sixteenth century in such areas as northern France, where customary law was under heavy Germanic influence.[142] Given that the law did not consider the child's maturity or experience, in practical terms, whose decision and consent carried more weight—the father's or the child's? It was the father, the one with age and experience, the possessor of the *patria potestas*, who surely was the prime agent behind most emancipations.

If the father were the prime agent in most emancipations, it seems, according to legal historians at least, that the same cannot be said in the case of tacit emancipations. Legal historians place great store on the fact that the son could literally move out of the house and thus figuratively escape paternal authority. In concurring with the view that emancipation was a benefit for the emancipatus, Pier Silverio Leicht says:

> We observe that medieval emancipation preserved the character it had in the last evolution of Roman law, that is, it was considered as a largess granted to the son more than as a separation from his paternal family. For some time it had not borne damaging consequences for the emancipatus in the area of inheritance. The fact that emancipation was seen more as an advantage than as a loss is seen by the fact that it was accorded tacitly to the son who carried on trade even though he remained in his father's house. . . . This provision was evidently taken in order to favor the lad and make his activity easier, certainly not to punish him.[143]

Leicht (like Besta and Tamassia) sees tacit emancipation as the result of something the child did on his own merits (for example, engage in trade, move away from home). If, however, the *patria potestas* were so awesome, indeed sacred, according to medieval jurists, we are justified in questioning whether the child's merits carried any legal weight even in tacit emancipation. After all, who was the tacit party?; was it not the father?

When lawyers discussed tacit emancipations, they placed their emphasis on the father, on his knowledge of, and consent to, his son's activities. Baldus, for example, declared that it was necessary for a period of ten years to intervene before a son who lived apart from his father could be deemed truly tacitly emancipated; it was not enough for the son to leave his father's house. The time interval indicated that the father had chosen not to exercise his *potestas* over the son, that he tacitly agreed to the state of affairs in which his son acted as if his father did not exist.[144] Baldus took the same position with regard to the tacit emancipation of a son who did not necessarily live apart from his father, but who acted legally as if he were emancipated. If the father knew and suffered this state of affairs, said Baldus, then after a period of ten years during which the son acted as if emancipated, one could consider the customary pattern of activity as legally indicative of emancipation. Interestingly, these statements follow a discussion of how a father might dispute, deny, or revoke his son's emancipation.[145] In both cases, the father's silence was seen to imply consent; furthermore, the passage of time turned his consent into a legally binding contract that he could no longer deny or reverse.[146]

The jurists' emphasis on the extent of paternal power and on the father's role in tacit emancipations is, finally, indicative of the fact that in their eyes, the emancipatus' relations and obligations were not completely severed by emancipation. Emancipation enabled him to act legally; it did not make him act. The emancipatus could remain at home, doing nothing differently than before, and that home was still run by the father whom he was used to obeying and honoring. In fact, it can be argued that emancipation cemented the relationship between the two parties by creating a nexus of obligations.[147] The commentator to the notarial formulary of Passaggieri declared that an emancipatus owed his father even more reverence and honor than a child *in potestate*, basing this opinion on the fact that emancipation was an *honor*, a favor undeserved by the emancipatus, and a *beneficium*, a gift that placed the child in his father's debt. The addition of a *praemium* only increased the size of the *beneficium* and made it material in part. The illustrious Florentine lawyer, messer Antonio di Vanni di Francesco Strozzi (1455–1523) wrote in his legal glossary that the *pater emancipans* need not give the son or daughter a *praemium* since "the son is more obligated to his father, because he is emancipated, than if he were under paternal power."[148] He, too, saw that emancipation established an even greater obligation than the one inherent in the *patria potestas*.

Emancipation changed the legal relationship of status (that between a *pater* and a *filius*) to a contractual relationship generated by the nature of emancipation itself (not to mention any subsequent contracts between father and child to fashion legal ties).[149] It did not necessarily, and of itself, bring about change in residence, wealth, or activity; we cannot, in fact, talk about wealth, household, age, or other factors without first looking at actual emancipations and other relevant documents.

CHAPTER TWO

Florentine Laws

To determine what treatment emancipation received in Florentine communal legislation, it is necessary to wade through a morass of statutes and *provvisioni* where there is the same disorganization that made contemporaries despair in the face of the mutability and ambiguity of Florentine legislation.[1] The Florentine statute redactions of 1322 and 1325 and that of 1415 exist in printed editions. A third redaction of 1355 is found only in manuscript in the Archivio di Stato of Florence, as are the over 200 volumes of *provvisioni*, legislation of *balie*, and the statutes of the Mercanzia and the guilds.[2] The archives also contain numerous statute books of *comuni soggetti*, those cities of Tuscany that fell under Florentine dominion. The subject communities' statutes were, however, made to harmonize with those of Florence,[3] so that any attempt at comparison must be based on those statutes that were less affected by the Florentine model.

Florentine statutory law "took for granted many of the principles of Roman law, especially in matters regarding property, contracts, rebellion, the position of the father, and aspects of civil status";[4] therefore, the statutes do not bother to define or describe emancipation. They are concerned with only a limited range of questions involving procedures, validity, and effects.

That Florence or any other commune should have enacted procedural guidelines for emancipation is not surprising in view of the fact that civil law left matters of judicial competence to communal administration and local custom. It was the individual commune that provided the administrative machinery and officials who were to lend public authority to emancipations. In Florence, as in most Italian communes, all notaries who were matriculated in the guild of lawyers and notaries were *iudices ordinarii* (ordinary judges). As *iudex ordinarius* a notary could clearly preside at an emancipation, for he had the prerogative of lending public authority to issue decrees in matters of voluntary jurisdiction.[5] The notary represented the commune at an emancipation as, in an earlier era, an imperial official (*missus*) had

35

represented the emperor at emancipations.[6] For their services, the notaries were allowed by guild statute to charge a fee of five *soldi*, which
was the highest fixed rate they could charge for any legal service.[7]

Florentine law did not indicate the exact form that an emancipation
was to take, nor did it specify any requirements, unlike the legislation
of other communes. The legislation of Florence, and the cities of Tuscany in general, also did not set age limitations on emancipation. Bellomo, Besta, and Antonio Pertile all found statutes of other communes that fixed a minimum, and occasionally, a maximum age for
emancipation;[8] at Como, for example, there was a minimum age of 14.
Each commune, of course, established an age of majority (the age
when emancipated children and those whose fathers had died were
deemed to be full adults), and it is important to keep in mind that the
age of majority in Florence was 18;[9] however, these ages were legally
unrelated to emancipation.[10]

In the Italian city-states, emancipation was not performed in a prominently public place such as the cathedral steps or the main piazza of
the city or neighborhood as it had been formerly. Generally, the only
people present at an emancipation were the principals, the judge, and
the witnesses. The communes, therefore, had to establish means of
publicizing the fact to interested parties and of proving it;[11] each city
was left to coin its own solution. One common method was to have the
emancipation proclaimed by the town herald in the same way that
communal legislation and other matters were made public. At Bologna, the herald was required to publish the details of an emancipation
on both stairways of the communal palace, in the family's neighborhood or village, and before the family's home or homes. Failure to
have statutory requirements observed (which was the responsibility
of the father and the emancipatus) nullified the emancipation, and
this was true in every commune.[12] Florence resorted to a publication
procedure for emancipations similar to that of Bologna: Emancipations and other matters of law were broadcast by heralds at the palace
of the Podestà, at Or San Michele, and at two places in each quarter of
the city.[13]

There can be no doubt that the notarial charter of emancipation was
admissible as proof of emancipation. Some cities, Florence among
them, also admitted as proof any complete mention (that is, including
the date, father's and son's names, and the name of the notary) of the
emancipation in any contract properly drawn up by a notary.[14] In Florence, it was also possible for anyone who wished to prove an emancipation to go to the notary and have him furnish a copy of the emancipation charter. These procedures for verification remained a feature
of Florentine law throughout the period covered in this study.[15]

The most common solution to the dual problems of publicizing and verifying an emancipation was to register all emancipations. This practical step allowed the announcement of an emancipation while, at the same time, maintaining a convenient written record that could serve as proof. Florence turned to this expedient later than most cities,[16] for by the time the commune passed legislation in 1355 that mandated registering emancipations, Siena had had such a law for a century.[17] The Florentine law prescribed that all emancipations occurring in the city or its *contado* or district had to be reported to the judge of the Mercanzia within 15 days or one month of the emancipation, depending on one's place of residence, or within two months if the emancipation occurred outside Florentine territory. Notification to the Mercanzia was to include all particulars: names of father and child, name of notary, date of emancipation. Any emancipation not duly reported was to be "of no effect or moment." The officials of the Mercanzia were also required to have these reported emancipations recorded in a book and each entry was to contain the appropriate information in a clear hand and the book was to be shown gratis to anyone who asked to see it.[18]

The Mercanzia, as the tribunal of merchants and commercial affairs, received jurisdiction in registering emancipations because emancipation affected financial liability in Florentine law as well as the ownership of property, rights, and legal abilities.[19] The government was concerned with emancipation in so far as it affected third parties who might have financial or other dealings with the father or with his emancipated offspring.

The Mercanzia began recording emancipations immediately after passing the law. Care was taken to keep the registers up-to-date, organized (by marginal notations), and legible. In 1410, the Mercanzia found it necessary, however, to warn its notaries to stop making errors and overcharging those who reported emancipations.[20]

In 1421, matters became confused by the adoption into law of a second, different registration law. This second *provvisione* was much like the first but with some important differences: A person who lived in the city itself had one month in which to report an emancipation (the previous time limit had been 15 days); in addition, a tariff of one florin for every emancipatus was set. The *provvisione* of 1421 also incorporated an important change in legal language that had previously appeared in the statutes of 1415 and had been enacted into law in the first years of the fifteenth century: An unregistered emancipation would henceforth be invalid "with regard to the benefit and convenience of the emancipatus."[21] This language had not been part of the original *provvisione* of 1355 concerning the registration of emancipations, but it was to play an important role for lawyers who were called on to render opinions in cases affected by this law, because the wording left open what constituted benefit and convenience.

The most obvious change worked by the legislation of 1421 was that the commune itself began to register emancipations. The previous law of 1355 was not suspended, so the Mercanzia continued to register emancipations; however, the commune ran its own parallel registration, encroaching on the jurisdiction of the Mercanzia.[22] Notification of the facts of an emancipation was to be given not only to the judge of the Mercanzia but also to the priors of the commune, who thereby delegated to themselves a measure of power and information. The Signoria retained its control over emancipations until 1534, when administrative and legal reforms of the Duke Alessandro returned registration once again solely to the hands of the Mercanzia.

By charging one florin for registration, the commune had escalated the cost of an emancipation from ten *soldi* (five for the notary, five for registering with the Mercanzia) to one florin and ten *soldi*, an increase of roughly tenfold. The law may have thus, intentionally or unintentionally, created a financial deterrent to emancipation and compliance with the registration requirement—with all its legal consequences.[23]

Legislative Intent: The Problem of Fraud

There was an important reason for establishing procedures for announcing and proving an emancipation: They were intended to prevent misinformation and misunderstanding that could and did result in defrauding creditors. Emancipation was always potentially open to use as a means of defrauding creditors in a manner similar to that outlined by Baldus in his commentary. Registering emancipations, however, gave creditors or potential creditors protection by informing them of who was liable for whom and who owned what property. It was no accident that the first *provvisione* mandating registration was passed in 1355, just seven years after the plague had left social and economic chaos in its destructive wake.[24]

The law of 1355 made its motivations very explicit. It began by stating that the priors were desirous of preventing Florentine citizens from being cheated and decreed that unless an emancipation were properly reported, "it should be presumed to have been fictitious and simulated and done in fraud of creditors."[25] The very same law also required registering repudiations of inheritance for the same expressed reason—to preclude fraud. These measures, in fact, followed by less than one month four petitions received from creditors who sought the right to seize and sell the property of their debtors who had fled the city to avoid payment. Although none of the four petitions mentioned that emancipation had been used to deceive the creditors, at least two of the cases involved sons of living parents. The Mercanzia, the body made responsible for registering emancipations, was also the administrative organ charged with enforcing the commune's statutes against delinquent debtors who had fled the city to escape their creditors.[26]

The law of 1421 had the same intent as that of 1355—to put a stop to the fraudulent use of emancipation or, in its words, "so that the road to fraud may be made more difficult."[27] The repetition of registration legislation in 1421 indicates that the law of 1355 had not been fully effective but the legislation was also rewritten in 1421 because at that time, the question of fraud was tied to a pressing problem of economic stagnation, a cause for political concern among the ruling elite. The emancipation law of 1421 can, therefore, be seen as the response by the city's rulers to the problem of economic stagnation resulting from illegal and unethical business practices.

It may have been part of a legislative program that created the magistracy of the Sea Consuls only nine days earlier on 13 December 1421. According to Gene Brucker, the legislation creating the Sea Consuls marked the beginning of a "campaign [designed] to strengthen the Florentine economy by means of subsidy and supervision."[28] The fact that the Sea Consuls were empowered to intervene in areas formerly under the jurisdiction of the guilds parallels the commune's encroachment upon the jurisdiction of the Mercanzia in registering emancipations. The detailed survey of persons and assets that formed the cornerstone of the *catasto* of 1427 was also designed to cope with fraud and evasion of fiscal obligations. The number of delinquent taxpayers in the official list, the *speculum*, had increased dramatically, so that tax evasion was a huge problem for the government and an indication of the economic troubles besetting Florence. Since emancipation could affect an exemption from the *speculum*, it was also for this reason in the interests of the government to keep track of emancipations.[29]

Fraud, real or imagined, was a constant feature of business life in Florence and elsewhere. The tales of Giovanni Sercambi of Lucca, for example, were peopled by robbers, cheats, forgers, and other thieves. The writer was almost obsessed with the omnipresence of fraud and theft, and Florentine businessmen shared his concern.[30] And uncollected debts, one result of fraud, were a major cause of business difficulties in Florence.[31]

Yet, in a real sense, Florentines were their own worst enemies. In a world that they saw as hostile, they considered it permissible to fight fire with fire, to meet fraud and deceit with fraud and deceit. Christian ethics were tossed aside at times in favor of the demands of honor and profit. Francesco Guicciardini, perhaps a more astute observer of his society than any other Florentine, openly assigned deception a prominent place in the conduct of one's affairs. What mattered was that the deception remain hidden, that the appearance of honorable and honest dealing be maintained; in his words:

> It is much praised in men and it is pleasing to everyone to be by nature free and forthright and, as they say in Florence, sincere. On the other hand, deception is despised and hated; but it is nevertheless much more useful in itself, while forthrightness works more immediately for others than for oneself. But because one cannot deny that it is not good, I would praise anyone who ordinarily acted freely and sincerely, using deception only in some important thing, which things rarely arise. Thus you would acquire a name for being free and forthright, and you would attract that favor that belongs to one who is held to be of such a nature; and nevertheless, in the things that matter most, you would derive benefit from deception, and so much the more as, having a reputation for not being a deceiver, your artifices would more easily be believed.[32]

Honesty could, quite frankly, serve the purposes of dishonesty; simulation and deception were established patterns of actions even if Guicciardini relegated them to important matters only. Leon Battista Alberti and Matteo Palmieri similarly endorsed the use of extralegal, underhand methods in conducting one's affairs.[33] To defraud another or not to meet one's obligations was dishonorable, to be sure, but dishonor was and is relative.[34] Besides, it was also dishonorable to be poor and miserable in late medieval Florence;[35] one had to do everything possible to avoid poverty, and one did not owe the same loyalty and honesty to others that one owed to relatives.[36]

Fraud harmed its victims and gave the city and its citizens a bad name, which, in turn, had both economic and psychological effects.[37] Throughout the fifteenth century there was, in fact, a constant effort on the part of the government to thwart attempts to defraud both the commune and private citizens. More often than not, the government took legislative action to counter fraud from an expressed desire both to protect the honest and innocent and to stimulate a lagging economy. Material and moral welfare were so closely connected as to be hardly distinguishable by the legislators and their advisers.

A review of just some fifteenth-century enactments to counter fraud indicates the continual and persistent nature of the problem and the measures taken to solve it. One measure arising from this concern with fraud was enacted into law in 1408 at the request of the Mercanzia.

The six officials of that body complained that Florentine custom, contrary to custom elsewhere, allowed one partner in a firm to obligate the other(s) not solely for the quantity of money put in his hands for the purpose of the firm's business but for all of his partners' property. This situation, it was alleged, caused people to withdraw from trade and many young men and "other virtuous persons" to lose initial capital, resulting in general loss of trade "on which the city of Florence is founded." For the sake of the merchants and the good of the city, then, the six requested that a law be passed requiring all who were entrusted with the funds of others for business purposes to register their names and the amount as well as the identity of those whose money was involved. Thus, the liability of others could be limited to the amount involved. The Mercanzia also requested a second paragraph in the law that similarly required registering names and sums involved if fathers, grandfathers, brothers, or paternal uncles gave business capital to their sons, grandsons, brothers, or nephews. The amount they turned over was subject to subsequent claims arising from business ventures without regard to whether or not the relative lived in the same house and practiced the same trade in the same shop.[38]

Another enactment concerned with fraudulent practices dates from 30 October 1458. On that date, a *provvisione* was passed by the Signoria ordering the registration of all *compromissa* (arbitration agreements) that were to last for more than three years, so as to preclude their use as a means of deceiving and cheating others.[39] Such a *compromissum*, for whatever reason it had been established, could suddenly be invoked to redistribute property ownership to the detriment of an unwary creditor.[40] Another law of 20 March 1477, written in the vernacular, spoke with impassioned eloquence of the way in which many were victimized by secret contracts (*contracti occulti*) that tied up property in a web of legal entanglements, safe from the claims of creditors. So many were cheated that people became reluctant to engage in business dealings even when the other party was acting in good faith; therefore, it was not only honest but necessary to remedy the situation. The cure hit upon was registering all alienations of property and all obligations imposed on property by means of a contract. The officials of the *gabella* on contracts were required by law to keep an accurate record and to index it, so that the mass of information did not defeat the purpose of the law.[41]

It is doubtful if such steps were successful, since economic crises continued despite these administrative efforts.[42] The laws, too, show that the problem of financial fraud and its prevention remained a lively and active concern. It is interesting to note that the regular means of preventing contract fraud was a form of registration modeled on that used for emancipations and cited as a precedent and exemplar by the law of 1458.

In general, registration laws designed to prevent the use of emancipation as an artifice of deception and fraud were common in the statutory enactments of the Italian communes. In addition to asserting that an improperly fulfilled emancipation was not valid, the laws also frequently specified that creditors were not to be hurt by such an emancipation.[43] The measures taken by the government of Florence, therefore, were fully consonant with prevailing legislative practice.

Extended Liability

Alongside the various registration laws that attempted to prevent fraud was a second set of laws that attempted to right its wrongs. This second set of laws, which dealt with the question of liability, remained rather constant throughout the fourteenth and fifteenth centuries and, most importantly, formed the context within which emancipation took on a peculiar legal meaning for the Florentine citizenry. As the complaints of the Mercanzia on the occasion of the law of 1408 indicate, the custom in Florence was to widely distribute and extend financial liability over kinsmen and business associates and their property. In the case of emancipation, the area of significance is the extension of liability over kinsmen.

A Florentine father was liable for the debts and obligations of his son or grandson if the son was a merchant or artisan—that is, if he were a member of a guild or acted like a businessman. In such a case, the son's manifest activities led to a supposition that he acted with his father's knowledge if not consent. The father could avoid liability on his son's behalf by one of two means: He could declare before his son's guild that he refused to be held liable any longer for his son's debts; or he could emancipate his son and thereby terminate his liability. Normally a Florentine father was not liable, however, for any contracts made by a son who was not a merchant or artisan and who entered into obligations without paternal consent,[44] since there was no basis for assuming that the father knew of, or condoned, his son's activity. The sons were, of course, liable for their obligations in any case.

The reverse situation also applied in Florence: A son or grandson was liable for his father's debts and obligations unless he had been emancipated. For daughters, dowry and marriage constituted exemption from liability.[45] The liability itself was of most immediate concern when the father had defaulted on his obligations and fled the city to escape his creditors. Since he was then not available to face up to his obligations, the law made his children face them. In fact, Florentine statutes stated that a son not emancipated could be jailed at the request of his bankrupt father's creditors and a similar fate awaited the brothers of a bankrupt who lived together with him after the death of their father. For sons who had been emancipated prior to their father's default, however, liability extended only to that property, if any, in their possession that may have belonged to the father at the time of his default and flight.[46] Given the liability of unemancipated sons for their fathers in Florentine law, it is clear that emancipation carried definite advantages for the emancipatus,[47] since it limited and mitigated the effects of the statutory principles.[48]

The severely punitive Florentine legislation that extended the liability of delinquent debtors rested on the equivalence drawn between judicial contumacy and flight and crime. Contumacious debtors were criminals; their contumacy was taken as evidence of criminal and fraudulent intent, so they fell subject to the same judicial ban as criminal and political exiles. Extension of liability and penalties to kin were based on the view of kinsmen that lay behind vendetta, which plagued Florence and other cities, especially in the thirteenth century. In other words, a view of kinsmen as a group aware of, consenting to, and responsible for the actions of any one member. Such an extension of liability, however, clearly ran contrary to the principles of civil law and the ideals of those trained in it.[49]

The statutes defining extended liability, first gathered together in the redactions of the first quarter of the fourteenth century but actually of considerably older vintage (1252–1286), were incorporated in all later redactions with appropriate additions and corrections. They also appeared in the statute books of the Mercanzia, which enforced them after 1309.[50] The only change included in the communal statutes of 1355 was the addition of the requirement of registering all emancipations to the statute on the obligations of sons and fathers.[51] The redaction of 1415, undertaken by the jurists Paolo di Castro and Bartolomeo Vulpi, effected a far more extensive and logical reorganization of the material; the substance of the law, however, was little changed.

The 1415 redaction clarified the extent to which emancipation applied in terminating liabilities between father and son by furnishing precise temporal parameters. Emancipation had to precede the time of the contract that established a father's obligation to a third party by six months. If a child were not yet born at the time the contract was drawn up, he or she had to have been emancipated at least six months before the father's default and flight. Property given to an emancipated son had to have been in his possession for at least one year before his father's bankruptcy in order to be immune from seizure for paternal debt.[52] The use of temporal intervals as proof of intent in the Florentine statutes parallels the use of temporal factors in establishing intent by the jurisconsults Giovanni d'Anagni and Pietro d'Ancarano, who considered objective temporal factors indicative of underlying subjective motivations.

Finally, in 1477, an amendment to the statutes declared that a *filiusfamilias* (therefore not emancipated) could obligate himself in his father's property and prerogatives only if he were 25 years of age and had paternal consent.[53] By placing an age limit (the age of majority in Roman law) on the son's ability to obligate his father and requiring the father's consent (further limiting the son's ability to obligate and thus possibly harm his father), this revision clarified doubts concerning the legality of such obligations. As a result, the father's position was less vulnerable when his son was not emancipated.

In general, Florentine law on debts was in conflict with Roman law as understood in the schools. In Roman law, the debts of an unemancipated son could be realized from the father's property—from the patrimony, in other words, upon which the son as future heir had some claim and was considered a sort of owner. But this liability only extended to that share of the patrimony due the one son (the *pars filii*);[54] Florentine law set no such limit. Furthermore, provisions in Florentine law for detaining, jailing, and exiling an unemancipated son for his father's debts and seizing the son's property for those debts were totally outside Roman legal precedents. The conflict between Florentine law, which considered the interests of the city's bankers and merchants whose livelihood depended on the fulfillment of credit obligations, and Roman law created problems of interpretation for the city's legal experts. Nonetheless, the fact that emancipation terminated liability made it important in the eyes of Florentines, for whom it became urgent to register the legally relevant facts of an emancipation in order to determine if liability existed in any given case.

Delinquent taxpayers' names were entered on a list, and until they met their obligations, they were prohibited from holding political office. In taxation, as in matters of private debt, liability extended to the delinquent taxpayers' sons along with the corresponding political disabilities. However, a law passed on 11 September 1409 absolved sons from political disabilities incurred by their fathers if they were emancipated, lived apart from their fathers, and were assessed separately from their fathers. The same three conditions also exempted fathers from political liabilities incurred by their sons. The legislators, in employing all three criteria—legal, physical, and fiscal—to determine if a son were "separated," thus created the narrowest and most valid possible exception to the political disability occasioned by the *speculum*.[55] At least with regard to taxes, emancipation alone was not enough.

In the area of criminal liability, Florence's statutes conformed to the norms of Roman law, which established a system of individual liability for crimes. In Florence, therefore, a father could not suffer for a son's crime. If the son were not emancipated, the father could be forced by the courts to hand over that share of the patrimony destined to the son (the *pars contingens*) as reparation for the son's crime. If, on the other hand, the son were emancipated, the father was in no way liable for him;[56] extending criminal liability to sons if their fathers fell under the judicial ban was, however, contrary to civil law.

Florentine criminal legislation was consistent in this regard with that of many other communes. Florentine law, however, did not go so far as that of other communes that held the father responsible for the crimes of his emancipated sons in order to insure that he would make the son's property available for reparation.[57] In general, as far as paternal responsibility for filial actions was concerned, the difference between the father's civil and criminal responsibility for his son lay in the fact that the son was seen to be acting freely in criminal matters.

In those areas of civil law founded on natural law (according to the jurists), Florentine statutes conformed with the legal principles that demanded a son's reverence and respect toward his father; here, emancipation made no difference.[58] When a son acted contrary to natural law, when he attempted to harm his parents or lead an evil life—playing dice, frequenting taverns, and associating with disreputable persons—his father could request that the *Podestà* incarcerate his son until such time as the boy should return to a good and obedient form of life. Such dishonorable and disgusting behavior was subject to punishment at the discretion of the father whether or not the son was emancipated. In no case was the word of the son, emancipated or not, accepted over that of his father.[59] Emancipation made no difference in these matters, except that it raised the question of who was the father—the holder of the *patria potestas* (in which case it could be the paternal grandfather) or the natural father.

In a similar manner, sons were compelled by Florentine law to supply their parents with *alimenta* if their parents were in need. This legal obligation applied to both emancipated and unemancipated children.[60] (At no point was emancipation a punishment for filial prodigality, disreputable behavior, or failure to give parents *alimenta*—in contrast to the treatment of emancipation in Bolognese law.) A final area where emancipation made no difference in Florentine law was inheritance, in fact none of the many Florentine statutes dealing with inheritance made mention of emancipation. Here, the city's statutes rested perforce on what civil law had to say about emancipation and perhaps also on the civil law's dictum regarding intestate succession that "today the difference between *patria potestas* and emancipation is overcome."[61]

The Nature of Emancipation in Florentine Law

As set out both implicitly and explicitly in the Florentine statutes, the *patria potestas* was generally durable, strong, and far-reaching.[62] Taking perhaps as point of departure such a vision of the *patria potestas* as that expressed by the jurists who said that a father and his son were one flesh and one voice, the statutes of Florence reached beyond Roman law to give legal substance to the *patria potestas*. As a result, the Florentine *filiusfamilias* faced certain disabilities and incapacities in addition to those incorporated in Roman law. A Florentine father had the option of avoiding liability for his son's debts by making a declaration to the guild council; the son had no corresponding option. If he were not emancipated, he was liable for his father's debts. In order to be emancipated and thus free of financial responsibility for his father, the son needed his father's consent; otherwise he had to prove that his father was prodigal (as the Roman law specified), but the burden of proof was on the son, and the law was weighted in favor of the father in such matters. Likewise, the statute of Florence made explicit the children's obligation to feed and care for a needy parent, but it did not mention the reciprocal obligation, which was contained in the Roman law. In fact, at some point in the thirteenth century, Florentine law had absolved the father from the necessity of feeding and clothing a son who had reached the statutory age of majority of 18.[63] The law mentioned the father's right to have peace and tranquility and to discipline his child, not the child's right to have peace and freedom from the parent's unnatural and unlawful behavior.

In Florentine law, emancipation must, indeed, have been an honor for the child, whom it made jurally a person, not merely an extension (*per lineam masculinam*) of the father. Emancipation, in fact, carried more weight in Florentine law than in Roman law because in Florence it also brought freedom from liability for paternal debts. Given the volatile nature of private fortunes in the fourteenth and fifteenth centuries, even an astute merchant could become financially strapped.[64] Emancipation furnished a potential means of mitigating the effects of financial disaster on either the father or the child by terminating their mutual liability.

The prime agent in emancipation must, however, have been the *pater emancipans*; at least everything in Florentine law relevant to emancipation favored him. He was the one charged with reporting the emancipation to the communal authorities. If he failed to do so, the child thereby lost the benefits of emancipation (a fact that was especially apparent after the terminological change limiting negation of emancipation to areas of convenience for the emancipatus). The period of 15 days or a month could also give the father an opportunity to reconsider and, in effect, revoke the emancipation by not registering it.

Tacit emancipation, which has often been cited as an indication of *patria potestas* weakening in the later Middle Ages, was more or less obviated by Florentine statutes. In Florence, a *filiusfamilias* was not legally prevented or prohibited from engaging in business or practicing a trade. Laws concerned with the liabilities of fathers for sons were predicated on the son's ability to enter into business contracts, and his engagement in such activities in an institutionally regular manner was taken to imply knowledge and consent on the part of the father.[65] Any contractual engagement by a son who did not belong to a guild or similarly act in a socially recognized businesslike manner and who operated without his father's consent was ipso facto null and void.[66] What Florentine law was concerned with was whether, and to what extent, a son's business activities could reach beyond his shop to touch property in the hands of his father (the family's patrimony). In this regard, the father's denial of his confidence in his son or emancipating him absolved the father and his property from liability on the son's account.

Emancipation must be seen not so much as a commercially, but as a patrimonially enabling act. It gave the emancipatus the right to manage directly his wife's dowry (if married) and his own *peculia*, and it gave him access to the legal means to do so, especially by empowering him to write his own last will and testament and enter into contracts not directly related to his business and trade. Emancipation in Florence was, therefore, not associated with such conditions generally indicative of tacit emancipation as professional activities and separate residence; rather, emancipation was associated with independent legal control of the patrimony.[67]

The emancipatus continued to be part of the family, as Bellomo, for one, has argued. Although he "left the subjection to the *patria potestas* and the more restricted familial community [a doubtful point], he did not thereby become estranged from the house."[68] Emancipation did not necessarily mark the breakup of the family; it did mean the legal loss of some of its patrimonial unity. Emancipation introduced flexibility into familial and patrimonial relations by freeing father and son from mutual liabilities. A son could, in legal theory at least, administer and acquire his own patrimony; he could enter into legal arrangements previously unavailable to him or not available without his father's consent. His father, on the other hand, could rest assured that the emancipated son's business activities would not create liabilities extending to the rest of the patrimony on which other family members depended. And the father had further legal assurance that his own affairs would not result in material or legal harm to his son after emancipation.

In Florentine law as in Roman law, emancipation was a form of freedom; it was also an adjustment in, and of, the child's rights and obligations. The city's lawyers were left to answer legal questions raised by the adjustments, especially those resulting from the contrary principles of patrilineally extended liability and freedom from such liability introduced by emancipation. Florentine fathers and sons, however, looked at emancipation not only from the perspective of the law but also from the perspective of the family.

CHAPTER THREE

Emancipation
in Florentine Culture

The discussion of emancipation in Roman law and Florentine legislation gives a partial answer to the question of what emancipation meant
to a Florentine. Consideration of the law is warranted because as a
legal institution, emancipation operated within the conceptual grid
erected by the overlapping legal systems. In addition, emancipation
operated within a conceptual grid of intersubjective cultural meanings
related to domestic life and kinship relations. Thus, the full meaning of
emancipation will not be uncovered without considering extralegal
cultural constructs existing in fourteenth- and fifteenth-century Florence. Emancipation was, in other words, endowed with meaning
not only for the jurists who saw it as part of a whole complex of jural
symbols but also for the laymen who used emancipation and encountered it in their lives.

Few historians have analyzed the wider cultural and social dimensions of emancipation; and most of those who have, have minimized
its functional and symbolic significance in the context of the family.
They have produced one-dimensional accounts, linking emancipation
to a single function or meaning. The most pervasive interpretation
treats emancipation as a *rite de passage* celebrating the onset of physical and mental maturity at the age of majority. Perhaps the first to formulate this interpretation was the great historian of Florence, Robert
Davidsohn, who declared that emancipation did not occur before age
18 (the age of majority in Florence): "At fourteen years the boy put on
the 'trousers' and from then on belonged among the young men; at
eighteen he was considered in majority if his father was dead, and the
living parent could emancipate him from that year, declaring him,
that is, mature in actions and in rights." Thus, Davidsohn and those
who have followed his lead have associated emancipation with some
form of age limit. Davidsohn himself went on to declare that the age

of majority (25) in Roman law functioned as an emancipatory age of majority (and, therefore, as a maximum age for emancipation).[1]

Interpreting emancipation as a transition to adult status has been influential. It has recently been argued that at Genoa, emancipation was expected at age 25;[2] yet, this interpretation has met with problems. The art historian, Richard Freemantle, has subscribed to it, but, as a result, he was puzzled to discover that the painter Masolino was not emancipated until he was about 45 years old.[3] Other variations on the theme of emancipation and maturity have attempted to identify a more circumscribed and functional significance in emancipation. One view is that emancipation was often, if not exclusively, linked with marriage for men, at least among the upper echelons of society.[4] Another view, advanced by Herlihy and Klapisch, is that emancipation was intended to put both legal abilities and some amount of property as initial capital into the hands of sons about to embark on a career. By this account, emancipation was still age-related but related to ages other than those at which a son could expect to be married or at which he could anticipate becoming the head of a family.[5]

All of these views of emancipation as related to age can be termed positive in contrast to several other interpretations that view emancipation as an expression of paternal power or prerogatives, not intended for the benefit of the emancipatus. Gina Fasoli has argued that emancipation was a form of punishment.[6] That she took such a position is not surprising, in view of the fact that she coedited the statutes of Bologna, which treated emancipation as a form of punishment. Richard Trexler has claimed that for males, emancipation was the functional equivalent of placing unmarried daughters in convents: sacrificing the child to the exigencies of familial economics.[7] Paolo Cammarosano, finally, has crafted another negative interpretation of emancipation that rests on the distinction between day-to-day business activities and properly patrimonial affairs. He claims that in patrimonial affairs, sons took no part while their fathers lived. Emancipation simply figured as a way sons could be used by their fathers as tools in managing the patrimony.[8]

This array of interpretations rests on a small number of examples drawn from emancipatory practices. No attempt has yet been made to determine the contemporary conception of emancipation or to relate that conception to the larger ideology of the family with which it, as an institution, formed a singular functional moment.

The typical sources that historians have used to delve into cultural meanings in Renaissance Florence are generally, and unfortunately, silent on the matter of emancipation. Perhaps this is why emancipation has been so largely neglected. In any case, emancipation did not attract the attention of those humanists (for example, Leon Battista Alberti, Matteo Palmieri, Agnolo Pandolfini), merchants (for example, Giovanni Rucellai, Giovanni Morelli, Goro Dati, Buonaccorso Pitti), and novelists (Franco Sacchetti and Giovanni Sercambi) whose writings have been published and widely read. Such overall silence on the subject suggests that emancipation held a common meaning, so common, in fact, that it need not be explained or expressed. Certainly, these writers were not ignorant of the existence of emancipation; some of them made use of it. Yet, those who did so did not bring up the fact in their writings. Rucellai, who began writing his *Zibaldone* in 1457, addressed his work to his two sons, one of whom he emancipated in the following year, the other, in 1465. But in this work, Giovanni Rucellai did not include a word for his sons about the institution that would affect all their lives. Similarly Pitti, Dati, and Morelli all emancipated sons or daughters but left no thoughts on the matter for them or for us.[9]

Some of the unpublished *ricordanze* housed in the Florentine archives do mention emancipation; however, the entries are unexpressive. Typically the entry simply states the date of emancipation of one or more children, lists the property, if any, transferred to the emancipatus, and perhaps gives the name of the notary and the date of notification of the emancipation to the authorities.[10] Such matter-of-fact recording would seem to offer little clue to the cultural meaning of emancipation or emancipatory behavior. However, the fact that emancipations were so recorded is itself significant. For one thing, the recording shows that emancipation was at times deemed important enough to be remembered and inscribed beside the births, deaths, and marriages of family members and familial property transactions. The notation of the relevant facts in a legal proceeding such as emancipation served much the same function as the modern custom of placing important papers in safe-deposit boxes or other secure places.[11] Fathers who had emancipated their son(s) or daughter(s) recognized the significance of what they had done, which is why, it would seem, they entered the facts in their records. What was it then that they had done or thought they had done?

The first clue to the meaning of emancipation lies in the content of the emancipation ritual that father and child acted out before the judge or notary. The exact content of the ritual can be reconstructed with some difficulty from the rather meager information contained in a few notarial charters. According to one Florentine source, which gives a singularly extended description in the first person, the father took his child by the hand, then released his hand while saying: "I, Testa, free and absolve you, my son, Giovanni, from my hand and power. . . . Be henceforth a Roman citizen and a man of your own right and under your own power." There are indications from other sources that the child knelt during this time. In most notarial charters, however, the nature of the emancipation ritual was reduced to, and hidden beneath, the reigning legal formulas.[12]

Both within, and beyond, a strictly legal context, the ritual of emancipation can be seen as a commentary on the society of which it was a part: It reaffirmed values and symbols of the culture; it told the participants something about themselves. By celebrating the *patria potestas*, the ritual made it clear that the *paterfamilias* held his children *in potestate*, in which state they lacked legal capabilities. The *paterfamilias*, in contrast to his children, could act in the public forum—make contracts, write a will, take part in a judicial process. Above all, the ritual told the child what was happening to him: His father, who clearly performed as the active agent in the ritual, was freeing him from subjection to that all encompassing *potestas*, whose existence had deprived him of any legal capacity, to enter the exalted status of *paterfamilias*, *civis romanus*, and *homo sui iuris*. When the ceremony ended, the once subordinate child stood on his or her own and was no longer *filiusfamilias* (or *filiafamilias*), but the *legal* equal of the father. The emancipatus had undergone an elevation in status to that of the *patres*. In fact, the emancipatus now had a dual status—*filius* and *pater*—which was symbolized by his designation thereafter as *filius emancipatus* (*figliuolo manceppato* in the vernacular).

The *praemium* further bolstered the sense of paternal generosity and gave concrete meaning to the father's action and to the child's new status. The value of the gift was not emphasized, for the *praemium* represented more than the utility or disutility of a material gift: It affirmed the child's new status. The *praemium* was, in fact, every bit as generous as the gift of legal capabilities the father had just given his offspring.[13] The gift *qua* gift symbolized the father's commitment to the child's interests as well as the new contractual relationship between the parties, and it affirmed their social relationship (as father to son and son to father) in the new ambience of legal equality between giver-emancipator and receiver-emancipatus.[14]

The gift also amounted to a partial restoration of the previous relationship between father and child of dominance and subservience. By giving the gift, the father reenhanced his own status in relation to that of his child's, but in the context, it was the father's moral rather than legal status that was reenhanced.

Emancipation ritual incorporated the themes of dominance and subservience, generosity, legal capacity, and the relationship between *pater* and *filius* and arranged them in order to throw into relief the relations between the parties, both in their content and in the modification of that content. Emancipation highlighted the fact that more was involved therein than material property and functional power.

The emancipation ritual made no reference to maturity, and no inquiry was conducted into the child's physical and mental abilities. The disregard for maturity in the emancipation ritual is reflected in the practices of the Florentines, who emancipated children when very young as well as in more mature years and also when relatively old —far past the onset of maturity or puberty. As pointed out, Masolino was 45 at his emancipation in 1428. Other examples of age at the time of emancipation are: Francesco di Giovanni Baldovinetti, who was 16 in 1494; Lapo di Giovanni Niccolini, who was 23 when emancipated in 1379 and who, in turn, emancipated his sons at ages 23 and 16; Valorino di Barna Curiani, who in 1399 emancipated his four sons aged 24, 19, 18, and 11; Giovantommaso di Francesco Giovanni, who was a tender eight in 1433, the same year that Dietisalvi Neroni, then already married, was emancipated.[15] Emancipation was similarly unrelated to the child's marital status or to his or her place of residence. Dietisalvi Neroni was married and living at home when emancipated; Priore Sassetti did not marry until six years after his emancipation. Niccolò di Zanobi lived in the *popolo* of San Lorenzo in 1405, the year that he emancipated Lorenzo, who lived in the *popolo* of San Pier Maggiore.[16] Evidence points to the fact that emancipation (the attainment of full legal rights) was separate from, or at least not necessarily attached to, maturity and ability.[17]

This brief analysis of the emancipation ritual, then, reveals that the spotlight was directed not on the child (that is, not on his or her maturity, marital status, residence) but on the father. The two points of radiance in the ritual were the active generosity of the father and his status as father. The latter served to bring home to the child and to all present the status he or she was gaining and the true depths of the father's generosity.

What Florentines emphasized when they got around to recording an emancipation in the family was likewise the generous acquisition of a new and equal status; quite often, they did so by linking emancipation with liberation. For example, Valorino di Lapo Curiani in 1329 wrote that he had "emancipated and liberated" his sons;[18] almost two centuries later, in 1512, Marco Parenti used the same terms to describe the emancipation of his children. These two men were by no means the only Florentines to find emancipation and liberation synonymous.[19]

When viewed as an act of liberation, emancipation appeared to be something positive—a set of rights and powers granted by the liberator. In Florence, however, liberation through emancipation unavoidably had a second meaning—one that may have been far more important to many Florentines. Instructive here is the account of his own emancipation by Lapo di Giovanni Niccolini. On the one hand, Lapo emphasized the freedom he gained through emancipation to do as he saw fit. In his words, "On the seventeenth day of May 1379, I, Lapo di Giovanni Niccholini, was emancipated and released [*disoblighato*] from every tie that I had with Giovanni di Lapo Niccholini, my father, . . . And I can make my will and obligate all my goods, movable and immovable, as it suits me."[20] He emphasized the character and object of his new legal abilities (that is, his property, including a farm bought for him by his father after the emancipation).

On the other hand, Lapo was at least as concerned with the important negative freedom he had also gained, namely, that he was no longer obligated on his father's account. It was also this second significance that was uppermost in Lapo's mind when he emancipated one of his sons years later

> Memory and remembrance that on the twenty-fourth day of September 1409, I, Lapo, emancipated and released from obligation [*disobligai*] my son Niccolaio. . . . Thus, from this day forth, I am not liable for any obligation he should make, nor is he liable for mine; and he can make his will, if he should have anything, and obligate himself, his person and his goods; and, if he should make a profit, it must all be his, and, if he should lose anything, neither I nor others are obligated for it.[21]

In this instance, Lapo played up the discontinuity of obligation (that aspect of emancipation most prominent in the Florentine statutes) because he was intent on freeing himself from obligations created by a son who was gullible, prodigal, and an incompetent businessman. Lapo continued to have dealings with his son, and he made the same remarks on the emancipation of his other son, Giovanni, a son about whom he did not complain.[22] Whether or not a son was a spendthrift and a general legal and financial liability for his father, emancipation carried with it the important freedom from mutual liability; but it did not sever affective or economic ties, nor did it prohibit voluntary contractual ties.[23]

In terms of freedom, rights, obligations, and the property affected by them, emancipation involved many areas of family life and relations, especially those areas directly concerning a father and his offspring. As a legal institution operating within the context of familial life, emancipation found its ultimate meaning and function in that context; so we must eventually turn to cultural conceptions of the family in order to understand emancipation.

The Cultural Context: Fathers and Sons in Florence

No discussion can hope to exhaust the polysemic nature of the Florentine concept of *famiglia*, a concept that has been the object of considerable historical attention, and I do not propose to recapitulate all the important findings of the excellent studies by Kent, Herlihy and Klapisch, and many others. What follows is merely an account of the more salient features of *famiglia* and father-son relations relevant to the study of emancipation.

To begin with, as Kent notes, *famiglia* was given two distinct operative definitions by at least one Florentine, Leon Battista Alberti, in his *Libri della famiglia*. One definition equated family with the domestic unit—the family as *casa*; the other was a more physically and quantitatively extensive definition of a group of blood- and marriage-related kin living "under the shadow of a single will."[24] The *casa* was feminine, filled and perpetuated by men, for only they (and not women) were capable of erecting the agnatic structural beams considered necessary to support the metaphoric edifice.[25] Indeed, it was the metaphoric power of the term *casa* that made it more an equivalent than a definition of *famiglia*, for it could cover simply those living under a single roof (a physical *casa*) or those living under a single will or even all of those bearing the same name.[26]

Alberti utilized two definitions of *famiglia* because they presented two different ways of stressing what he, above all, meant by the family—a body of people acting together and in unison in such a way that they truly formed a single body. In this context, his (somewhat longwinded) definition of *famiglia* from another of his dialogues, *De iciarchia*, is instructive:

> It seems to me that just as the city is made up of many families . . . the family is a kind of small city. And if I am not in error, the existence of one as of the other is derived from the congregation and conjunction of many joined and held together by some necessity and utility. . . . This habit of living together and remaining under a single roof is called familiarity; and this number of people thus come together is called family. . . . And it seems to me that at the origin of the family the first step was love, and thus the primary tie to hold them together was reverence and love and a certain duty demanded by nature toward one's own.

In this first section of his definition of the family, Alberti was really speculating on the origins of this important social body. These origins were at once functional and affective; however, as he in fact saw it, functionality was more significant, since nature had already brought these people together through consanguinity. Alberti, therefore, went on to expand his definition of the family into an ethical imperative:

> It is fitting to conceive of the family as a body similar to a republic, composed of yourselves and of this [love]: And you are to the family as innate instruments and members of this body. The first obligation of whoever is part of this family will be to become active and diligent so that in truth all together form one well-united body, in which all the mass, just like an animated body, feels the movements of any of its parts, even the last and furthest. . . . Therefore, the duty of all together will be to bind and tie themselves to one intention with firm good will. Next will follow the dedicating of themselves with every effort, labor, and diligence, as any family member is capable of, so that the name and condition of the family be greatly honored and honorable with much peace, tranquility, and strength. And so each of you on his own, and all together, and I with you, will be solicitous so that neither through our error nor that of any other might the family sustain harm, even in the least of its affairs. On the other hand each of us will lend every effort with all our genius and ability so that each person of our name may be as blessed and happy as the human condition permits.[27]

As Alberti developed his image of the family, all of its constitutive elements, all of its defining characteristics—blood ties, residence, name, and needs—coalesced in a single body, a single action, and a single intention. The *casa* was thus linked with the history of the family and with the practical observance of a code of honor and a pattern of responsibility binding the members in a close and positive relation to one another.

As in any body, the control of its members and the single goal to which they were directed came from the head, and the head of the family (*capo di famiglia*) was the father. One definition of the *famiglia* was, therefore, all of those subjected to the will of the father.[28] His word was law. As Alberti put it, the father "has over his children a just domestic power similar to that of a king," and as husband, he "rules over his wife." The father's role was to give orders, the children's and wife's duty was to obey them.[29] However, the role of father, which was crucial to the family's welfare, was not easy. A father could expect to be judged by others in the community for how well he fulfilled his domestic role.[30] What status and esteem he had outside the home rested in good part on how well he was seen to perform his domestic role. To have recourse once again to the words of Alberti:

A different light of prestige and authority will emanate from one who is accompanied by his own people, whom there are many reasons to trust and many reasons to fear, than from one who walks with a few strangers or without company. The father of a family followed by many of his kinsmen will be more eminent than one who is alone and seems abandoned.[31]

It is in this light that Alberti can assure his audience of present and prospective Florentine fathers that "what is useful to all the family certainly will also be useful to you, and in the first place the reward for the effort will fall to you."[32]

The material and spiritual well-being of the father and the whole family under his control rested on his performance. Thus, the father was seen as the central figure in the family, and the central relationship was between him and his sons, in whom lay the hopes and perpetuation of the *casa*. The various handbooks, dialogues, and *ricordi* of Florentines like Alberti, Morelli, and Rucellai were directed at this central relationship. They presented a picture of how fathers should teach their sons (a crucial aspect of that domestic role by which fathers could be evaluated by others) and how sons should treat their fathers. The controlling image of the father-son relationship was expressed succinctly by the Pseudo-Pandolfini:

> We believe our consolation most [lies] in seeing you, father, surrounded by us all, a master loved and revered by all, and [in seeing you] teach the youth, which is a very great joy, because virtuous sons bring their fathers much help, much honor, and praise. In the father's care stands the virtue of the sons. The solicitous and dutiful fathers instill their families with gentility.[33]

Antonio Pucci, too, depicted the father's responsibilities and the respect and obedience accorded him as a result.[34] The father's stature and responsibilities were such that respect was the proper attitude to be taken toward him. And the respect owed to fathers was commonly assumed; it served as a yardstick for determining the respect owed to other relatives and elders.[35]

Marsilio Ficino went so far as to compare the father to God, calling the father a second God because he gave his children life, nourishment, and commands. To this earthly god was owed respect, obedience, and reverence similar to that owed to the celestial diety. The *reverentia* shown to fathers was a "fearful love," arising from a fear "composed of shame and obedience." Fathers were to be spoken to with a low and humble voice and with gestures of respect. In sum, one "should use every act and manner that designates love and submission."[36]

Florentine sons generally accorded their fathers the reverence due them. Not all were so expressive or hyperbolic as Bernardo di Lapo da Castiglionchio, who addressed his father in an almost subservient manner, but they indicated their filial piety in a variety of ways.[37] For one thing, they quite commonly named their own children after their fathers. In this fashion, they could ensure a continuity between generations, even claiming at times to have "remade" a deceased ancestor by having given his name to a child.[38] Piero di Carlo Strozzi, for example, made no secret of the fact that he had named his son Carlo in honor of his father.[39] Florence was, in fact, populated by men whose names reflected the custom of giving sons fathers' names: Piero di Lorenzo di Piero de' Medici, Francesco di Tommaso di Francesco Giovanni (whose first son was named Giovantommaso), and Giovanni di Lapo di Giovanni Niccolini, to name just a few. Sons also addressed their fathers in the polite plural, *voi*, in order to show their respect. In such culturally determined actions, they expressed their reverence for the "second God."[40]

Fathers may have received reverence and obedience from their children, but they, in turn, had obligations toward their offspring—to provide for them and teach them. The tragedy of Giovanni Morelli's life was that he was orphaned at an early age and did not receive the instruction and care his father would have given him. He pointed out at length in his *ricordi* how he had been harmed by the lack of proper parental instruction and by his vulnerability to his guardians. He thereby showed his sons the inestimable advantage they enjoyed in having a father living and caring for them.[41] Morelli's *ricordi* were an expression of his care, for they contained the teaching he wished to pass on to his sons. In his *Zibaldone*, Giovanni Rucellai gave his sons advice on such diverse matters as how to treat employees and partners, kin, friends, and servants; how to conserve their wealth and manage their domestic and business affairs; and how to raise their own children, choose their wet nurses and their spouses. He counseled his sons to restrain the passions of youth in their offspring and, above all, not to do or say dishonorable things in the presence of their children in order to give them the proper example. The good father should teach his children, in short, as Giovanni Rucellai had taught his, the things that were useful to them.[42]

As can be seen, the education of the young consisted not only in the formal education advocated by humanists but also in the practical insights valuable to a person in life. Here, the father was the primary teacher. He had to set a good example, restrain his children from bad actions and habits, and awaken in them the love of good and honest things.[43] Alberti, the most eloquent writer on domestic affairs, placed great stress on the father governing the family and on his authority to inspire and correct his children.[44]

The cultural emphasis on the father's domestic responsibilities and on the respect and obedience owed to him reflected the underlying conception of father and son as a single substance. Ficino articulated this belief when he declared that a father had a natural love for his son because the son was "his own work," produced from his substance and, therefore, similar to his father in looks, in form, and in habits; and because the father, through the son, sought to leave behind something of his "substance, likeness, name and glory and memory." The fact that the sons were of the father's substance was the basis for the joy fathers took in seeing their sons well disposed and their justification for keeping their sons with them in a common residence.[45] The cultural belief that father and son shared a single substance also lay behind the close association of the two in Florentine legislation concerned with debts and fiscal responsibility—an association that one historian has termed a "communion, almost a personal unity between father and son."[46]

The writers who theorized on the family were not content with singling out reverence, obedience, and love as a father's reward for performing his paternal duties and raising his children well. These writers also pointed to the important material benefits children could bring to their families. As summed up in a charming story in Franco Sacchetti's novelle, a well-raised and successful son could be a source of honor and material profit for his parents.[47]

The material advantages to be gained from one's children were seen to be especially important for the elderly. Alberti, for one, declared that children were "the natural and reliable crutch of the old." He frankly exhorted children to care for their aged parents: "Visit them, comfort them, succor them, give them renewal by your presence, with your action and reverence, help and maintenance against the oppressions of old age." If an exhortation based on the positive moral worth of caring for sick and aged kin was not sufficient to remind children of their function within the family, it was possible to impress them with a more negative argument—that it was their duty to care for aged parents. They owed it to them. As Alberti said, "If your friends ought to enjoy a good portion of your possessions and goods and wealth, far more ought your father, from whom you have received, if not your goods, still life itself, and not only life but nurture for so long a time, and if not nurture, still being and name."[48] Ficino posed the relationship of support between father and son in terms of debts and credits. The son, he claimed, was eternally bound to his father in gratitude and bore the obligation to repay his father some day for the innumerable gifts he had received from him.[49] Giovanni Cavalcanti, too, said that children were the debtors of their father, although he saw the debt as the obligation to care for their children just as their father had cared for them.[50]

With all that sons meant to their fathers, it is no wonder that it was considered important and desirable to have sons. The loss of a son, therefore, was tragic, especially the loss of a son in whom one had placed much hope. When his eldest, Alberto, died, Giovanni Morelli paraded his grief and loss through the pages of his *ricordi*. In part, his show of sorrow was intended to demonstrate to his other children that he was a loving and caring father. But his loss and grief were also quite genuine, for his son had been stricken while his future still lay before him. The loss of children must have been quite common in an era of high infant mortality, but not all deaths met with such extreme grief. Morelli himself was far more stoic at the passing of his second son; he simply prayed that his other children would have long lives and that he would not live to see them die.[51] The deaths of those who had lived a rather full life, who had married and fathered children, were accepted with more equanimity than those of adolescents;[52] older children had already contributed, or not, as the case might be, to the family's honor.

Florentines defined the *famiglia* substantively and metaphorically by reference to both the *casa* and the authority of the *capo di famiglia*. Paternal authority defined relationships of status and dependence between members of the family, and by extension, the father's "image" and "single will" came to stand for the family. The *casa* likewise was the physical site of family life, and by extension, it stood for the family's entire symbolic and material capital—its patrimony.

The *casa* was not simply a monument to family honor and a sanctuary for its members; it was a cornucopia filled with the fruits of its labor.[53] As many late medieval jurists maintained, "The family is its wealth [*substantia*]";[54] in fact, the *capo di famiglia* exercised most of his power maintaining and managing the patrimony. It was wealth that preserved the family, while its loss threatened a family's survival.[55] And one of the most important means of preserving a family's wealth was its sons, since its property, honor, and name passed to them. Hence, it was a father's most important duty to administer his patrimony well and pass it on to his sons, along with extensive and careful instructions for its preservation and increase. The advice contained in the third book of Alberti's *Della famiglia*, therefore—to cite the most prominent literary example—was widely circulated in the writings of others, like Giovanni Rucellai and the Pseudo-Pandolfini.

Material wealth and honor were closely related. Property was not only an economic asset but also a symbolic extension of an owner's, or a family's, character. As the anthropologist J. Davis has argued, honor is a system of social stratification that determines individual access to resources and is, in turn, determined by it. The father of a family is deemed honorable as a result of performing his role as father. That role involves feeding and housing his family, establishing his sons in good careers, and dowering his daughters, for all of which material resources are necessary, if not merely helpful. Success in the domestic role then gives the father even greater access to resources by placing him higher in the hierarchy of honor within the community.[56] Therefore, a father bequeaths to his sons both his material wealth and his claims to honor with all its moral and economic value.

In Florence, too, honor and material interests were closely intertwined in father-son relationships, which were described in terms of honor and shame (*onore* and *vergogna*) and in terms of profit and loss (*utile* and *danno*). What was honorable was often also useful.[57] So, fathers like Giovanni Rucellai went to great pains to instruct their sons in wise management, advising them to act with honor toward all, to take care that "no one consider himself cheated or be unhappy, because this would rather be a loss than a gain."[58]

Property was, of course, important in meeting the family's daily needs; it was also the means of surmounting adverse situations. Paolo da Certaldo urged his readers to increase their wealth, so that they could meet expenses occasioned by such contingencies as fines, taxes, sickness, natural disaster, or the dowering of daughters.[59] But beyond practical interests, wealth added to the family's prestige, honor, and reputation (which were themselves useful and concrete additions to the family's patrimony).[60] Wealth, in other words, was part of the accumulation of symbolic capital.

Wealth was not only to be gained, it was to be preserved through moderation and careful investment.[61] Indeed, the injunction to conserve one's wealth was interpreted by people like Paolo da Certaldo to carry more weight than the injunction to increase one's wealth.[62] Rucellai told his boys, "Above all, govern yourselves in such a way that it cannot be said of you that you are in over your head etc. And it is enough for you to conserve [your wealth] etc."[63] His ideal of the prudent manager was the person he called *massaio*:

> One finds that conserving and spending one's wealth with prudence is greater than prosperity, industry, or profit. Those who use things how,

when, and as much as is necessary, and not more, and serve to increase
them are the ones I call *massaio*: They are those who know how to keep
the median between too little and too much.[64]

The opposite of the *massaio* was the *avaro* (the avaricious man).
Rucellai advised his sons that "nothing is so contrary to the fame and
grace of a man as avarice; there is no virtue so clear and excellent that
it would not be obscured and forgotten beneath avarice."[65] The *avari*
included those who spent too much too often and those who spent
not at all, even in necessity. They were so intent on either gaining or
spending money that they would do anything: They were without
shame.[66] Because the *avari* acted irrationally, they were subject to the
biasimo (disdain, ridicule) of the rest of society. Proper moderation
and avoiding avarice, moreover, were recommended in dealings with
kin and friends: One should not be generous beyond one's means,
nor should one give to those who were prodigal *spenditori*.[67]

In hopes of teaching their sons to be *massai*, some fathers gave their
boys a form of allowance so they could learn to manage money.[68]
(Such sums may have shown up in the *peculium profectitium* of emancipati.) In general, however, the young were considered to be especially prone to prodigality and greatly in need of parental supervision
in using wealth.[69]

One way to transfer wealth to children yet avoid the possible consequences of filial prodigality was to place legal conditions and qualifications on the future disposition of the property. The *fideicommissum*, a testamentary stipulation binding on the heirs and affecting
their ability to dispose freely of the contents of the estate, was increasingly used in the fifteenth century. In his will drawn up in 1465, Rucellai gave Pandolfo and Bernardo his *palazzo* with the condition that
they not alienate it except within the family or lineage of the Rucellai.[70] Such a restriction served to keep important pieces of property,
especially houses, within the family, which, according to Kent, identified itself with such important symbolic property.[71] Gifts made during
one's life such as the *praemium emancipationis* as well as testamentary
bequests were also liable to these restrictions and conditions.[72]

Finally, instruction in preserving material resources and honor included guidance on handling friends and kin—an important source
of support. Rucellai recommended to his sons that they practice a calculated generosity to build up and maintain a network of *amici* as
people whom they could trust and who would owe them favors.[73]
(His sons, in fact, may have learned a great deal about such patron-
client relations from simply being sons, for in that position they were
like clients to their father, the patron.) The asymmetry of the father-

son relationship was deeper and more thorough because it was based on concepts of nature and natural moral duty, yet as in patron-client relations, the relationship rested in part on a material nexus of goods and services and on a sense of kinship.[74]

The advice of Florentine fathers like Rucellai had an important, though often unvoiced, dimension to it, playing against the backdrop of the ever present threat of financial disaster. Mismanagement of the patrimony or outrageously dishonorable behavior could destroy the family itself. As a result, the sons who were the bearers of the family's hopes were also the locus of its fears.

The Florentine patricians who wrote family *ricordi*—men like Alberti, the Pseudo-Pandolfini, Morelli, and Rucellai—did so not simply because they valued highly the place of the *famiglia* in their lives and desired to celebrate its virtues. They also wrote with an urgent and practical end in view, as their advice on wealth makes clear: They were concerned with preserving honor and resources; in other words, with preserving the family in the face of many real threats to its continued existence.

This sense of urgency in the face of threats to the family's very existence is perhaps nowhere clearer than in the preface to Alberti's *Della famiglia*, where he remarks on the passing of many formerly great and wealthy Florentine families.[75] As a member of another of those families but recently returned from exile, Alberti sought to provide the kind of instruction that would allow the family to avoid the fate of so many other illustrious houses. The fate of the family, he said, lay in the good governance of the *padri* and in the good and honest customs and practices they inculcated in its members. His book, therefore, was intended to study those things that would lead the family to "supreme happiness" and allow it to escape the blows, however temporary, of a cruel and malevolent fortune.[76]

One source of potential disaster for a family lay in the world around it. This sense of perpetual evil and danger on the outside was well expressed by Sacchetti, who said in the moral to one of his stories, "In this life one cannot be too much on guard, because from every side come tricks and betrayals designed to make one's own another's."[77] Much of the advice of Morelli, Alberti, Rucellai, and others was directed at the problems the family and its *capo* faced from others. Outsiders were a source of concern not only because they were perceived to have designs on the family's resources but also because, as the source of public opinion, they could reverse their estimate of a father and his family. Not only honor but dishonor (shame) resulted from the opinions of others.

Furthermore, the threat presented by the outside world could be compounded by incompetence and mismanagement on the part of the head of the family, and a single misfortune could destroy a mismanaged *casa*. In the words of one popular source of advice on domestic management, negligence would make a *casa* "full of ruin," and negligence itself was likened to a perpetually lit blaze in the midst of the *casa*, ever ready and capable of consuming it.[78] A father who failed to live up to the social ideal of the *padre di famiglia* could be the source of grave misfortune for the family.

The readily proffered advice on how to be a good *padre* was, of course, designed to put out this dangerous fire within the *casa*. However, such advice was also aimed at the way the father handled his wife and children, for they, too, and perhaps most of all (paradoxical as it seems), constituted a powerful threat to the very family of which they were members. Preserving the family meant in good part preserving proper relationships within the family. In the context of emancipation, the threat posed by children, especially by sons, is of interest.

Florentines were well aware of the threat children could become. The dialogue structure of the *Della famiglia* allowed Alberti, for one, to explore both sides of the issue of children. There, he weighed the joy, honor, utility, and naturalness of having children against the pain and suffering involved in raising them correctly. Children were a mixed blessing; if there were many powerful reasons for having children, there were also arguments on the other side of the issue:

> It is a much greater sorrow to have them than not to have them: in not having them is a passion, in having them so many torments. If they are bad, they live too long, and one never has anything but bad from them; if they are good, they die early; and everyone tries to have [children], and most of the time [in having them] one merely seeks his own bad fortune.[79]

Not all Florentines looked on the prospect of having children with such a jaundiced eye, but many regarded them warily, and with good reason: Bad sons or daughters brought shame and grief to their fathers and their families. Giovanni Sercambi touched a resonant chord for parents in both Lucca and Florence with his story of a man whose only son, despite advantages in wealth and background, did not want to enter a trade but spent his life wooing and wasting.[80] The eventual sorry fate of the son illustrated what disobedient children could expect. They brought shame upon themselves and their fathers—as Alberti put it—"Every undisciplined son brings his father no small shame."[81]

This shame accrued to the father because it was his job to train his sons to be properly obedient and virtuous. It was his duty to keep the family united and functioning properly, as Alberti said:

> Being a father consists in having the things proper to a father and in act-ing like one. . . . And his first duty will be that the family be without any disunifying discord. I don't deny that it is useful for a family not to be united on things from which harm results; but not being united on those that are useful harms it beyond measure.[82]

The disobedience of sons born of vices like greed and selfishness was one cause of disunity, disorder, and loss of reputation and wealth. Such sons followed their own desires and opinions only and did not value wealth, honor, or friendship. It was, therefore,

> an important duty of the father to begin in early youth to dry up and to stop so great and so dangerous a vice in his children as this stubborn-ness. It threatens anyone who is subject to it. It also promises prestilence and death to his whole family. In nothing, not even very minor matters, should the elders permit obstinate wishes or dishonorable plans to harden in their children.[83]

Clearly, loss of honor and property were the consequences reaped by fathers who were not sufficiently attentive to preventing or removing vices in their children.

Correcting and disciplining children was an important and deli-cate matter. Alberti advised fathers to use reasonable rather than unworthy language, authority rather than commands, but yet to be severe if necessary.[84] Carefully supervising children would prevent vices, but in case they should take root, Alberti cautioned against cut-ting them off in such a way that damage to fortune and reputation might result. A father should

> not separate his son from himself or send him out of the house as some uncontrolled and irate fathers do. Thus do young men already bursting with wickedness and filled with indulgence fall to doing vile things un-der pressure of necessity, committing dangerous deeds, and living in a way that disgraces them and their family.[85]

Not all Florentines were so moderate as Alberti in their opinions of how to deal with children. Some, like Paolo da Certaldo and Antonio Pucci, held to a more traditional view whereby a father strictly con-trolled his sons, using appropriate forms of force rather than words and examples.[86] But for both moderates and traditionals, the ultimate recourse was the same, since in Florentine law (as discussed in Chap-ter 2) disobedient sons could be imprisoned at their fathers' request. Both Pucci and Alberti pointed to this final remedy. A son who had gone so far as to merit prison obviously did not want his father any-more, so the father had no reason to treat him as a son any longer and thus harbor an enemy in his house.[87] With some pride, Giovanni Ca-valcanti wrote of a relative who not only had his miscreant son put in prison but eventually had the lad spirited out in order to kill him with his own hands in the family's home.[88]

Imprisonment figured in a father's plans only when his son's mis-behavior had gotten out of hand; but contemplation of this ultimate step shows, if nothing else does, that continual vice or shamelessness by a son was an affront and a challenge to paternal authority. In fact, that authority over family members and familial wealth was often both the source and object of conflict between fathers and sons—Floren-tines held no illusions on this score. It was in order to avoid such con-flict that Rucellai proposed a moderate regime of childrearing, ad-vocating an age-related relaxation of the paternal grip on the family purse. Up to age 18, he said, a father should treat his sons as sons and demand reverence and obedience from them. From 18 to 30, however, he should treat them as brothers, take them into his confidence, and seek their advice in his affairs. After 30, the father should be the son and allow his sons to control the patrimony. Many Florentine fathers gave considerable economic freedom to their sons and allotted prop-erty to them, but it was also not uncommon for fathers to keep eco-nomic control in their hands alone.[89]

Fathers had to face the fact that their sons were potential enemies who might even desire the parent's death in order to be free.[90] The competition between father and son for authority in the family and control over its resources was most marked when the father was con-siderably advanced in years. The exhortations of Florentines to the young to care for their aged parents indicate by their frequency and repetitiveness that the ideal was too frequently ignored. The aged parent, who was also likely to be sick and feeble, was thoroughly de-pendent on the offspring's goodwill and highly vulnerable as a result. A common piece of wisdom was that when one approached old age, one was best advised to commit oneself to God rather than to a son.[91] The humanist Palmieri found the only defense for the elderly was to have properly raised good children who would not desert them.[92] Paolo da Certaldo, on the other hand, tried to make aged parents ap-pear useful for their experience and wisdom, since if they in some way could still contribute to familial welfare, they would not then be so despicable and helpless.[93] Paolo da Certaldo, in fact, took a stance directly opposite that advocated by Rucellai. He advised a regime of strict control over sons and patrimony; the danger of the opposite course was obvious to him:

The son stands subject and subservient and humble to his father so long as the father holds the control of the house and of his property; and when the father has given his son the control to manage his property, he stands above his father and hates him, and it seems to him a thousand years before he will see the day when his father dies: And from the friend that he was before, he has become your enemy on account of the trust you had in him.[94]

The problem for Florentine fathers was that their adult sons demanded some measure of autonomy and responsibility, with the result that fathers might be pushed to retire, to relinquish control of the family and its property, especially if they were no longer capable of productive activity.[95] If, however, fathers met this contingency by giving property to their sons, the division of property weakened the family; the choice was not easy. Alberti was opposed to division on principle, even as a means of dealing with an obstinate son, and expressed amazement at sons who desired some property for themselves. In so doing, they were opting for momentary gain against eventual loss, and they were violating the "religion and sanctity of the innate brotherhood" that was the family.[96] But fathers did not escape his condemnation either, for Alberti recognized that a father could so foolishly insist on his authority and prerogatives in the home that he would drive his sons away, jeopardizing the honor and esteem of the united family.[97] Alberti's implied solution, similar to Rucellai's second age-related stage for dealing with sons, was that the father retain official authority in the family—a public and even ceremonial authority—but that sons participate in decisions and be active on the family's behalf where the father's presence was not required.[98]

The pose of a unified and peaceful family was a means of reducing conflict or at least a mechanism for disguising it from others, including historians. Occasionally, conflicts exploded beyond the confines of the *casa*, but even then, fathers were able to petition the commune to have public legal proceedings dropped, so that the matter would remain within the family.[99] Yet, conflicts did, indeed, arise, some of which have left traces for the historian to follow.

One example of conflict can be found in the testament of Simone di Rinieri Peruzzi in 1380. In no uncertain terms, he disinherited and anathematized his son Benedetto, who had constantly gone wrong, been disobedient, and had placed the family in grave danger because of his political escapades.[100] In this conflict, the patrimony remained intact, at least physically, but the family effectively lost a member.

Not all conflicts went to such lengths, however. Baldassare di Simone degli Ubriachi had a run-in with his son Benedetto (*non benedetto ma maladetto*) when the boy demanded a larger income. Two years later, father and son had reconciled, although Baldassare retained the clause in his will enjoining his executors to give his sons nothing unless they were upright and obedient.[101]

Another conflict less overtly political in nature was that between Lanfredino d'Orsino Lanfredini and his son Remigio. The latter, incensed by the fact that his father had made peace with a family enemy without his knowledge (thus shaming him, as Remigio thought), left to live and work in Venice. In a dramatic gesture, he also changed his name, symbolically terminating his filial relationship with Lanfredino. In Remigio's eyes, the incident merely proved what he had suspected for sometime—namely, that his father was a "strange man" and a "traitor" to the family.[102] In this case, it was the son who accused the father of failure.

There was in Florence, then, an active concern with conflict between family members, including conflict between a father and his children. And these conflicts did occur, perhaps more regularly and frequently than historians have been led to suspect, given the presentation of a unified and consistent familial facade to the rest of the world. Such conflict may well have been endemic to Florence, for it arose from the very structure of the family and society and not simply from occasionally aberrant psyches. The root of the problem was, in fact, the system of authority and control over resources within the family. In the words of Herlihy and Klapisch:

> The father or the aged mother has the moral weight necessary to draw the respect and the aid of the children whom they have raised, but the needs of the young are the source of conflicts between generations, above all in the cities and the social ranks in which it is necessary to dispose of some capital and to be able to administer in one's own right in order to undertake an independent career. The prolonged control of the property by a sick or old man, the absence of means resulting from this for the young, engendered discussions and disputes between parents and children.[103]

This vision of generational conflict requires only minimal elaboration and specification. The "needs" of the young in this domestic system were not solely, and perhaps not even primarily, economic. Control over one's resources meant that a son would have the chance to establish his own reputation, to demonstrate his abilities at meeting the responsibilities of a *capo di famiglia*. The fact that property remained in the hands of the father, ordinarily not to be dispersed until his death, meant that the son would spend his most productive years without the requisite resources, dependent upon, and subject to, his father.[104]

Between fathers and sons, then, quarrels could erupt over matters of honor, authority, and access to resources. In material terms, the property that in some way touched the son—his earnings, his wife's dowry and other possessions, and eventually his share of the patrimony, for example—could become the occasion for discord. In addition, whatever might concern the honor and prestige of the family—vendettas (as with Remigio Lanfredini) and political activities (as with Simone Peruzzi)—could also lead to problems. Daughters, too, threatened family unity, since they could turn on aged parents. And a daughter's dowry and the task of concealing her shame could provide sufficient headaches for her father, although in other matters, there was less likely to be friction between them.[105]

That status was the central issue in the conflicts between fathers and sons is indicated by the fact that a father's old age was a factor in the discord. There was, indeed, no more propitious moment for sons to contest the status and authority of their fathers, for old fathers were no longer the providers and managers they had been, and one who failed to provide for his family was no longer a father.[106] (Recall Rucellai's change in terminology for the role of the father as he gave his sons greater responsibility.)

Conflict within the family was also influenced by such important external factors as the existence of economic options in the society as a whole. Realistically, sons could set out on their own only (or at least more easily) if there were opportunities for employment. If they could not make a go of it outside the *casa*, there was really no reason to leave unless the financial position of the family was so weak that there seemed to be nothing to lose;[107] the obverse also held. A son in a family of great wealth might be content to remain where he was, subject to the tutelage of his father, because he hoped eventually to gain control of a considerable portion of that wealth, including the prestige that went with it.[108] The emphasis on preserving the patrimony, as opposed to its increase, worked to fix the son's gaze on the resources in the family's possession rather than on the resources to be gained or found elsewhere.

In general, the relationship between economic opportunities and a son's close allegiance to the *casa* seems to have held true in Florence. The households of the wealthy were larger and more complex than were those of the poor, since greater wealth could not only support greater numbers, it could retain their allegiance and their hopes. Moreover, increases in the average size of the household throughout the fifteenth and sixteenth centuries, an era of declining economic activity according to Herlihy and Klapisch, may, indeed, indicate that there were fewer opportunities to entice sons away from *casa* and patrimony. The greater tendency toward generational extension of the household in rural areas as opposed to urban likewise indicates the relative scarcity of alternative economic opportunities where land was the key resource. The rural *filiusfamilias* would have to turn to the city to find other employment.[109]

Wedded as they were to the ideology of the family, Florentines did not attack the structure that created so many domestic problems for them. In their more frank moments, they revealed that they were well aware of the endemic character of generational conflict within the *casa*, yet they viewed this conflict as a moral problem. The proper virtues, they claimed, would prevent economic matters from causing domestic discord. Poverty itself, they said, was the result of vice, and disputes over wealth were really manifestations of lack of love and proper regard for kinship.[110] As for generational conflict, according to Alberti, the problem generally lay in the fact that the young were just naturally at odds with their elders. Again, the solution was moral instruction of a kind calculated to instill respect for the family and its *capo*:

> Families are not divided only through competitions and discords, nor will they be united only through living together. Some other things, useful to know, give families no less unity than one would like. It seems that by nature the desires of the young are dissimilar from those of the old. . . . the dissimilarity prohibits and prevents that complete unity that is required in true love. . . . For our need, here is this competent and suitable strategy for one and all, that the elders place themselves often in easy familiarity with the young, especially at dinner. I don't know whence it is that this pastime of bantering at a meal inculcates such grace and domesticity. And here it will suffice if the young would have as much modesty and reverence toward their betters as good customs require, and if the elders put aside that severe gravity and conduct themselves as humanely, easily, affably as is necessary to equate themselves to the youth without undue levity.[111]

The common meal, the point where a true bond between old and young became possible, demonstrates why the phrase *ad uno pane e uno vino* was seized upon as the metaphor for familial coresidence. The family meal was, in fact, viewed as a quasi-ritualistic event, a form of communion, whose participants would come to esteem each other as fellow worshippers at the altar of the family.[112]

Communion through the meal was one way of coping with what was, in fact, a fundamental ambiguity in the Florentine family: While children were necessary to form and perpetuate the family, they could also bring it to ruin.

Fathers had to be constantly aware of the ideal and the functional duality that children represented. They had to develop strategies and manipulate relationships to protect themselves and their families.[113] They had to prevent or minimize losses due to a recalcitrant son, but without totally alienating him, if possible, because he was still a relative and a potential source of support. Likewise, fathers had to make use of a good son, but without provoking the jealousies of other children. And fathers had to cultivate relationships beyond the home with *parenti*, *amici*, and *vicini*, who were at times more useful and more trustworthy than family members, though no relationship was fully secure.[114]

On important political and economic issues, *amici*, *vicini*, *parenti*, and even members of the same *casa* could find themselves on different sides;[115] perceived interests could, therefore, result in emphasizing or downplaying any particular relationship, in cultivating ties or denying them. Kinship, even kinship within the *casa*, was defined by only very general and amorphous rights and duties (for example, respect, obedience, aid) and could not enforce specific rights or duties. It was left to the individual (or groups) to invoke them and make them active. Manipulating kin ties served various purposes and strategies: acquiring or disposing of a piece of property, a marriage alliance, holding political office, a favorable judgment, and emancipation figures among the strategies and purposes involving fathers and their children.

Emancipation in Florence

In some societies, including modern Italy, a man does not become an active and full member of the community until he is head of his own family; and he becomes head of a family by marrying and establishing a separate residence.[116] Extensive paternal power in Florence, however, ensured that marriage and separate residence, neither singly nor together, would of themselves make a man the head of his own family. Short of his father's death, only emancipation could provide the legal attributes necessary for being head of a family. However, in view of the dual meaning of emancipatory liberation in Florentine law and the ideology, structure, and multiple functions of the *casa*, it seems justifiable to insist that emancipation did not necessarily confer *effective* paternal status on the emancipatus. Whether it did or not and the degree to which it did varied with circumstances, with the strategies emancipation was serving.

When both aspects of emancipatory liberation were at play and relatively substantial property rights were in question, emancipation implied a general restructuring of the father-son relationship in terms of legal rights and responsibilities. Dysfunctional conflict or tension, among other things, could, thus, be managed by a peaceful and acceptable legal maneuver. One graphic example of this restructuring of the father-son relationship is that of Dietisalvi di Nerone Neroni. In his account of his own emancipation, like other Florentines before and afterward, he stressed the conjoined verbs *liberare* and *mancipare*. He also recorded the details of an agreement between himself and his father that was reached by means of a third party acting as arbitrator, an agreement that realigned their relationship:

> And furthermore, on the same day, we . . . made a compromise through the aforesaid messer Giovanni, and he proclaimed and decreed that Nerone should allot me my [wife's] dowry, which is 1,300 florins of gold in the shop, that is, that everything that is in the shop is understood to be mine, except for 100 florins . . . and all things in my room and the clothing of myself and my wife, and all my books. And although all these things do not amount to the aforesaid sum, nevertheless I was content to let the matter drop, and I gave receipt and declared that I had received all the aforesaid amount. And furthermore, I obligated myself in that every year that I remain in the house with Nerone I would give him 50 gold florins for the expenses of myself and my wife, and I did not want to be liable for anything more.[117]

Now that Dietisalvi held all his property in his own name, now that all he gained went to himself and not to his father, it was necessary to stipulate how much he had to contribute to household expenses. It was not unusual for a relative to pay room and board; payment was, however, a sign that living together was not involuntary.[118] To Dietisalvi Neroni, emancipation meant, moreover, that he was free from his father's control over his business and patrimonial affairs. In place of that control, he and his father had defined their relationship in terms of contractual rights and duties.[119] In his case, then, emancipation amounted to a form of adulthood (understood as patrimonial competence). He controlled his property (his *peculium*), here mainly his wife's dowry. Mollified by this arrangement, Dietisalvi could, henceforth, treat his property as his own, as he did when he later lent his father a book and made note of it in his accounts along with his other transactions.[120] His father, however, remained the official head of the household, charging his son room and board.

Another Florentine, Lodovico di Paolo Niccolini, who was emancipated at age 27 in 1466, after a year of marriage, also sought and received autonomy from his emancipation. In fact, he sought greater autonomy than did Dietisalvi Neroni because Niccolini wanted to move out of his father's house at the same time. Since, in his father's opinion, he was a good son and knew how to manage his affairs, he was given his wife's dowry and his share of the patrimony.[121]

The emancipations of Neroni and Niccolini may have masked a degree of conflict between them and their fathers, a conflict that took the form of agitation for independence. In any case, these emancipations resulted in independence; other emancipations, however, conferred little or no status or authority on a child. They were undertaken to deal with adverse moments in familial fortunes (often utilizing the negative aspect of liberation from mutual liabilities) or to utilize the new legal abilities of the emancipatus in the service of father and family.

Lapo Niccolini's precautionary emancipation of Niccolaio is an example of a father coping with economic misfortune, in this case brought on by the son. Lapo clearly hoped to preserve his patrimony from any further claims from his son's creditors.[122] Consiglio di ser Ventura Monachi likewise used emancipation to "avert loss," but in this case, it was a matter of losses from his own business dealings.[123] It is not surprising, moreover, in view of the Florentine legislation's concern with fraud that not all fathers used emancipation licitly in this regard. Matteo di Niccolò Corsini emancipated six young sons and a daughter to protect the property he gave them when he found himself in financial difficulty. But the transfer of property in emancipation remained largely fictive, for Matteo later sold a farm ostensibly given to one of his sons.[124] Another glaring instance of the fraudulent use of emancipation occurred in the family of Luca da Panzano. When his granddaughter Mea was emancipated by her father Antonio, Luca coolly noted that the emancipation was performed so that she might legally acquire the estate of her dead mother. This acquisition was intended "in truth to protect the wealth of Antonio her father, because his bank is in bad shape."[125]

Other Florentine fathers turned to emancipation as a means of involving their children in family affairs. Bartolomeo di Niccolò Valori, for example, was emancipated on the eve of his father's departure for Hungary on business. As a result, he was later called on to handle a business transaction for his father and to act on the family's behalf in a lawsuit.[126] Guido Baldovinetti found a variety of uses for the emancipations of his sons: One was emancipated so that the property given him could be protected from scheming maternal kinsmen. Two years later, two other sons, following emancipation, were able to help him meet some debts, in return for which they received the casa as their inheritance 15 years later; a fourth son was disinherited.[127]

Finally, it is also important to keep in mind that emancipation was legally valid not merely for a single act but it dissolved the *patria potestas* irrevocably. As a result, emancipation carried a potential that might not be manifested until well after its enactment. The original purpose served, other and quite different purposes could later arise. To cite a fairly simple case, Niccolò di Giovanni dei Giraldi, an emancipated son, made a petition to the Signoria of Florence to be absolved of any liability for his father before the *speculum*. Because he was not only emancipated but (at least patrimonially, if not residentially) separated from his father, his petition received favorable action.[128] The emancipation that may originally have been intended to free a frustrated son from paternal control later became an emancipation whose central feature was the protection afforded by having terminated liability.

Because emancipation entailed both aspects of freedom (from paternal control and from reciprocal liabilities) and because fathers (and sons) were simultaneously concerned with preserving the family and avoiding internal conflict, not all emancipations admit as simple an interpretation as that given to the emancipation of Niccolò di Giovanni dei Giraldi. In some cases, the meaning and use of emancipation varied with time in a more complex fashion. The case of Domenico di Niccolò Pollini is instructive; he was emancipated in 1411 at age 18. He continued to live with his father but renounced his right to his mother's dowry. His emancipation thereby aided his father in managing the patrimony. Domenico was later married, and his father received the lavish 1,300-florin dowry. His wife's death led to a second marriage in 1418, this time a political alliance that produced only a modest dowry of 480 florins. This second marriage, said Domenico, was only for his father's convenience: "I obeyed him in everything and took the small dowry to his advantage and my loss to be useful to him." Finally, Domenico's resentment at being exploited by his father not only provoked Domenico to move out of the house, but to bring suit against his father before the consuls of the Por Santa Maria guild (which he could do because he was emancipated). Domenico demanded his wife's dowry and that of his maternal grandmother. Niccolò claimed that he had used this property to support Domenico and his family. Domenico, however, won the judgment, having used his legal independence to bring suit to gain more effective control of himself and his property, despite the fact that "one cannot see anything in the world more abominable and dishonorable than a father and son in conflict."[129]

These few examples must suffice for the moment to show how pliable a tool emancipation could be in familial strategies. With its dual sense of freedom (*liberare* and *disobligare*), it was a potential instrument for dealing with functional or dysfunctional moments in father-child relations and familial fortunes. It is clear, nonetheless, that no one explanation offered by the historians considered at the beginning of this chapter has completely explained the function and sense of emancipation in Florentine society. Emancipation was not unequivocally and inalterably connected with maturity, although the age of an emancipatus could be an important factor. Emancipation was not solely a means of exploiting children for the sake of father and family, as Cammarosano argues, for it could also serve the designs of sons like Lodovico Niccolini. Emancipation was truly an instrument whose function varied with the state of the family and the relationships within it, even as these changed well after the emancipation itself. In any particular instance, circumstances both legal and extralegal were present to dictate courses of action, and these circumstances changed continually throughout the fourteenth and fifteenth centuries.

CHAPTER FOUR

Emancipatory Practices
in Florence

Having located the various norms, legal and cultural, affecting and defining emancipation, it is now possible to investigate emancipation, not as a cultural construct or as a legal institution, but as an event. By looking at a number of emancipations, we can isolate various factors —who was emancipating, who was being emancipated, what types of property were involved in emancipations—throughout the fourteenth and fifteenth centuries in order to determine the reasons for emancipations; in other words, its uses.

The Sources

There are two main sources of data on Florentine emancipatory practices: the registries of emancipations and the chartularies of the notaries. The registries survive almost intact. The aggregate data for this chapter come from the registry kept by the communal government from 1422 until 1534 and from the registries of the Mercanzia from before 1422 (back to its inception in 1355).[1] Since registration with the Signoria was required for validity, the continuous records of the Mercanzia after 1421 were not systematically exploited. There is some discrepancy between the two registries, but the range of discrepancy decreases over time.[2]

The state of the records, especially those of the Mercanzia, varies from one point in time to the next, largely depending on the diligence of the notary who had charge of the records at that time. The usual entry in the registries would, as the law proscribed, provide the names of the father, of the emancipatus(i), and of the notary as well as the dates of the emancipation itself and of its notification. Often, the father's place of residence (that is, the urban *popolo*, the rural commune or parish, the appropriate administrative division within another city) and occupation were indicated. Occasionally, there is some indication of the age(s) of the emancipatus(i). The Mercanzia registry has two large gaps of about a year each (22 May 1416 to 22 December 1417 and 8 January 1393 to 30 January 1394). In both the Mercanzia and especially the communal registry, there is a stray notification of repudiation of inheritance. It appears that the same notary kept both registries (repudiations of inheritance were also registered) and may at times have conflated his books. Finally, the later volumes of the commune's registry reveal a more casual approach to record keeping (for example, placing two or more entries on one page contrary to previous practice) and provide less information about age, residence, and occupation, probably because the notary suppressed such trivia in favor of saving time and space.

The style of the Mercanzia entries was less formal than that of the communal registry. In some of the former's entries, emancipated sons were depicted as the actual notifiers of their own emancipations. The fact that the son could perform the notification means that he could protect himself and his new status from an intentional or unintentional lapse on the part of his father. In general, however, Florentine fathers were well aware of their legal obligation to notify the authorities of an emancipation. Fathers often made a record of the notification alongside their record of the emancipation in their domestic account book, and they noted when an emancipation was invalid because they had failed to register it.[3]

One of the curious features of the registries is the repetitive entries—notifications that had already, days, months, or even years before been entered in the books.[4] These duplications point to a desire to fulfill the precepts of the law. The long-term duplications may indicate, too, that the original emancipation had a pressing, immediate motivation, especially if the child were very young. In later years, a second emancipation and registration may have been deemed necessary to publicize the emancipation to others whose memory of the first emancipation may have faded; in such cases, the emancipation was repeated. I encountered, in fact, several instances where an emancipation had been performed twice or even three times.

Another indication that emancipation was often performed in order to meet some pressing legal need, usually signaled by other legal actions immediately following it, is the fact that notarial records do not always agree with the emancipation registries. Some of the emancipations found in the notarial books simply were not registered, and most of them were followed by other legal acts.[5] This observation leads to a conjecture about the law. The civil law, as has been seen, declared that an emancipation could not be performed for the purpose of executing a specific act enabled by emancipation. The law said that emancipation was general and permanent; it enabled all possible legal acts whenever they might occur. Paradoxically, however, the statutory registration requirement offered a way around this tenet of the civil law. A valid emancipation could be undertaken, allowing the emancipatus appropriate legal abilities, and the efficacy of that emancipation could later be revoked for failure to register it after the lapse of the requisite time period. The rule in the statutes was that such unregistered emancipations were invalid in matters that benefited the emancipatus; it would seem, however, that any benefit to the father or to third parties was not lost. (Here, the decisions of judges and the opinions of lawyers would be decisive if suits were brought.) For example, Bernardo d'Andrea di Bernardo dei Brandellini emancipated his sons Giuliano and Andrea in 1492 so that they could participate with him in the sale of a piece of land. The boys also acceded to their shares of their mother's estate. Bernardo did not register the emancipation. Since the alienation of the land was not to the sons' benefit, nonregistration did not affect the validity of their role in the sale. Nonregistration also meant that they were unable to make use of the property they had gained by accepting their shares of the maternal estate; in other words, they were unable to use the land legally to their advantage in a transaction. In effect, they could not alienate or obligate it.

The notarial records reveal much more than an occasional unregistered emancipation; they provide a legal record of all the particulars of an emancipation. They reveal the contents of the *praemium* and the substance of any other legal act completed before the notary at, or around, the same time by the emancipator, the emancipati, and other relatives or associates. The notaries' books also provide additional data on such matters as ages, residence, and occupation. Taken together, the data in the registries and notarial chartularies make it possible to discern any pattern in emancipatory behavior and to discuss the function and meaning of individual emancipations.

An Overview

The registries provide a point of departure for viewing the vicissitudes of emancipation in an aggregate sense. Table 1 shows the distribution of acts of emancipation by decade, calculated by the Florentine year (not the modern) in which they occurred (not the year in which they were registered), beginning in 1355 when the Mercanzia began registering emancipations.

The registered emancipations came from all over the Florentine do-

TABLE 1.

Emancipations by Decade

Decade	Emancipations	Total emancipated	Multiple emancipations	Females emancipated	Percentage of multiple emancipations	Percentage of females emancipated
1355–59[a]	172	204	26	40	.151	.196
1360–69	778	936	117	202	.150	.216
1370–79	1,047	1,290	174	231	.166	.179
1380–89	1,173	1,512	245	249	.209	.165
1390–99[b]	1,208	1,599	276	267	.228	.167
1400–1409	1,126	1,417	198	254	.176	.179
1410–19[c]	1,149	1,505	243	203	.211	.135
1420–29[d]	528	680	109	86	.205	.127
1430–39	369	478	71	49	.192	.103
1440–49	487	598	78	49	.160	.081
1450–59	579	727	102	46	.176	.063
1460–69	756	960	154	55	.204	.057
1470–79	777	933	117	59	.151	.063
1480–89	751	879	98	61	.130	.069
1490–99	652	774	93	72	.143	.093
1500–1509	599	678	65	52	.109	.077
1510–19	728	833	82	52	.113	.062
1520–29	689	800	103	66	.149	.083
1530–33[e]	179	209	22	18	.123	.086
TOTALS	13,747	17,022	2,373	2,111	.173	.124

[a]Mercanzia registry begins 13 August 1355.
[b]Gap in registry from 8 January 1392 (1393 modern style) to 30 January 1393 (1394 modern style).
[c]Gap in registry from 22 May to 22 December 1417.
[d]Communal registry begins 24 January 1421 (1422 modern style).
[e]Communal registry ends 20 February 1533 (1534 modern style).

minion, whatever its extent, in a given year. There were, however, relatively few emancipations from the other major Tuscan cities subject to Florentine rule—Pistoia, San Gimignano, Arezzo, Pisa; in fact, cities like San Gimignano continued to register their emancipations themselves. Those citizens and residents of such cities who had their emancipations recorded in Florence were generally those who had some professional, commercial, or political connection with the Arno city. In the Florentine registries, therefore, we find the emancipations of men like the jurist Nello da San Gimignano, the canon of Arezzo messer

Donato di ser Mino, the son of Filippo di Francesco di Duccio of Pistoia, who was a notary, and the sons of the Pisan messer Raynerio di messer Gherardo de' Gambacorti.[6] Some few emancipations, in addition, came from beyond Florentine territory, as the law allowed, involving Florentines away in other cities, such as Venice;[7] otherwise, there is no discernible geographic bias in the registries. Registered emancipations occurred in every parish and throughout the rural areas.[8] Time and again, we run across the names of rural towns or areas like Sesto, Settimo, Quinto, Borgo San Lorenzo, Carmignano, Castel Fiorentino, Terra Nuova, Barberino, Scarperia. There does, however, appear to have been a decrease in registering emancipations from outside Florence in the course of the fifteenth century. Actually, it would be more accurate to say that the percentage of emancipations identifiable as those of a father residing outside Florence decreases (Table 2).

Emancipations took place all over Tuscany, but they did not take

TABLE 2.
Residence and Emancipation

Decade	Emancipations	Emancipations outside Florence	Percentage of emancipations outside Florence
1355–59	172	53	.308
1360–69	778	300	.386
1370–79	1,047	484	.462
1380–89	1,173	527	.449
1390–99	1,208	500	.414
1400–1409	1,126	553	.491
1410–19	1,149	542	.472
1420–29	528	226	.434
1430–39	369	131	.361
1440–49	487	132	.272
1450–59	579	157	.271
1460–69	756	151	.200
1470–79	777	158	.203
1480–89	751	126	.168
1490–99	652	115	.176
1500–1509	599	80	.134
1510–19	728	66	.091
1520–29	689	77	.112
1530–33	179	18	.101
TOTALS	13,747	4,396	.320

place in every family. The total number of emancipations and of those emancipated clearly indicates that emancipation was not a legal institution that touched everyone in the Tuscan population. It is not possible to tell exactly what portion of the Tuscan population was emancipated at any one time; it is even harder to tell what portion of that population was emancipable. It seems, however, that the portion of the population involved in emancipation was small; the reasons for this fact are many. As Herlihy and Klapisch have shown, a large portion of the Tuscan population consisted of children, and all children under seven were ineligible for emancipation without imperial rescript. The same historians have also demonstrated that men were of relatively advanced age at marriage; many of them, therefore, may have died before emancipating all or some of their children. The fact that Florentine law allowed sons to practice a trade without being emancipated and the cultural bias in favor of the father's dominant position and the unity of the family must also have been powerful disincentive factors. Perhaps most important was the relative wealth and social position of the family: As a patrimonially enabling act, emancipation would have meant very little to the poor. The proportional decrease in emancipations in rural areas also shows that its attractions were greater in the more mobile and diversified social and economic environment of the city.[9] Finally, it is impossible to tell what role, if any, was played by tacit emancipation, for it is simply impossible to gather any data concerning it. A tacit emancipation would only be recognized if one sued to have it recognized, and I have found no such suits. The fact that sons who lived apart from their fathers were sometimes formally emancipated makes it seem that few would have pressed such a suit. We cannot assume that all children not formally emancipated were tacitly emancipated.

With an understanding of the extent of the coverage of the emancipation registries, I turn to the aggregate figures yielded by those registries. The first point of interest is the year-to-year fluctuation in the figures in comparison to overall trends. These fluctuations seem to be pinned to a number of political and demographic factors. The total number of emancipations was relatively low in the last half of the 1350s, when the effects of the great plague and famines of the 1340s were still in evidence.[10] The number of emancipations rose during the 1360s and 1370s and remained high until 1422. Throughout the period before 1422, there were short-term fluctuations reflecting social and political events. The years of the War of the (so-called) Eight Saints (1374–1376) saw a relatively low number of emancipations (84 in 1374 and 81 in 1376, as opposed to 107 in 1373 and 105 in 1377). The total was also low in 1378, the year of the Ciompi revolt (84 emancipations) and, interestingly, very high in 1382 (153 emancipations), the year of the return of the oligarchy. The war year of 1402 also saw a rather substantial drop in the number of emancipations. The wars and sweeping political events in the fifteenth and early sixteenth centuries continued to be faithfully reflected in emancipation totals as short-term, generally negative fluctuations (for example, only 34 emancipations in 1494 in contrast to 86 in 1493).

Whereas war and political disruption affected emancipation negatively, the effects of plague epidemics in the short term were uneven. The plagues of 1363, 1374 to 1375, 1423 to 1424, and 1449 may be accountable for decreased numbers of emancipations; but the epidemics of 1390 and especially that of 1400 appear to have stimulated emancipatory activity. There were more emancipations in 1400 (175) than in any other single year. Other known years of marked plague mortality have left little real trace.[11] In any case, the data reveal that emancipation was bound up with practical considerations. Events like wars and plagues that could terminate, change, or create opportunities—or temporarily dismantle the administrative machinery—contributed, directly or indirectly, to the decision to emancipate.

The most salient feature in the overall data is the precipitous decline in the number of emancipations from 125 in 1421 to only 33 in 1422 and the continued lower number of emancipations thereafter. Why this sudden and radical drop, and why did it persist? It is perhaps easier to point to reasons for the continual depression in emancipatory activity. The peculiar compounding of wars, plague, and economic problems in the 1420s and 1430s may account for much of this statistical pattern. The continued low levels of emancipations after 1440 (low in relation to the figures before 1422) may be indicative of a general economic stagnation, although the relative increase in emancipations may be related to some degree of demographic growth in those years. The increase in average household size in the fifteenth century documented by Herlihy and Klapisch, moreover, may have been both cause and effect of less emancipation.

As for the dramatic difference between 1421 and 1422, it seems that since the change coincides with the entry of the Signoria itself into the process of registering emancipations, this fact must be interpreted as a reason for the change. A good deal of the sudden reluctance of Florentines to emancipate their children may be attributable to the higher fee charged by the Signoria for registration. If the higher fee did, indeed, have an effect, we would suspect it to result in emancipation becoming an instrument more exclusively for the use of the wealthy. To some extent, as will be seen, this was, in fact, the case. But the increased cost of emancipation was probably not the sole factor; the new fee of one florin for each *emancipatus* was not necessarily an insurmountable sum. The communal government in the 1420s was arrogating more power to itself, stripping functions from bodies like the Mercanzia, and becoming involved in such ventures as the Sea Consuls, the *Monte delle doti*, and the *catasto*. Given its need for liquid capital, the commune was intent on regulating and controlling commercial affairs and promoting a healthy economy in order to generate revenue through taxes and forced loans. The type of studied suspicion and distrust that temporarily thwarted the dowry fund and generated fraudulent evasions of the *catasto* may have become a general lack of activity when a question of registering emancipations.[12] This lack of activity may, however, in this case be indicative of the law's success. Emancipation could not be used fraudulently if it were not used. The success of this registration law may have been the reason the government turned to registration procedures again to deal with arbitrations (1458) and the *contracti occulti* (1477). It is likely, at least, that emancipation was being used for purposes generally related to the legal severance of mutual liability (as opposed to patrimonial and familial adjustments), because the number of emancipations in the first two decades of the fifteenth century remained quite high while the plague- and war-ridden population was declining.[13] Also, the available data on ages at emancipation indicate that half or more of these *emancipati* (especially from 1400–1409) were below the age of majority and so incapable of legal action on their own (see Table 4). These were not sons agitating for a measure of responsibility; a number of them may have been used in a fraudulent emancipation like their contemporary, the daughter of Antonio di Luca da Panzano.

Fraudulent use of emancipation could not be halted totally by the 1421 law, but it appears that the law did have some effect. Emancipations performed largely from the desire to terminate legal liabilities and to transfer property that could be protected by terminating liability certainly continued. After the 1420s, however, emancipation also came to be used increasingly in ways (some of them new) designed to cope with other domestic problems.

Closely related to the number of emancipations is the number of children emancipated. In the great majority of emancipations, only one child was involved; but many emancipations included two children, and the number went as high as seven. Table 3 shows the percentages of multiple emancipations by decades. It reveals that from the 1380s through the 1430s, multiple emancipations accounted for around 20 percent (actually 20.6 percent) of the total number of acts of emancipation. Both before and after this period, multiples amounted to only around 15 percent (15.9 percent before 1380, 15.4 percent after

1440); the 1460s being a glaring exception. In the last decades of the fifteenth century, the percentage fell below 15 and even lower in the first decades of the sixteenth century. Table 3 does not take into account a phenomenon apparent in the registry that should be mentioned here. There were instances when a father emancipated one or more children and soon after, within a matter of days or perhaps a month, emancipated another or others. These "soon after" instances could be construed as a type of multiple emancipation. There were also a few instances when brothers or cousins emancipated children within a brief interval, sometimes on the same day, and before the same notary. These instances cannot, however, be properly termed multiple emancipations. Both types of instances occur sporadically and are too few to affect markedly the trends established in Table 3.[14]

TABLE 3.

Multiple Emancipations

	EMANCIPATIONS		EMANCIPATI		
Decade	Multiple emanci- pations	Percentage	Emancipati in multiple emanci- pations	Emancipati per multiple emanci- pation	Emancipati per emanci- pation
1355–59	26	.151	58	2.23	1.19
1360–69	117	.150	273	2.33	1.20
1370–79	174	.166	417	2.40	1.23
1380–89	245	.209	584	2.38	1.29
1390–99	276	.228	666	2.41	1.32
1400–1409	198	.176	489	2.47	1.26
1410–19	243	.211	599	2.47	1.31
1420–29	109	.205	260	2.39	1.28
1430–39	71	.192	180	2.54	1.30
1440–49	78	.160	189	2.42	1.23
1450–59	102	.176	250	2.45	1.26
1460–69	154	.204	358	2.32	1.27
1470–79	117	.151	273	2.33	1.20
1480–89	98	.130	226	2.31	1.17
1490–99	93	.143	215	2.31	1.19
1500–1509	65	.109	142	2.18	1.13
1510–19	82	.113	187	2.28	1.14
1520–29	103	.149	225	2.18	1.16
1530–33	22	.123	52	2.36	1.17
TOTALS	2,373	.173	5,643	2.38	1.24

The low rate of multiple emancipations in the period from 1355 to 1380 could well be the result of the ravages of the recurrent plagues on the younger elements of the population. This impression is strengthened when we look at the average number of emancipati involved in multiple emancipations, for then we see that the average was also low prior to the 1380s. In the following decades, from the 1380s through the 1450s, the mean remained near or over 2.4 emancipati per multiple act, higher than the average from 1355 to 1380. The 1460s saw an average below 2.4, but the lower average number of emancipati per multiple emancipation must be balanced by reference to the higher percentage of multiple acts of emancipation in that decade. If we turn to the average number of emancipati per act (not per multiple act), we see that a downward trend began in the 1430s (actually 1436), when the percentage of multiple acts of emancipation also began to fall. Thereafter, children were more often emancipated singly.

Finally, in the latter decades, the averages show a decline both for the number of children per emancipation and for the number per multiple emancipation. This occurred at the same time that the total number of emancipations and the proportion of multiple acts were falling. The causes for these declines are not to be found in demographic contraction or in a greater incidence of plagues striking the younger cadre of the population. If anything, the total population of Florence must have been above the total of 1427 and even growing.

The decrease in the use of multiple emancipations may, therefore, be another indication that emancipation after 1421 was less a matter of terminating legal liability than it had been previously and more a matter of adaptive familial strategy in which a particular child was involved. With household size increasing in the fifteenth century, there was no shortage of children to be emancipated in groups. The decline in multiple emancipations must have been the result of a familial strategy dictating a different use of emancipation. There are a number of factors, in fact, that point to a different use of emancipation beginning in, and around, the 1420s. In addition to total emancipations and the frequency of multiple emancipations, variables like sex, age, property, and residence underwent significant changes in trend around 1421.

We would expect any change in the use of emancipation to be reflected in a change in who was being emancipated and, perhaps, in who was doing the emancipating. Age might provide one indication of a different population among the emancipati. Ages were not systematically indicated either in the emancipation registry or in the notarial records; they were occasionally given, however, and more frequently, in notarial charters. When the age of the emancipatus was furnished (the age of the father never being given), it was not rendered precisely but put in broad terms of legal significance. In other words, the usual practice was to cite an age of legal importance as a minimum age of the emancipatus (for example, *maiorem septem annis, maiorem septem annorum minorem tamen quattuordecim, maiorem quattuordecim annorum, maiorem annorum vigintiquinque, maiorem duodecim annis*). Phrases like *ut dixerat* appended to the age make it clear that the notaries simply took the party's word and did not ask for evidence or corroboration by witnesses. The notarial records and the emancipation registries, then, provide a relatively vague and random insight into the ages of emancipati. This information is assembled in Table 4.[15]

A second source of data on ages has also been utilized. This source is the registration of birth dates of politically eligible Florentine males, a practice begun in 1429 and supervised by the magistracy of the Conservatori delle Leggi.[16] This second source is more satisfactory because the ages of emancipati can be calculated very exactly (I have rounded them to the half year); however, the data pertains to only a limited segment of the population. The data derived from this second source

TABLE 4.

Ages of Emancipati by Sex

MALES

Decade	AGES					PERCENTAGES			
	0–7	7–14	14–18	18–25	25+	7–14	14–18	18–25	25+
1340–49		4		3		.571		.429	
1350–59		2	1	2		.400	.200	.400	
1360–69		25	3	7		.714	.086	.200	
1370–79	5	25	13	31	3	.325	.169	.403	.039
1380–89		39	9	36	5	.438	.101	.404	.056
1390–99		37	21	28	9	.389	.221	.295	.095
1400–1409		55	13	30	12	.500	.118	.273	.109
1410–19	1	50	22	70	13	.321	.141	.449	.083
1420–29		17	7	26	10	.283	.117	.433	.167
1430–39	3	25	11	17	17	.342	.151	.233	.233
1440–49		11	13	58	10	.120	.141	.630	.109
1450–59		10	12	54	23	.101	.121	.545	.232
1460–69		14	20	80	29	.098	.140	.559	.203
1470–79		9	12	72	34	.071	.094	.567	.268
1480–89		2	5	76	21	.019	.048	.731	.202
1490–99		5	2	35	20	.081	.032	.565	.323
1500–1509		2	2	22	2	.071	.071	.786	.071
TOTALS	9	332	166	647	208	.244	.122	.475	.153

supplements that from the registries and notarial chartularies and is summarized in Table 5.

Taken together, the two types of age data reveal some interesting facts about emancipatory practices in Florence. Table 4 indicates that from the 1370s through the first decade of the fifteenth century, less than 40 percent of male emancipati whose ages were given were adults (that is, over 18). After 1410, the percentage of adults among the emancipati was usually over half; and by the end of the fifteenth century, adults accounted for almost 90 percent of those whose ages were given. The ages of emancipated women show a similar increase. Before 1390, less than 20 percent of emancipatae were 18 or over; after 1410, adult women accounted for well over half of the women emancipated, while the number of emancipatae under 12 declined from over 40 percent to 20 percent by the 1430s. In sum, then, with regard to the ages of both males and females, the data in Table 4 point to increasing emancipation of adults beginning in the decade from 1410 to 1419.

The data in Table 5 provide another perspective on the problem of

Table 4 (*continued*)

FEMALES

Decade	7–12	12–18	18+	7–12	12–18	18+
	AGES			PERCENTAGES		
1340–49		1			1.00	
1350–59		1			1.00	
1360–69	6	6	1	.462	.462	.077
1370–79	9	7	2	.500	.389	.111
1380–89	8	9	3	.400	.450	.150
1390–99	9	8	12	.310	.276	.414
1400–1409	19	11	12	.452	.262	.286
1410–19	10	3	20	.303	.091	.606
1420–29	4	2	12	.222	.111	.667
1430–39		3	3		.500	.500
1440–49	3	3	9	.200	.200	.600
1450–59	2	4	4	.200	.400	.400
1460–69		1	3		.250	.750
1470–79	1	2	7	.100	.200	.700
1480–89			6			1.00
1490–99			4			1.00
1500–1509			3			1.00
TOTALS	71	61	101	.305	.262	.433

the ages of emancipati, a perspective that revises some first impressions garnered from Table 4. In the first place, Table 5 shows a much flatter distribution of emancipati between the 18-to-25 age group and that of the over-25 group. The discrepancy between Tables 4 and 5 here indicates that people who gave ages to be entered in the notarial charter or in the emancipation registry generally desired only to establish the legal majority of the emancipatus (in which case, they only needed to claim that the emancipatus was over 18, even if he were over 25). The analogous observation holds for the two tables with respect to younger emancipati. Table 4 shows a marked bias toward the 7-to-14 age group, at least for the years between 1410 and 1449—the result of doing no more than certifying that the child was of age for emancipation.

Table 5, then, displays a somewhat more consistent distribution of emancipati among the various legally significant age groups, with an average age between 22 and 25 years. This second table, however, confirms the first, insofar as it also shows that three-fourths or more of the emancipati were adults after 1422 (with a slight continual in-

TABLE 5.

Tratte Ages of Florentine Males

| Decade | AGES | | | | | PERCENTAGES | | | | | |
	0–7	7–14	14–18	18–25	25+	0–7	7–14	14–18	18–25	25+	Average
1416–21[a]		19	9	26	8		.306	.145	.419	.129	18.5
1422–29	2	3	7	22	18	.038	.058	.135	.423	.346	23.0
1430–39	3	17	15	41	42	.025	.144	.127	.347	.356	22.0
1440–49	1	8	10	54	61	.007	.060	.075	.403	.455	24.9
1450–59	1	13	11	32	52	.009	.119	.101	.294	.477	24.2
1460–69	1	16	22	77	60	.006	.091	.125	.438	.341	23.3
1470–79	1	14	27	87	62	.005	.073	.141	.455	.325	22.4
1480–89		20	31	120	81		.079	.123	.476	.321	22.4
1490–99	2	17	25	107	99	.008	.068	.100	.428	.396	23.5
1500–1509	2	12	24	104	103	.008	.049	.099	.424	.420	24.6
1510–19		21	42	116	120		.070	.140	.388	.401	23.6
1520–29	2	18	60	128	106	.006	.057	.191	.408	.338	23.1
1530–33		4	16	47	25		.043	.174	.511	.272	21.9
TOTALS	15	182	299	961	837	.006	.079	.135	.419	.365	23.2

[a]Dividing point of 1421–22 used here because it coincides with change over from Mercanzia to communal registry.

crease from 77.1 percent in the 1450s to 84 percent in the first decade of the sixteenth century). The relatively low percentage of adult
emancipations (70.4 percent) in the 1430s, moreover, may be ascribed
to the notoriously difficult political situation in the first years of that
decade (the war with Lucca, the factional strife between the Medici
and the Albizzi, the increase in fiscal delinquency), or so it would
seem, given the fact that of the 25 emancipati of the 1430s who were
not adults, 20 were emancipated in the period from 1430 to 1433.

At this point, a precautionary note is in order regarding Table 5.
While it seems to confirm the impression that the percentage of adults
among the emancipati began to increase precisely around the time of
the establishment of the communal registry in 1422, this confirmation
may owe something to the nature of the data. Because declarations of
birth dates were collected only from 1429 on, as we go further back in
time through the emancipation lists, the ages of the emancipati who
can be located will necessarily decrease. To minimize the resulting
distortion, I have gone back only as far as 1416. Some distortion must
remain, however; and, in any case, there are only six years on which
to base a comparison of ages before and after 1421.[17] Until it is possible
to calculate a good number of exact ages for the decades before 1422,
we must admit a degree of uncertainty about the purported increase
in adult emancipati beginning in 1422.

In general, the age data confirm that emancipation was not a ritual
marking maturity. Significant numbers of minors and adults well along
into their 30s and 40s were always being emancipated. In my opinion,
an increase in the ages of emancipati points, not to a greater emphasis
on maturity, but to a greater emphasis on the positive or instrumental
aspects of emancipation. Emancipation in a negative sense—to avoid
financial liability, for example—could be undertaken any time after
age seven. Indeed, if a father wanted to protect his child, we would
expect him to emancipate the child as soon as possible. If, however,
the father were intent on the rights and abilities conferred by emancipation, then emancipation would have to be delayed until the child
had reached an age at which he or she could make use of those rights
and abilities.

The increasing age of emancipati also raises another point. If the
emancipatus was becoming older, so was his father, and paternal age
was not an unimportant consideration in some emancipations. In addition, postponing emancipation to a later age accounts, in part, for
the lower number of emancipations in the fifteenth century. Quite
simply, the longer the father waited, the greater the chance that he
would die before emancipating. As Herlihy has determined, the aver-

age age at marriage for men was quite old;[18] a man who married at age 30 would be 48 or 49, at least, by the time his first child (if the child survived) reached 18.

A decline in the incidence of female emancipations also set in in the second decade of the fifteenth century. This decline occurred in both married and unmarried women more or less equally (Table 6). Until the sixteenth century, married and widowed women rather consistently accounted for about one-quarter of all women emancipated.[19] The establishment of the *Monte delle doti* in 1425 and its subsequent growth in the 1430s may have further fueled the reluctance to emancipate daughters. A father could hope to control the dowry of his unemancipated daughter whose husband was deceased, and this control could be especially important if the daughter's marriage ended without issue, in which case her dowry was by law to be returned to her from her husband's estate.[20] Another factor that could have con-

TABLE 6.
Emancipation of Females by Marital Status

Decade	Total females emancipated	Married and widowed	Percentage of married and widowed emancipated
1355–59	40	6	.150
1360–69	202	35	.173
1370–79	231	46	.199
1380–89	249	53	.213
1390–99	267	66	.247
1400–1409	254	59	.232
1410–19	203	44	.217
1420–29	86	26	.302
1430–39	49	12	.245
1440–49	49	12	.245
1450–59	46	15	.326
1460–69	55	14	.255
1470–79	59	14	.237
1480–89	61	16	.262
1490–99	72	17	.236
1500–1509	52	5	.096
1510–19	52	19	.365
1520–29	66	22	.333
1530–33	18	11	.611
TOTALS	2,111	492	.233

tributed to the decline in female emancipations was the emphasis on the instrumental side of emancipation. Both women and minors were burdened with a number of legal disabilities and could not operate without a guardian. For whatever reason, emancipation of such children was considered of less service to the family.

In contrast to trends evident in age and sex, a decline in the incidence of emancipations involving fathers residing outside Florence becomes apparent only in the 1430s. As already noted, this decline was continual, until only around 10 percent of all emancipations in the early sixteenth century originated in the *contado* or district. In some few emancipations, fathers and sons were not coresident; if the son lived in a different parish or a different town, it was noted in the charter and the registration.[21] Formal emancipation in these circumstances shows that the son was not considered emancipated merely by virtue of his separate residence.

The data indicate that the variables of age, sex, and residence all underwent changes in the second, third, and fourth decades of the fifteenth century. Another variable that can be isolated, namely, the emancipation gift (the *praemium*), likewise displays some mutation beginning in the 1430s, although a truly dramatic shift was evident only 20 years later. Fewer *praemia* were being given; a greater portion of property transactions at emancipation took other forms, but in general property transactions decreased.

The *praemium* gives some indication of the use of emancipation in relation to wealth, but it is not a thoroughly accurate barometer. For one thing, the *praemium* could take many forms. Bellomo has declared that the *praemium* was usually the emancipated son's portion of the family estate and that it was, therefore, always a substantial amount of property. An analysis of notarial records (where it is possible to find information on the *praemium*), however, shows that in practice, the *praemium* was much more complex in nature.[22] In the first place, the *praemium*, like emancipation, was not limited to males; females, too, received *praemia*.[23] In the second place, the *praemium* was not omnipresent: A large percentage of emancipations were unaccompanied by a gift. The lack of an emancipation gift may indicate poverty or temporary financial distress, but the fact that many wealthy men, like Gino Capponi, emancipated sons and gave them no *praemium* shows that there was always a strong element of paternal choice.[24] On the other hand, a child given nothing at emancipation might later receive something from his father, if not by means of a direct gift, then perhaps as a result of an arbitration proceeding.[25]

Even if there were a *praemium*, we can never be assured by that fact alone that true control over the property had also passed to the emancipatus; we must always keep in mind the case of Matteo di Niccolò Corsini, who gave three farms to his son Piero but later sold all three of them.[26] Many a substantial *praemium* may only have been a paper gift; on the other hand, many an emancipation unaccompanied by a *praemium* may, in fact, have contained a substantial transferal of property. All emancipations contained among their legal formulas one stating that all *peculia* passed to the full legal control of the emancipatus; the contents of such *peculia* were unspecified. There is usually no way of knowing the value of the son's wife's dowry or of his portion of his mother's dowry, except in fortuitous instances (like that of Dietisalvi Neroni) where the exact contents had to be arbitrated or rendered in an equivalent value. The *peculium profectitium* may have amounted to little or nothing, or it may have consisted of all the emancipatus' bedding and furnishings.[27] It is also difficult to tell if a son's earnings, whatever they may have been, were considered to form part of the *peculium quasi castrense*; in some cases, it seems that they were so treated.[28] Yet, here as elsewhere, it is not usually possible to determine what value they had or whether real control accompanied the legal formulas in the emancipation charter.

Even where *praemia* appear, they were not always substantial. The contents of the *praemium*, moreover, seem to have undergone a change in conjunction with its decreased use in the fifteenth century. If there were an element of choice in giving a *praemium* at all, there was certainly an element of choice in what would go into it. In the fourteenth century, when the *praemium* was far more prevalent than it was in the fifteenth, many of the *praemia* were small, token monetary gifts or consisted of small pieces of land.[29] It is impossible to say what portion of the patrimony was involved in such small gifts, just as it is impossible to say what portion was involved when the gift was not small.[30] The prevalence of token-size gifts points to a symbolic rather than a real value, much as the customary 50 *lire donatio propter nuptias* (a husband's wedding gift to his bride) may have been symbolic.[31] Perhaps the modern birthday gift is the best comparison to the *praemium*. Like the birthday present, the *praemium*, at least in the fourteenth century, was seen as a normal accompaniment of the occasion and as something of value, though not necessarily of great value.[32] It was a gift appropriate to the occasion and, as many transactions of small, almost useless pieces of property, a transaction signifying the nature of the relationship between giver and receiver.[33]

The use of money in the *praemium* was usual in the fourteenth century, although real property (lands, vineyards, houses, mills) and movable possessions figured in the *praemia* of some emancipati. Gifts of specie were relatively less frequent in the fifteenth century, when

more of the *praemia* consisted of property. The trend away from money
was due, perhaps, to the general scarcity of specie in the fifteenth
century coupled with the government's voracious appetite for cash.[34]

The *praemium* was not the only way to transfer property. Table 7
takes account, therefore, of any form of property acquisition by the
emancipatus and not only of those property transfers from father to
child designed as *praemium* or *donatio*. The emancipatus could receive
something from someone other than his father; in the case of a woman,
for instance, an unmarried daughter could be given property as her
dowry. The emancipatus could undertake an *aditio hereditatis* (acces-
sion to an estate left to him) to acquire direct title to his share of his
mother's or grandmother's estate (probably primarily the deceased's
dowry). The emancipatus might also purchase property or come into
property by means of an arbitration, and a father might even rent

TABLE 7.

Praemia by Decade

Decade	Praemia	Other types of transfer to emancipati	Total acts consulted	Percentage of *praemia*	Percentage of all transfers
1300–1309	16	0	20	.800	.800
1310–19	13	1	17	.765	.824
1320–29	32	1	46	.696	.717
1330–39	45	2	58	.776	.810
1340–49	37	3	62	.597	.645
1350–59	26	3	36	.722	.806
1360–69	43	5	71	.606	.676
1370–79	31	7	79	.392	.481
1380–89	52	5	89	.584	.640
1390–99	36	5	77	.468	.532
1400–1409	34	15	77	.442	.636
1410–19	35	14	88	.398	.557
1420–29	29	6	62	.468	.565
1430–39	23	5	61	.377	.459
1440–49	31	3	82	.378	.415
1450–59	26	10	89	.292	.404
1460–69	16	6	118	.136	.186
1470–79	40	10	141	.284	.355
1480–89	13	32	135	.096	.333
1490–99	14	24	120	.117	.317
1500–1509	7	12	58	.121	.328
TOTALS	599	169	1,586	.378	.484

something to his emancipated child. With the decline of the *praemium* came an increase in these other forms of acquisition; there was an especially notable increase in the use of *aditio* to the maternal estate in the fifteenth century. I suspect that maternal estates consisted of a larger portion of disposable property and thus loomed larger in patrimonial strategies.

The direct transfer of property at the time of emancipation was more regular and more frequent in the fourteenth century than in the fifteenth. The society of fifteenth-century Florence appears to have been less inclined to pass property on to children before testamentary transferal. The incidence of property transfers of any kind at emancipation fell quite sharply after 1430, just as changes were taking place in the use of emancipation in terms of age, sex, and residence. The general problem remains, then, one of explaining why *praemia* and residence outside Florence declined from the 1430s, why the ages of emancipati rose, and the numbers of females emancipated went down from around 1410, and what the relationship is between these factors and between them and the precipitous drop in emancipatory activity beginning in 1422. All of these changes through the period from 1410 to 1440, stimulated to some degree by the law of 1421, appear to indicate a change in the use of emancipation. Before 1410, emancipation was more likely to involve a young child who would receive some kind of *praemium*, probably a small amount of money. After 1440, however, the child was usually older, the *praemium* was often absent, and the child was also more likely to live in Florence and less likely than before to be female. The earlier paradigm of emancipation was not concerned with the emancipatus' legal abilities. Women and minors were not fully capable legally even after emancipation, and small symbolic donations were not objects for the exercise of legal rights. Emancipation before 1410 may, therefore, have been more often concerned with dissolving legal obligations and liabilities than with creating legal rights and abilities. Later, emancipation came to involve such legal abilities more, abilities tied to the availability of economic opportunities and to the possession of property on which those abilities could be exercised. In this vein, however, the strong negative correlation between increased age at emancipation (the strongest indicator of a link to rights and abilities) and the decreased incidence of *praemia* is surprising at first sight.[35] If these later emancipations were concerned with rights and abilities tied to property, why was property less often given at emancipation?

The answer to this question may lie in the *peculium* and must also take account of the token nature of many *praemia* in the earlier period. Token gifts were generally abandoned as the age of the emancipatus increased. Older children were either given substantial gifts, received property by means of other legal devices (whose incidence increased), or already had something of value in their *peculia*, as the result of bequests from relatives, earlier extralegal gifts, support from parents, or their own earnings or marriages. The older emancipati may have needed less from their fathers or may already have received a substantial property settlement; they may also have been less willing to accept only a token. In a depressed economy undergoing severe stresses in the second and third decades of the fifteenth century, it may also have been imperative to retain legal control over one's children longer in order to be able to claim their wages, to use their earnings to add to the family income and provide dowries for the girls.

From the trends in evidence, we can see that the 1430s marked a watershed in the history of emancipation in Florence. The structural parameters of emancipation did remain the same. Both before and after the 1430s, emancipation carried implications regarding liability, and it could be either a strategy serving the perceived interests of the family as a whole or a means of resolving competitive tensions within the family by fragmenting it to some degree. The strategic use of emancipation in the interest of the family appears to have been most adaptive and to account for most of the change evident in the two decades before 1430. The first changes were in the incidence of emancipation of minors and females, both of which decreased. Emancipations of minors and females would have been most at a father's discretion, as he chose which, if any, of his children to emancipate. It appears that fathers began to move from a strategy of severing obligations and liabilities to a strategy of utilizing older emancipated children and their legal rights and abilities. By the 1430s, when this new tendency was confirmed, the disposal of wealth began to change in conformity with the older ages and greater number of male emancipati. The exact strategies varied widely case by case.

The declining incidence of emancipations in the *contado* and district of Florence must, on the other hand, be related to the complex political relationship between Florence and its countryside: the exclusion of *contadini* from various public-debt funds and the private and public exploitation of the rural area by predominantly urban forces.[36] Decreased use of emancipation in the countryside meant that there, legal liabilities for debts and taxes were not dissolved. Someone would pay the taxes, just as someone in the larger families of the *mezzadri* would do the work. And the *mezzadria*, the urban public debt subsidized by taxes raised in the rural areas, and debt in general kept the country subjugated to the city while exploited by it.

Urban wealth came to figure more prominently in the use of emancipation just as economic initiative and opportunity were vanishing in the countryside. The trend in this direction could have been greatly aided by the registration law of 1421, whose effect may have been to turn emancipation (more so than before) into the legal plaything of the urban wealthy. What evidence there is on this point may not be statistically conclusive, but it does seem to point toward greater use of emancipation by the wealthy. At least, a comparison of emancipatory activity of the rich before and after 1421 points tentatively in this direction.

Evidence available from the *prestanza* (forced loan) assessments of the city in 1403 provides the names of 351 males from the 308 wealthiest households. A search in the emancipation registries reveals that in the 24-year period from 1393 to 1416, these men emancipated 159 children in 110 emancipations (Table 8). Thus they accounted for roughly 4 percent of emancipations in that period, although they and their households were almost certainly not 4 percent of the population.[37] There was a continual slight increase in their emancipatory activity over the period, related, in part, I suspect, to the fact that fathers were wealthiest and ruled the largest households around age 55.[38] These households would have been at their wealthiest and largest in 1403 when they appeared at the top of the assessment; and thereafter, more emancipations were likely to occur. The role of wealth in promoting emancipation is further indicated by the internal performance of this group. Of the 80 males who performed the 110 emancipations, 26 (32.5 percent) came from the wealthiest quartile, 21 (26.3 percent) from the second quartile, 18 (22.5 percent) from the third, and 15 (18.8 percent) from the fourth.

A comparison of the *prestanza* group of 1403 with a group taken from the 1427 *catasto* is very illuminating (Table 9). This comparison lends some support to the idea that the law of 1421 and the subsequent overall decline in emancipations left emancipation more than before in the hands of the wealthy. The 600 wealthiest households in the city in 1427, containing 666 *patres*, produced an even more disproportionate number of emancipations across a similar 24-year period from 1417 to 1440.[39] While only 84 of these 666 performed emancipations (versus 80 of 351 in the earlier group), their 110 emancipations were 9.1 percent of all emancipations in the period, and the 182 emancipati were 11.7 percent of all emancipati. Yet, these 600 households were only 6.1 percent of those in the city of Florence and its territory.[40] The emancipatory activity of this second group also increased at a rate over four times higher than the rate of increase for the first group from 1403.[41] Of the 84 emancipators, 35 (41.7 percent) appeared in the top quartile of household assessments, 18 (21.4 percent) in the second, 15 (17.9 percent) in the third, and 16 (19.0 per-

TABLE 8. Assessment of 80 Emancipators, 1403 *Prestanza*

	NUMBERS				PERCENTAGE OF TOTAL EMANCIPATIONS			
Year	Emancipations	Emancipati	Multiple emancipations	Females	Emancipations	Emancipati	Multiple emancipations	Females
1393	—	—	—	—	.040	.047	.067	.069
1394	5	8	2	2	.038	.036	.036	.038
1395	5	6	1	1	.042	.038	.028	.032
1396	6	7	1	1	.035	.058	.107	.061
1397	5	11	3	2	.067	.054	.029	.143
1398	8	9	1	3	.007	.005		
1399	1	1	—	—	.023	.019		.029
1400	4	4	—	2	.033	.048	.100	.030
1401	4	7	2	1	.024	.020		
1402	2	2	—	—	.064	.069	.118	.087
1403	7	9	2	2	.010	.008		
1404	1	1	—	—	.088	.140	.250	.100
1405	8	16	4	1	.045	.033		
1406	5	5	—	—	.042	.031		
1407	4	4	—	—	.016	.058	.077	.074
1408	2	10	2	2	.063	.078	.096	.111
1409	7	11	2	2	.060	.080	.136	.071
1410	8	13	3	2	.015	.011		
1411	2	2	—	—	.039	.029		.038
1412	6	6	—	1	.070	.073	.100	.040
1413	7	9	2	1	.042	.038	.042	.091
1414	4	5	1	1	.035	.042	.071	
1415	4	7	2	—	.038	.033	.033	
1416	5	6	1	—				
TOTALS	110	159	29	24	.039	.043	.049	.041

TABLE 9. Assessment of 84 Emancipators, 1427 *Catasto*

	NUMBERS				PERCENTAGE OF TOTAL EMANCIPATIONS			
Year	Emancipations	Emancipati	Multiple emancipations	Females	Emancipations	Emancipati	Multiple emancipations	Females
1417	1	1	—	—	.022	.018		
1418	1	4	1	—	.008	.025	.043	
1419	5	9	2	—	.042	.064	.111	
1420	3	4	1	1	.024	.025	.034	.059
1421	6	7	1	1	.048	.046	.050	.048
1422	1	1	—	1	.030	.019		.333
1423	3	3	—	1	.143	.120		.167
1424	1	2	1	—	.050	.091	.500	
1425	2	2	—	—	.054	.048		
1426	3	4	1	1	.071	.078	.143	.091
1427	3	5	1	—	.083	.106	.143	
1428	4	9	2	1	.095	.155	.200	.167
1429	4	8	2	—	.098	.136	.154	
1430	5	11	2	1	.172	.289	.400	.333
1431	4	6	1	—	.174	.222	.500	
1432	10	21	6	1	.263	.382	.545	.250
1433	5	6	1	1	.091	.086	.083	.125
1434	13	22	6	3	.351	.407	.750	.600
1435	8	14	3	—	.186	.241	.333	
1436	3	3	—	1	.088	.073		.250
1437	9	12	3	1	.281	.324	.750	.125
1438	9	15	6	1	.243	.294	.750	.500
1439	2	2	—	2	.057	.049		.500
1440	5	11	2	2	.122	.208	.250	.286
TOTALS	110	182	41	19	.091	.117	.174	.102

cent) in the fourth, thus displaying an even more marked relationship between wealth and emancipation. The 1427 group produced more multiple emancipations, accounting for 56.1 percent of them in that period, a sign perhaps that only the wealthy could easily afford the florin-per-child charge for registration. Most astounding, however, is the activity of this group in 1427 and after, when they accounted for around 10 percent or more of all emancipations; from 1431 to 1440, in fact, these 600 households performed 18.1 percent of all emancipations. They were especially active in 1432 and 1434, perhaps because they were in danger of falling into the growing list of delinquent tax-payers.[42] This increased activity cannot be accounted for solely in terms of the relationship between wealth and the age of the head of the household. We are faced with a situation where the wealthy enjoyed greater power to utilize devices to protect their property and their political position.[43]

Insofar as wealth coincided with political eligibility, it seems, in fact, that there is further evidence of the increasing predominance of the wealthy among the emancipators and the emancipati. The politically eligible males, whose ages have already been discussed, also accounted for a relatively large percentage of male emancipati between 1416 and 1533 (Table 10). By the 1480s, when emancipations outside Florence had declined, these men accounted for a third or more of male emancipati. It would seem that to a great degree, emancipation followed wealth, power, and ambition.[44]

However, emancipation was not exclusively for the wealthy. Florentine emancipation data reveals a wide range of occupations and professions in every era; we encounter the more exalted professions (for example, notary, lawyer, doctor), noble statuses, the title *mercator* often proudly coupled with the designation *civis*, linen and wool merchants, shoemakers, druggists, various agricultural laborers and other less skilled tradesmen, and even a self-proclaimed pauper in 1387. Emancipation was available to all and utilized by all; moreover, the fact that the wealthy were proportionally more involved in emancipation is not of itself surprising. Typically, just about every legal mechanism came to be used more by the wealthy, who could both afford to employ it and had possessions and interests to be activated by legal devices. In this regard, emancipation is no different from any other Florentine legal institution. But it is also clear that the law of 1421, coupled with the financial problems of the government and the economic problems of Florence in general, produced a situation where the rich predominated more and more in the use of emancipation and took a hand in shaping the institution to meet new exigencies. The typical emancipation of the 1430s, in other words (if we can be justi-

TABLE 10.

Emancipation of Politically Eligible Florentine Males

Decade	Emancipati in *Tratte*[a]	Total males emancipated	Percentage of emancipati in *Tratte*
1416–21	62	745	.083
1422–29	52	318	.164
1430–39	118	429	.275
1440–49	134	549	.244
1450–59	109	681	.160
1460–69	176	905	.194
1470–79	191	874	.219
1480–89	252	818	.308
1490–99	250	702	.356
1500–1509	245	626	.391
1510–19	299	781	.383
1520–29	314	734	.428
1530–33	92	191	.482
TOTALS	2,294	8,353	.275

[a] Totals from Table 5.

fied in speaking of a typical emancipation), not only involved an older child, more often male, who received no *praemium*, but it also more often involved members of the wealthiest ranks of urban society. These people employed emancipation in a variety of ways, many of them creative, in order to exploit opportunities or to develop ways of meeting domestic needs. The aggregate data provide clues that important changes were taking place, but the substance of these changes was contained in the individual emancipations themselves and, therefore, can only be understood by analyzing them.

Varieties of Emancipation

Most emancipations do not provide any clue to their motivation. The notarial charters merely convey the fact of emancipation clothed in the requisite legal language, with information about date, place, and the parties involved. Even if the charter indicates the emancipatus' age and the contents of the *praemium*, there is no way of determining what was the underlying motivation of the actors (though transfer of property and the bestowal of legal capacity could themselves have been the motivation).

Other emancipations were, however, followed or accompanied by other legal acts on the part of the parties involved in the emancipation. In these instances, we can hazard an interpretation about the reason for the emancipation by looking at its immediate legal effects. But there is a limit to how much can be extrapolated from notarial documents. The legal text, a chain of interlocking symbols synchronizing a whole complex of social and cultural traffic, cannot be taken as defining the spatial and temporal boundaries of what happened. The legal text was a communicative act, concealing as well as revealing.

Leaving aside the emancipation of females, which will later be treated separately, I turn to the emancipations of sons to examine the types of property adjustments, legal activities, and adjustments in familial responsibilities resulting from the emancipation and the variations in these elements over time.

All sorts of property were involved in emancipations throughout the fourteenth and fifteenth centuries, although the variety seems greater in the fourteenth. In the 1340s, for example, we find *praemia* consisting of real property (rural and urban), money,[45] feudal rights and dues,[46] and tools and craft supplies.[47] It is not possible to determine exactly why the particular property was given to the person who received it, and it is almost impossible to determine if real control over the property also changed hands with the transfer of title. Some of these *praemia* may have been fictitious, designed either to mollify a son's desire for responsibility or to deceive the authorities and creditors about the exact extent of one's assets. What reason can be assigned, for instance, to the property transactions between Fano di Baldese and his son Bono in 1337? Fano gave his son at emancipation a piece of land with a house and half a *capanna* near Fiesole, which Bono, who lived in the *popolo* of Santa Maria in Palchetto in Florence, rented back to him for a three-year term at a rate of half the harvest per annum.[48] Fano continued to reside on, and to work, the land, but Bono was now titular owner. The annual rent may or may not have been what Fano had previously contributed to his son's sustenance. For all the legal maneuvering, little may have changed in reality.

Property transactions similar to these took place with regularity after the plague of 1348, although the types of property involved underwent changes in the course of time. After 1348, for example, the *praemium* was occasionally used to sort out obligations and ownership left in abeyance by the sweeping mortality. In 1365, Nerone di Nigi gave his son Lottero as his *praemium* the right to seek payment on a loan of 30 florins made back in 1365;[49] collecting this long-standing credit was thus passed on to the younger man. The practice of including un-collected debts in the *praemium* continued after the immediate impact of the plague. In the fifteenth century, we continue to run across such instances, which came to include credits in the *Monte comune* as well.[50] However, while many *praemia* were fairly small in value, in some cases, sons were able to add to the emancipation gift by means of pur-chases, which were sometimes worth more than the *praemium* itself, indicating that the emancipatus had accumulated earnings prior to emancipation.[51]

In the fifteenth century, some *praemia* remained relatively insub-stantial,[52] but, in general, while *praemia* occurred less frequently in the fifteenth century, they were quite large. Here, the emancipatory ac-tivity of the humanist chancellor of Florence, Poggio Bracciolini, is exemplary. Poggio was an old man in 1455 when he emancipated Piet-ropaolo, who was 17, and gave him 600 florins. Over a year later, Pog-gio emancipated another son, Giovanbattista, and gave him a house, three farms, and numerous pieces of land that Poggio had been accu-mulating for a number of years in his native region of Terra Nuova.[53] Poggio himself continued to add to his patrimony, and he left a siz-able estate to his heirs when he died on 30 October 1459. Pietropaolo, however, was not among his heirs because having received 600 florins upon entering a monastery, he later renounced his share of the estate in favor of his brothers on the eve of taking his vows. Emancipation had both enabled Pietropaolo to make that later renunciation and pro-vided him with an income to support him in the monastery. The other emancipated son, Giovanbattista, was a canon of the cathedral in Flor-ence. His emancipation also furnished him with a handsome income, although he turned to his father as *procurator* to manage the property. Following Poggio's death, Giovanbattista also renounced his share of the patrimony in favor of his three younger brothers.[54]

Poggio used emancipation to provide a substantial endowment for two sons entering the religious life, sons who were also cooperative pawns in patrimonial strategy. Indeed, the willingness of sons to co-operate with their fathers and to aid them was sometimes rewarded by emancipation and a *praemium*.[55] In fifteenth-century examples of this practice, however, it was customary to specify what these ser-vices were and to align the *praemium* with their value. The *praemium* thus became a carefully computed quid pro quo. Matteo di Francesco da Ripoli, for example, gave various household furnishings to two of his sons to compensate them for the fact that "they had aided him in his needs and had earned by their labor and sweat the greater part of [those furnishings]" and for the fact that they had lent him money "for marrying his daughters." A third son, who had married and moved away 15 years before, was given no share in this property.[56] This third son had, however, already received his share of the patrimony at the time of his departure. In his case and in others, establishing a separate household was treated as an occasion for paternal generosity.[57]

Emancipations accompanied by such careful accounting of property arose when the father determined that a son had earned the right to a measure of responsibility or when there was a need to disguise or change property ownership to protect it from the claims of others or when sons sought to separate themselves from their fathers. Whatever the reason, a father always had a means of retaining some degree of control over the property in question and, thereby, some degree of respect from his son. Control and respect were retained, quite simply, by placing conditions on the property.[58] Such conditions appeared throughout the fourteenth and fifteenth centuries, but here, as in so many other areas, the range and type of conditions and their frequency increased in the fifteenth century.

Conditions attached to *praemia* affected the potential disposition of the property in a variety of ways. One fairly common condition invoked the prohibition "to sell, alienate, give, or rent for a long period"—to entail, in other words. At other times, fathers chose to call for the eventual collation of all or part of a *praemium* inherited with one's brothers.[59] Another common measure fathers had recourse to was retaining usufruct on the property in the *praemium*, so that fathers who gave sons productive lands retained a life interest in half of the revenues or fruits.[60] And fathers who gave their sons the family's *casa* were likely to spell out their right to live there for the rest of their days.[61] Finally, a relatively popular condition in the fifteenth century was the fideicommissary stipulation on the line of descent the property was to take. In this way, the father could retain a control on the property almost from beyond the grave. When Benozzo di Simone d'Antonio di Benozzo gave his son Antonio a farm in 1478, he not only kept usufruct and forbade its alienation, but he also ordered that it pass to his daughters if Antonio's sons died without male heirs.[62]

Conditions on the *praemium* in the fifteenth century were also often more complex and contained a more positive embodiment of duties toward other family members than a simple prohibition of alienation. Fathers used their sons' energies and abilities to cover domestic needs. Vieri di Francesco di Guccio da Borgo San Lorenzo, for example, worked out different arrangements with his two sons in 1472 and 1475. On Bernardo's *praemium*, he placed the condition that "he, Vieri, the donor, may during his life demand payment from [Bernardo's] debtors and make such credits his own as if he had not established the present gift," thus indicating a desire to retain active control and merely transfer titular ownership. With Antonio's *praemium*, on the other hand, went the stipulation that Vieri's widowed daughter was entitled to stay in his house and that "Antonio the beneficiary should keep her in said house just as it is customary for brothers to keep their sister in case of widowhood."[63] Each son also received half of Vieri's property, but their father kept the rights of usufruct.

Vieri was not content with the customary moral injunction to brothers to shelter widowed sisters; he spelled it out as a legal obligation in the contract of Antonio's emancipation. Similarly, other fathers did not leave matters with custom during the fifteenth century. They put in legal terms the obligations they passed on to their sons to see to the material well-being of male descendants and to the honor of females (in matters of dowry or provisions for widowhood).[64]

Not all property that came to sons at the time of their emancipation (with or without conditions attached) came from their fathers or came from them directly in the form of *praemia* and *peculia*. Other categories of property and other means of acquisition were involved—increasingly so in the fifteenth century. The maternal dowry became a very important piece of property in many emancipations especially beginning in the 1420s. The monetary value of these maternal estates was rarely specified,[65] so it is impossible to determine even approximately how large such maternal estates generally were. The sources do, however, allow a determination of the legal transformations that such property underwent as a result of emancipation.

In a number of cases, the emancipatus immediately turned over the maternal estate to his father or, less frequently, to other family members. By this means, the father (or other member) acquired direct title to the property. There was a variety of circumstantial reasons behind such title transfers. Sometimes the emancipatus was said to owe his father money;[66] at other times, sons about to enter a monastery were emancipated so they could leave their share of the maternal estate to their fathers or brothers; one such emancipation is described in the *ricordi* of Marco di Giovanni Strozzi.[67] The sons in these cases might openly express their concern for the family's financial needs.[68]

The gifts from emancipati about to enter a monastery were undertaken in a cooperative spirit: They put their property rights to the service of familial imperatives. In other emancipations, however, property rights were not a focus for cooperation but a point of generational friction and conflict. It could be that a son was demanding some autonomy and responsibility or that a father was trying to preclude friction by distributing shares of the patrimony fairly. In an attempt to prevent such unsightly friction among siblings, some fathers, in the fifteenth century especially, took advantage of the opportunity offered by emancipation to allocate shares in the patrimony;[69] Luca di Bartolo Riccardi did so when he took elaborate steps to deal with the situation in his household. He emancipated Bernardo, his 30-year-old son in 1455 and gave him land, money, and assorted cloths and clothing on condition that Bernardo seek nothing further from him. He also gave Bernardo one-third of all the *masserizie* in the house (the other two-thirds went to his two brothers), because he ordered his son hence-forth to live elsewhere unless his brothers allowed him to reside with them. Luca aligned himself with the other two boys, reserving usu-fruct to their two-thirds and the right to alienate any portion thereof, leaving Bernardo free of any such burdens.[70]

Fathers like Luca Riccardi were rare, however. Rather than work out a division of property on their own, most fathers and sons—at least among those whose cases appear in the notarial records—resolved their differences in arbitration. In fact, arbitration through a third party was one of the more important and frequent means, other than the *praemium*, by which emancipated sons acquired property, es-pecially in the fifteenth century. Often, the arbitrators called upon to settle such domestic disputes were kinsmen, but the arbitrator(s) could be any mutually agreed upon third party.[71] Arbitrators did not need legal expertise (although lawyers and notaries acted as arbitrators at times); the notary who recorded the settlement gave it the necessary legal standing by clothing it in legal terminology. Arbitration agree-ments (*lauda*) dealing with domestic disputes are a rich source of in-formation about the nature of familial wealth and attitudes toward it; they also reveal attitudes toward emancipation. The son, of course, had to be emancipated to be able to stand as a party separate from, and even opposed to, his father in such a proceeding.

Problems resolved by arbitration varied widely. There were cases where a son was awarded property when he had not been given any at his emancipation; Lapo di Paolo di Lapo, for instance, who had not received a *praemium* nor his share of his mother's estate, was adjudged 100 florins to be paid by Paolo and by Filippo (Paolo's brother), who had kept their holdings in common.[72] Such settlements in the four-teenth century seem to have arisen from a sense that a son should re-ceive a *praemium*.[73]

By the fifteenth century, the *praemium* was no longer a major bone of contention in arbitrations between fathers and sons. The focus of attention had shifted to two other forms, or sources, of property rights: the dowry of the son's wife and the estate of his mother. In some cases, arbitrators discovered that a father had paid for many of his son's living expenses, with the result that the son was either given no property or made to repay his father.[74] In other cases, arbitrators discovered that a father had, indeed, retained possession of his son's wife's dowry or his share of the maternal estate; and in these cases, the arbitrators stipulated some form of payment to the son from his father's property. Thus, an arbitrator "wanting to preserve the son's love for his father" gave Bingieri di Jacopo di messer Giovanni Rucellai a guarantee for payment of his mother's 500-florin dowry and the right to food and clothing from his father.[75] So, too, another arbitrator awarded Lorenzo di messer Tommaso Soderini his wife's and mother's dowries, as well as two houses and other property worth 1,000 florins; but he also ordered Lorenzo and his wife to leave Tommaso's house, which had been their home for the past 13 years.[76]

Another form of property, finally, that occasioned the intervention of arbitrators was the property that an emancipatus had earned before his emancipation. In both the fourteenth and fifteenth centuries, some emancipated sons found it necessary to rely on an arbitrator to retrieve such property, which they believed justly belonged to them. For example, Francesco and Antonio di Corsio Cioli, both adults, were awarded various holdings in 1375 because it had been their *labor* and *industria* that had allowed the family to acquire the properties. Their father and mother readily acknowledged their debt to their sons. In addition, the arbitrator enunciated the principle that in the future, each son was entitled to keep his wages and profits for himself.[77] In a similar action over a century later, Sandro, son of Pietro di Primerano Vanelli, was given half of a farm in arbitration because Pietro was in his debt for money that "was properly Sandro's and his by Sandro's industry and belonged to him as his *peculium quasi castrense*."[78]

To third parties, the family may have appeared as one unit—a group united in residence, income and consumption, and in possession of property—but within the family, ownership could be reckoned differently, it seems. Children had claims to what was theirs by inheritance, marriage, or their own labor, even though the law and custom projected an image of the father as representative of the group and sole owner and controller.[79] Family property was not monolithic; division or rearrangement of ownership, by either voluntary or involuntary means (that is, arbitration), occurred from time to time to deal with stresses and strains arising both from within and outside the house. Emancipation necessarily played a part in many such divisions and rearrangements. It certainly offered fathers an opportunity to use sons and their property to aid the family or to lessen tensions between fathers and their sons concerning property—even if the precise details had to be entrusted to an arbitrator.

LEGAL ADJUSTMENTS

In many ways, a distinction between legal activities and property with regard to emancipation is a false one. Property was involved in emancipation under the guise of a complex of legal rights, and legal rights and abilities were rarely, if ever, unconnected to property. Nevertheless, in some emancipations, there was clearly no immediate transfer of property rights but some legal adjustment affecting the future disposition of property. Over the 200 years of the fourteenth and fifteenth centuries, a variety of legal concerns led Florentines to emancipate their children; these concerns were embodied in the rich diversity of Florentine legal activity and in the changes in that activity over time.

The legal rights and abilities acquired by an emancipatus formed the focus of much legal activity. The preceding discussion of property considered, in effect, the legal rights to acquire property. The present discussion centers on the legal abilities of emancipati to dispose of property.

One ability gained by an emancipatus was that of writing a will. Predictably, there were times when this testamentary capacity figured prominently in emancipations. During the plague of 1348, for example, a dying son was able to draw up a will in favor of his father and leave pious bequests for the benefit of his soul.[80]

Composition of a will by an emancipatus was one means by which a father could gain title to his son's property; such a son, however, had to be in his majority. The property of underage children, on the other hand, could be subjected to legal guardianship (*tutela*) following their emancipation. By having himself designated as *tutor* for his son, the father became the legal administrator of the emancipatus' property, including the dowry of his mother if she were dead.[81] Though the *tutela* gave the *tutor* very limited control over his ward's property, it could give a father more direct control over dowry property.[82]

Formal paternal guardianship was actually rare, however, especially in the fifteenth century, when fewer young children were emancipated; at least, I have found no fifteenth-century examples of guardianship of emancipated sons.[83] The rights and abilities of the older emancipati of the fifteenth century were put to other purposes. The presence of emancipati alongside their fathers at the sale of family lands, for example, became fairly common. By having the sons present to renounce their rights to the property being alienated, fathers assured the purchasing party that the property would not be subjected later to claims by the sons under *retrait lignagier* (the right of members of a family to regain alienated family property by refunding the purchase price to the purchaser).[84] There are isolated examples from the fourteenth century of this practice of including emancipated sons in a sale,[85] but it was not until the end of the fourteenth century that the practice became a consistent feature of emancipation in Florence and its environs.[86] By the later years of the fifteenth century emancipation for the purpose of involving the son(s) in a sale had, in fact, become quite common.[87] In addition, it was often stipulated in such ratifications that other sons would also ratify the sale in turn when they reached the age of majority (and thus could do so in their own name).

The use of emancipated sons as sureties was yet another legal reason for emancipation. On occasion, emancipated sons obligated themselves as sureties on the dowries of a father's second wife or a brother's wife.[88] After 1400, a number of sons were emancipated in order to give their personal guarantee to an obligation of their father. So, emancipation allowed Bassiano di maestro Jacopo di Paolo del Bene to obligate himself for a paternal debt and to guarantee the same obligation from his younger brother when he reached the age of majority.[89] In these examples, emancipation, which by statute dissolved such obligations and liabilities, was, in fact, paradoxically being used to strengthen them. Instead of dissociating sons from their fathers, here, emancipation operated to associate sons more closely with their fathers as consenting, if not fully active, partners in the family enterprise.

The biggest single legal adjustment resulting from emancipation—any emancipation—was the endowment of the emancipatus with legal capacities. If these capacities could be, and were, used to a father's benefit, the fact remains that the emancipatus could also use them for himself. Not all emancipati made use of these capacities for their own purposes. Emancipated minors were unlikely to have any direct interests to worry about, and they could not act without some guardian; and many older emancipati, as must be obvious by now, merely put their legal abilities at the service of their father and the family. On the other hand, for many older emancipati, the legal capacities they acquired were of great benefit, either at the time of emancipation or afterward. Piero di Benevento di Michele Olivieri, for example, used his new legal right to stand as a party in arbitration to enter into such a proceeding with his business partners. The arbitration defined what and how much of the business belonged to him and what the rights and obligations of the various partners were. Piero sought such a definition because his *praemium* had been vaguely defined as whatever was his in the business.[90]

Tracing the later activities of emancipated sons becomes a difficult undertaking, but throughout the Florentine notarial records, there are many acts involving men who designated themselves as emancipatus. Florentines were accustomed to dealing with such people and often demanded from them some proof of their emancipation.[91] These emancipati actively utilized their legal abilities on their own initiative for themselves and others.

One of the most visibly active (in business and patrimonial affairs) after his emancipation was Vieri di Cambio de' Medici (1323–1395), who was emancipated on 8 April 1363. He was the only Medici truly active in trade and banking in the fourteenth century.[92] Vieri used his emancipation to gain title to some Medici family properties in the hands of female relations whose living expenses and dowries became his responsibility. He also wrote a will before leaving Florence on business. Four years later, he and his brother Giovanni contracted for an arbitrated division and separation of their property.[93]

Sons like Vieri de' Medici throughout the fourteenth and fifteenth centuries used legal abilities acquired through emancipation to accumulate and dispose of property. Such men, having reached legal adulthood, were able to act, as the emancipation charter's formula said, like any *paterfamilias*. But this fact did not necessarily mean that their fathers ceased to act like such, even with respect to their emancipated sons. In the fifteenth century, however (and even in the fourteenth, to a more limited extent), some emancipated sons did, indeed, obtain a more sweeping type of paternal power that spelled the end of their fathers' reign as *capo di famiglia*.

ADJUSTMENT OF FAMILY ROLES

Emancipation allowed two major forms of permutation in familial relations. Vesting legal capacities in a son or sons created a situation where the son could potentially either set himself up independently of his father or take over from his father, making the parent dependent on the child. Both options were used in and around Florence, but, here again, as in so many instrumental and positive aspects of emancipation, they happened with more regularity in the fifteenth century.

Sons who wanted a division of property and outright possession of their earnings (instances of which have already been examined) were generally intent on pursuing their affairs separately from their fathers. They were thereby establishing a new and legally separate family following emancipation. The examples of division and separation previously discussed deal with situations where a single son was given his property separately by his father or by an arbitrator. What has not yet been considered is those situations where domestic tranquility could be restored only by means of a fission of the family into numerous

legally separate entities. Such situations were often complex and required the considered judgment of a neutral third party; I cite the
example of Angio di Dino da Careggio of San Lorenzo and his sons
Francesco and Donato. In 1336, an arbitrator ordered "that said ser
Angio di Dino should emancipate and should do so today" Francesco
and Donato and give them their portion of the patrimony. Their emancipations followed immediately, and each was given a piece of land
and use for life of a house and its adjacent shop space. After Angio's
death, the sons would acquire the house, its contents, and 130 florins
that belonged to their wives' dowries. The *praemia* that were later to
be given to their brothers, Bartolomeo and Filippo, were also determined in advance.[94] These sons did not physically separate from their
father, but they had a token amount of land for themselves, the firm
promise of more, and, most significantly, the legal power to manage
their own affairs. The arbitration in this case is also interesting in itself
for its illegality. The sons were parties to an arbitration before their
emancipation, and the arbitrator had compromised the *patria potestas*
by ordering their emancipations—something that Baldus, for one,
was to declare invalid.[95]

An even more complex division of property occurred in the family
of Giovanni di Deo. Giovanni emancipated Antonio, Jacopo, ser Nad-
do, and Ormano (all over 18) on 12 October 1444. On 6 April 1445, he
emancipated his fifth son Matteo, a minor; and he and Matteo then
formed one party in arbitration against the other four sons. The arbitrator first had to achieve a balance between the familial assets and
liabilities of the four eldest, taking into account business capital and
dowries. All four brothers were also assessed contributions for the
dowries of Antonio's four daughters, with Antonio having to provide
a larger share. Having made these arrangements, the arbitrator could
finally declare that each would act on his own and manage his own
money and affairs. Because their father was still alive, however, the
property was not yet to be divided among them; and each was appor-
tioned his share of the household expenses, including taxes.[96]

Another form of separation between fathers and sons took place at
the infrequent emancipations of sons who were about to be married.
Separation in these cases was far less complex or acrimonious, because
it really occurred more or less in advance of the acquisition of property.
Emancipation at marriage did not even necessarily mean that a physical separation of households was being contemplated. The result of
such an emancipation might only be the designation of separate pa-
trimonies, dowries, expenses, and responsibilities for each "family."[97]

Even if a son and his bride were not necessarily going to set up their own household or even manage their affairs separately, the father could gain a degree of indemnity by the fact that his emancipated son could directly accept his wife's dowry and be primarily responsible for returning it. The emancipation of Ridolfo di Peruzzo di Bencivenni in 1329 appears to have had no other purpose than that of allowing him to take the dowry directly from his father-in-law;[98] similar emancipations occasionally occurred in the fifteenth century.[99] Many other sons were in a position to take direct responsibility for the dowry because they had already been emancipated before marriage. Of the husbands who received dowries from the *Monte delle doti* for subscriptions placed during the first 20 years of the fund, 85 percent of those who were ever emancipated were emancipated when they received the dowry. Unless other family members pledged surety with them, these *emancipati* faced the problem of dowry restitution on their own.[100]

The other major form of adjustment in family roles occurred when a son took control of the family from his father. While in the eyes of the law, strictly speaking, the son was establishing his own *familia*, in social terms it can be said that the son was taking over the family in the wake of his father's retirement. Paternal retirement as implied in such emancipations may not have meant total withdrawal from all productive activities. What was implied was withdrawal from control and oversight of the entire patrimony and its legal disposition.

Generally, the father's desire for such a change seems to have been dominant when the transfer was completed in the normal course of an emancipation. By way of example, I cite the early case of Dino di Cambio who, in 1327, emancipated those of his sons whom he had not previously emancipated. He gave these sons various holdings, and he gave additional properties to the already emancipated offspring. The sons, in turn, took over Dino's outstanding obligations, swore to demand nothing further from him, and affirmed their parents' right to stay in the family home for the rest of their lives and to enjoy the use of the properties they had given to their sons.[101] It would appear that Dino had retired to live out his days supported by his sons, who had taken over active direction of the patrimony. One of the key clauses in the postemancipation agreement was the retention of usufruct by Dino, for it was that clause that gave him a legal right to support. It is unclear how many of the frequent clauses establishing retention of usufruct in emancipations masked the cession of real power within the family (not merely over the property in question) to the sons. The reservation of *alimenta* also figured in paternal retirements. When Niccolò di Domenico dei Pollini finally retired in his old age in 1436, he emancipated his four remaining sons, gave them his property, and obligated them to dower their sisters and to feed and shelter him for the rest of his life.[102]

The occurrence of such paternal retirements was small in the fourteenth century, especially when we consider the greater overall incidence of emancipation before 1422. Perhaps most fathers in the fourteenth century took to heart the proverbial wisdom of Paolo da Certaldo who said that a man should not give in to his sons' desires to control the patrimony. And when fathers did retire, they did not rest content with the protection afforded them by the statutory obligations of children to support their hungry and needy parents. Instead, they spelled out this customary moral obligation in a manner analogous to spelling out filial obligations to dower the family's female members and to see to their care in widowhood.

Most retirements, in fact, seem to have been worked out by arbitrators. The extent of the conflict to be resolved by the arbitrator is difficult to determine in most cases. It may be that a father who emancipated sons for the purpose of arbitration concerning retirement had already agreed, or decided, to step aside, in which case, only the exact form the arrangement would take was in doubt. But some sons may have used the arbitrator to force their fathers into retirement. Arbitration may also have served to make the nature of the arrangement public knowledge, thereby giving the father a further guarantee of public censure of his sons if they failed to carry out their end of the bargain.

In one case, an arbitrator gave Giovanni di Bonino an annuity for life following the emancipation of his son Marco in 1443. Marco, the arbitrator decided, "Had acquired in his profession and trade, by his industry, many household goods and certain merchandise that Marco had in his shop," and these goods were judged to belong solely to him. Clearly, ownership and responsibility had passed to the son, whose father was no longer capable of laboring in his profession. Over a year earlier, another Florentine, Matteo di Zanobi di Michele Viviani, had been given all of his father's property and complete control over his business activities. Furthermore, because Zanobi had three sons and six daughters, "of whom two are at present of marriageable age," and because Zanobi was old and weak, the arbitrator decided that "said Matteo must and should provide for and aid his father in his needs and also feed his daughters and sisters and also provide for their dowries or part of their dowries." So Matteo became head of the family, charged with supplying each sister with 40 florins for her dowry.[103] In this example, then, the eldest son became head of the house. How well the arrangement worked or how long it lasted is impossible to say.

AFTER EMANCIPATION

The emancipated son enjoyed full legal rights if he were in his majority or when he reached it; whether or not a son chose to use those rights remains problematic. In most cases, the relationship between father and son was not totally terminated by emancipation; there remained room for further adjustments of property and responsibility. Fathers could and did give their sons something long after emancipation; fathers could sell or rent to their sons or conversely, buy or rent from them. Some fathers who gave property to their previously emancipated sons were motivated by a desire to equalize the shares falling to each or to reward a son for conspicuous service to his father. Other fathers sought to make use of an emancipated son's proven or potential ability to protect the property, while still others found the son's immunity from his father's debts to be attractive. Early in 1431, for example, Luttozzo di Jacopo di Luttozzo Nasi, one of the wealthiest Florentines in 1427, went before a notary without his two sons, Piero and Lorenzo, whom he had emancipated back in 1428. Luttozzo noted that at the emancipation, he had transferred to his sons title to their *peculia*, containing, among other things, the 800-florin dowry of his deceased wife, their mother. Luttozzo then confessed that "after said emancipation, he began to fall into bankruptcy," and, since he wanted his boys to have the dowry, in exchange for it, he gave them specified pieces of property.[104] Here, a father took advantage of the fact that his emancipated sons were free of his debts in order to place at least part of his property outside the reach of his creditors.

Fathers and emancipated sons also acted legally on each other's behalf. Examples of such activity abound throughout the period of this study. To cite but two of them, Bartolomeo di Niccolò Valori acted as *procurator* for his father in the 1370s[105] and Francesco d'Andrea Quaratesi acted as *procurator* for his son Piero in 1430.[106]

Yet, the relationships between fathers and sons and their respective activities after emancipation are perhaps revealed nowhere with more clarity than in the occasional arbitrations between them. As in arbitrations at the time of emancipation, these later arbitrations gravitated about property like wives' dowries.[107] But they also involved other property rights that had come to a family after emancipation of one or more sons. For example, Francesco di Vieri di Francesco del Bene was found in arbitration to be in debt to his brother for 23 florins. The two brothers had often acted on the other's behalf, and the arbitration amounted to an accounting between them. Francesco then sought a similar accounting from his father. Francesco, it appears, had for many years administered some of Vieri's property and had incurred expenses in the process for taxes, certain articles of Vieri's clothing, and for some interior decorating and reconstruction in the house. Francesco had also twice met the expenses of his own weddings and yet, all those years, had remained *ad unum pane et unum vinum* with his father. In total, Francesco was owed 320 florins by the arbitrator's reckoning.[108]

In these arbitrations, then, sons who had long since been emancipated finally sought economic independence and an accounting from their fathers. In another case, the son was already living apart from his father when he took him to arbitration. In 1467, an arbitration between Matteo di Morello di Paolo Morelli and his son Jeronimo determined that Jeronimo was entitled to two farms because "the father's substance should be the son's by the law of nature" and because Jeronimo "with the consent of said Matteo and his family remains by himself with his family and in another house of Matteo's and because said Jeronimo should be given some aid so that he can feed himself and his wife and children." Matteo was also in debt to his son for 819 florins. Matteo, naturally, had to promise to repay his debts. Clearly, the emancipation of Jeronimo had not negated the father-son relationship if Matteo was still seen as the natural provider for his son. Jeronimo Morelli was, in fact, seeking to have his father act more like a father than he had. Not all such arbitrations worked to the emancipated son's advantage, however. Orlandino di Francesco Bonachetti, for one, was awarded money from his son Francesco in compensation for the considerable sums he had spent on his son's behalf after his emancipation.[109]

The various arbitrations discussed thus far reveal the complex continuous relationships that could exist between a father and son following emancipation. Many of the arbitrations themselves occurred when either the son sought complete real independence from his father or the father sought to withdraw from active leadership of the family. Such arbitrations, which began to appear in the late fourteenth century, were more numerous in the fifteenth century, more detailed in their provisions, and more elaborate in their motivation.

In a settlement after emancipation between Leonardo di Bartolomeo Bartolini and his son Bartolomeo, who also represented his brothers Bernardo and Cosimo, the sons were granted full control of their father's property. Each received property in proportion to what he had given to help meet his father's debts. The sons had paid off these debts because otherwise Leonardo, in his need for money, would have been forced to accept the post of *capitano* of Livorno, a place renowned for its *mala aria* and in which Leonardo, in his sons' opinion, would surely have died. They had acted from a sense of filial duty and devotion to keep their father from what they saw as certain death. But, whatever their motives, the arbitrator determined that they were entitled to compensation; and the compensation amounted to full ownership and control over their aged father's meager holdings.[110]

A final example demonstrates that settlements involving a father's retirement were not always easy to reach. They could and did follow on a period of angry interchanges, the result perhaps of the fact that some fathers remained wary of placing themselves in their sons' hands. In April 1465, Matteo di Francesco di Giovanni di Tommaso da Gamberaia, a resident of Settignano, emancipated his two sons, Francesco and Giovanni. He then gave his sons the patrimony on condition that they supply him every year with specified amounts of grain, oil, meat, wine, and clothing. In the following November, however, the sons went into arbitration against their father; the arbitrator found that

> in truth, of the goods transmitted in the *praemium* by said Matteo to his sons, many were bought with his sons' money. And in view of Matteo's condition, the discord between him and his sons and their families is well known, and said Matteo is impatient and contentious and with innumerable diatribes he afflicts his sons and their families, and, therefore, there can be no quiet, peace, or agreement among them.

The aged Matteo was, therefore, ordered to live apart from his sons, who were assessed for their father's rent and provisions and for furnishings for his new lodgings, which he could not alienate. It was also threatened that Matteo would lose this income if he entered his sons' homes or pestered their families.[111] Matteo's unjust demands, vexatiousness, and false generosity cost him the respect his old age and position would otherwise have accorded him.

These arbitrations after emancipation illustrate in a direct manner how emancipation often did not of itself terminate active relations between a father and his son(s). After emancipation, a son was often in a subordinate position with regard to family decisions, even with regard to the disposition of resources that had been given to him or that he had brought into the *casa*. And after emancipation, a father might manage a daughter-in-law's dowry, use a son's earnings, and control the family business or farm. Yet, the arbitrations also demonstrate that if emancipation did not bring independence, some sons were later willing to use the legal abilities gained through emancipation to win their economic independence or even to take over active leadership of the family.

EMANCIPATION OF WOMEN

Women were emancipated in far fewer numbers than were men, especially in the fifteenth century; there would seem to be two reasons for the relatively smaller and less frequent appearance of women among the emancipated. On the one hand, women were not legally capable of complete independence—they had to have a male guardian; on the other hand, in accord with the strong cultural bias against female independence, men generally wanted to keep control over women and, thus, over the property that women nominally owned. As a result, the emancipation of a daughter or granddaughter was a relatively rare event and was not entered into lightly; it usually responded to some definite need or concern within the family.

In the fourteenth century, when emancipations of women were more numerous than after 1410, women were emancipated for some of the same reasons that brought about the emancipations of men, although at all times their gender imparted a peculiar character to their emancipations. Some women, like many of their brothers, were emancipated in order to receive property; their emancipations were no different from the many emancipations of males that record only the facts of emancipation and the ensuing *praemium*.[112] Some daughters received land that they, in turn, rented to a third party or to their fathers, usually for half of the yield.[113] By this means, they received some return from land they may not have been able to work or manage on their own. Also, as was true of some *praemia* given to males, women sometimes found their father's generosity burdened with conditions and restrictions.[114]

Due to the special legal position of women, gifts of land, goods, or money to them may have held one of two distinct meanings: Either the property was meant to form all or part of a woman's dowry (more likely if the woman was young and unmarried). Or since the dowry was actually a form of premortal inheritance for a girl, the property may have been intended as a bequest, perhaps supplementing the dowry.[115] In this way, a father might circumvent the statutory provisions excluding women from inheriting from their father if they had been dowered.[116]

The legal adjustments ensuing from the emancipation of a daughter were also prized by Florentines; some of these adjustments were the same ones they made after the emancipation of sons. Fathers, for example, might emancipate young daughters and then be appointed their legal guardians; the purpose here seems to have been to acquire a second and different form of power and authority over property, especially a maternal estate. The *tutela* over a daughter may also have been part of a ploy to disguise ownership and escape creditors. In 1372, Piero di Martino of Luchio in the Mugello became *tutor* for his daughter Lina and gave her two houses and 32 pieces of land. Some of the property was later transferred to his wife by an arbitration. The *laudum* maintained that the lands in question belonged to the wife by way of her parents and that they had come to Piero only because she had been a defenseless minor when her parents died.[117] Granting additional property to his daughter and advancing the claim of his wife may all have been intended to confuse the ownership issue and place the property where Piero could still manage it, while it technically belonged to women whose liability for him was limited at best. These uses of the *tutela* over a daughter remained attractive enough, so that the *tutela* continued to appear sporadically into the second decade of the fifteenth century.[118]

The *tutela*, however, took on a meaning for some women that it did not have for men. Emancipated men might find themselves placed under guardianships, but some emancipated women found themselves becoming guardians of their own children. One such widow was Fetta, daughter of Tani d'Aghinetti;[119] her experience was shared by other women in the fourteenth century and the first two decades of the fifteenth.[120]

Another legal adjustment involving women even more so than men took consideration of the fact that emancipated women could write a will. The *pater emancipans* was often not a disinterested spectator in such proceedings, for he could become the chief beneficiary of the will. The plague year of 1400 saw several emancipations of dying women who had their wills drawn up. This practice may account both for the large number of emancipations in that year and for the large number of women emancipated.[121]

After 1400, there were some significant changes in the uses of emancipation that corresponded to the decrease in emancipations of women. Such activities as the *tutela* and writing a will all but disappeared; in their place arose other legal activities, some of which were already evident in the fourteenth century and simply became more prevalent. The role that property played in women's emancipations also changed.

Fifteenth-century emancipations of women also exhibit an abiding concern with their legal rights and with their use for the benefit of the family. At the beginning of this period, there were a number of emancipations of women who were about to be married. These women watched as their dowries were turned over to their husbands, and then they were called upon to release their fathers from any further obligation toward them.[122] The fathers, in these instances, desired a guarantee that the remainder of their property would go to their other children. This desire may account for the fact that marriage seems to have occasioned the emancipation of the bride more often than that of the groom.[123] A related case of some interest took place in 1502, when Piero di Jacopo Guicciardini emancipated Dianora on the eve of her marriage. She renounced any claim to a farm that Piero had previously designated as part of her dowry. It appears that he had originally feared that the *Monte delle doti* would go bankrupt and not pay the dowry he had established for her.[124]

The type of property that figured most often in such renunciations was, however, the mother's dowry, a share of which a daughter was entitled to equally with all her brothers and sisters. Emancipation allowed a daughter to give up her share or to make some arrangement with her father. Already in the first half of the fourteenth century, the daughter's share of her mother's dowry figured in some patrimonial strategies. By the later years of the fourteenth century, this use of female emancipation had become relatively common.[125]

The cession by women of their rights to their mother's dowry was only one way that their emancipation could become a means of transferring rights or property directly to the father. Ceding one's right to the mother's dowry meant that it remained in trust for the other children, but actually giving one's share of the mother's dowry to the father made it his. Because women were unlikely to have earnings of their own, the only property they could give their fathers was their mother's dowry or their own; a few such gifts occurred in the fourteenth century. Noteworthy in this regard are the legal maneuvers of Loysio di Poltrone Cavalcanti, who used the emancipation of his daughters to alleviate his sad financial situation. Two of his daughters, Margarita and Lisabetta, ceded to him their shares of their mother's estate and released him from any further obligation in that regard. His other daughter, Piera, whom he had emancipated two months previously and for whom he was *curator*, did the same. Piera, however, unlike her sisters, was not married (and perhaps, therefore, closer to her father). She recognized "how Loysio her father was and is obligated for several, various, and diverse debts and usuries and quantities of money to certain creditors vexing Loysio to pay them the amounts owed to them." She realized that he faced poverty and the humiliating prospect of imprisonment because he lacked the cash to repay those debts. She, therefore, accepted her share of her mother's estate not from her father but from Dino di Lapo Cavalcanti, a kinsman,

who at that time bought a number of properties from Loysio, including the family palace.[126]

There are a number of examples in the fifteenth century of an emancipated woman giving her property to her father or to another male
member of the family. Women who made a gift of their mother's dowry
often did so with expressions of gratitude to the father for dowering
them and with concern for the responsibilities he had toward his
other children. In 1485, the daughter of Francesco di Bernardo del
Mare gave him (actually claiming to be obligating her future husband
to give to Francesco) half of the dowry of 1,000 florins he had set up
for her at the *Monte delle doti*. She did so, she claimed, because he had
been very generous to her but lacked the means to be anywhere near
as generous to his other two daughters. Francesco may, indeed, have
been in a financial pinch; at least the subsequent emancipation of two
sons in the following year brought them no *praemium*.[127]

Finally, yet another form of property transferal to one's male kin
involved returning the dowry to one's father. In 1408, for example,
monna Felice was given the right to remain in her father's house for
the rest of her life and widowhood after she gave her father, Nofri di
Roggieri di Federigho, title to her dowry.[128]

Such cessions of rights and property as undertaken by these women
required them to be of adult age. The generally older ages of emancipated females in the fifteenth century, therefore, goes along with the
renewed emphasis on their legal activities in emancipatory practice
and parallels a similar emphasis and age increase among emancipated
males. Another feature of the emancipation of females that parallels
that of males is the increasing incidence of arbitrations involving
women.

Some arbitrations settled immediately after emancipation may simply have been arranged in advance as another way of giving a daughter her dowry or of terminating any further rights she may have had
to her father's patrimony.[129] Other arbitrations may have embodied real
differences between a father and his daughter or even between a father
and his son-in-law. Arbitrations began to appear in the second half of
the fourteenth century and became progressively more numerous.

At issue in such arbitrations were the fathers' obligations to their
daughters, obligations that usually involved the dowry. In one case, a
daughter of marriageable age (*nubilis etatis*) was awarded her dowry
by arbitration;[130] in most cases where daughters were awarded property, however, the award was the result of the fathers' difficulties
in meeting their debts. A widow whose dowry had been returned to
her father was given property of equivalent value because her father
had spent the money to satisfy his creditors;[131] and two daughters re-

ceived compensation for the sums they had provided for their father's creditors.[132]

The reverse was also true at times, however—daughters could owe their fathers money. In these cases, the fathers were not awarded money so much as they were given legal absolution from any further obligations or expenses on their daughters' account. The father, for example, might be released from his obligation to give his daughter her share of her mother's dowry.[133]

In the fifteenth century, finally, some Florentine fathers used emancipation of a daughter to provide for their own retirement, which, in these instances, did not mean turning over familial authority but did entail provisions for old age. So Lisabetta, daughter of Matteo di Ceccho di Feo da Linari, undertook to care for her old and ill parents in life and bury them honorably in death.[134] Here again, the daughter assumed responsibility for her aged parents. Her new responsibility was not quite the same as that of a son, who also took over the role of primary breadwinner if he were given the position of *capo di famiglia*, but it was a responsibility of great importance to the parents. As a final example of such a use of a daughter's emancipation, there is the case of Antonio di Matteo Ciardi and his daughter monna Ginevra, emancipated in 1505; Antonio gave her three pieces of land because

> said monna Ginevra had helped Antonio in his needs and infirmities and [had used] her own money etc. earned by working as a servant and staying with others as a domestic and because Antonio had dowered and married other daughters, sisters of Ginevra, and wanting to discharge his debt, he should recognize Ginevra's services in a fitting manner.

A subsequent *laudum* determined that Antonio was quite old, unable to function naturally, and had a son "who treats him badly" and "refuses to feed and care for him and nourish him in his infirmities." Therefore, all of Antonio's property, along with the obligation to feed and care for him, went to his loving and generous daughter.[135] It appears that the father first thought of his son, but in this case, Antonio could say figuratively that he had no son. Since his status as father had not been sufficiently compelling for his son, Antonio had turned to a specific and contractual arrangement with his daughter.

Chapter 3 examined the meaning of emancipation for Florentines, discussing that meaning as conveyed by the phrases and formulas utilized to perform and describe it, and it looked into the structural significance of emancipation in the context of the family. The aim of this chapter has been to determine why fathers in Florence and its territory in the fourteenth and fifteenth centuries emancipated their children. To do so, it has been necessary to look at emancipatory activity both as a whole and in many particular instances.

Emancipation meant freedom—freedom from debts and obligations, on the one hand, and freedom from paternal control (and a corresponding acquisition of legal capacities), on the other. This freedom had meaning, moreover, in the context of the family and for the individual emancipatus; the precise meaning and function of any emancipation varied, therefore, with circumstances.

Analysis of the data derived from the emancipation registries and notarial records reveals that there were significant shifts in emancipatory practices between 1410 and 1440. Political, economic, and demographic factors all had a hand in producing shifts in the number of emancipations; the age, sex, and residence of emancipati; and the property rights transacted in emancipations. But the equation of the family with its wealth (*substantia*) and the use of emancipation in familial strategies indicate that shifts in emancipatory practices are perhaps best understood in terms of wealth.

Involvement of paternal property in emancipation was optional, and generally substantial portions of paternal property were not involved in emancipations. Its disposition was left to inheritance. *Praemia* were, therefore, small and symbolic in general prior to 1430 and increasingly infrequent thereafter. Only when it was expedient in terms of the family's immediate needs were substantial portions of paternal property liable to come into play in emancipation.

Changes in the incidence and forms of involvement of paternal property in emancipations, coupled with perceptible trends in other dimensions of emancipation, like the number and ages of emancipati, point to changes in familial strategies regarding wealth and emancipation. By emancipating fewer children at later ages in the fifteenth century, fathers retained control not only over their own property but over that of their children (earnings, dowries, maternal estates). When fathers did turn to emancipation, they used their children's legal abilities in the service of the family and kept at least indirect control over property subject to conditions and restrictions. By contrast, the more frequent earlier use of emancipation with younger children seems to have figured as a precautionary device. Fathers were more inclined to forego legal control over a child's earnings to protect themselves and their children from claims of creditors, at times in a fictitious and fraudulent manner.

The relative shift to an instrumental use of emancipation after 1430 had important consequences in terms of familial wealth. Children's property—what belonged to them at least nominally whether emancipated or not—became more prominent in the property dispositions occurring at emancipations. Some children claimed their property for themselves; some gave it to their fathers or other family members. Delaying emancipation also meant that a child had more interest in the management of family property, both because his own property was implicated and because as an unemancipated child, he was liable for all obligations incurred by his father. Resulting friction between father and child led to arbitrations and paternal "retirements" at the time of emancipation. By the instrumental use of emancipation, opportunities might be seized, problems solved, and tensions eased; but new problems might always arise, even as a result of emancipation.

The reasons for the relative shift in emphasis in the use of emancipation in the fifteenth century were in large part economic and demographic, but these reasons operated and were given formal expression only through the mechanisms of law. With the entry of the communal government into the business of registering emancipations (as one way to cope with fraud), use of emancipation declined. The shift in emancipatory practices also coincided with the appearance of a number of writings advising fathers and future fathers on how to fulfill the role of *capo di famiglia*. The works of Alberti, popularized by the Pseudo-Pandolfini, enjoyed particular success, so that many of his statements found their way into the stock of advice of men like Giovanni Rucellai. These writings contained much that was conventional and proverbial, similar to earlier writings like that of Paolo da Certaldo. Yet there was a pervasive, if subtle, difference: The accent later was more on preserving the patrimony than on its acquisition. Due to their interest in the careful management of family and wealth, later writers were reluctant to advocate measures like separation from a son and disinheritance. Leaving such measures as a last resort, these writers relied rather on the kind of shifting relationship outlined by Rucellai in his *Zibaldone*, a relationship which progressively involved sons with their fathers in patrimonial management. The uses of emancipation may, indeed, have responded to this new view of the best familial strategy, itself a response to economic conditions and cultural values.

The success of strategies involving emancipation was, however, determined outside the family, as was true for all primarily legal devices. Results were never assured, and some consequences were unforeseen or uncertain for any number of people. The resolution of problems arising from emancipation, the resolution of conflicts between theory and practice or between divergent interests and rights lay with the lawyers.

CHAPTER FIVE

Conflicts between Theory and Practice: Lawyers and Property

General Principles of the Practitioners

The revival of Roman law in medieval Italy led to the institution of the *consilium sapientis* where a judge, often a political appointee with little or no knowledge of the law, sought the opinion (*consilium*) of a lawyer (*sapientis*) and then aligned his verdict with it. *Consilia* were also written at the request, and in support, of one of the parties in a lawsuit.[1] The legal *consilium* was, thus, the institutional meeting point between legal theory and practice, between the singular civil law and the diverse local statutes, customs, and exigencies of daily life. Here, at the point of contact and conflict between conceptual systems of varying complexity, we can see how those trained in the law drew on their substantive and methodological training to resolve problems or to reconcile the issues raised by a clash between different legal tenets. The legal experts did not encounter institutions like emancipation in the serene isolation of abstract legal speculation; they encountered it in the midst of the complexities generated by life. In their opinions, the lawyers attempted to establish the legal meaning of the facts of a case, to impose legal meaning where none was evident. They had to contend with not only the legal meanings of emancipation but also with the meanings given emancipation by those who used it.

Florentine lawyers were trained in the university, where they learned the principles, methods, and substance of what they termed the *ius commune* (the canon and civil law). They practiced their profession, however, aside from teaching it, within the territory circumscribed by the *ius proprium* of Florence as embodied in the city's statutes and the legislative decrees of its councils. They attempted to overcome conceptual chaos and to assimilate the *ius proprium* to the *ius commune* by a variety of means. They could, for example, take charge of compiling a city's statutes, as Paolo di Castro and Bartolomeo Vulpi did in Florence in the early fifteenth century. In general, however, they were left with the option of interpreting civic statutes according to theories of interpretation crafted around legal, moral, and logical principles they had learned in school. Their interpretations could take the form of a commentary on the statutes, but the tool most available to them, which served as the basis for statute commentaries, was the *consilium*. In Florence in the fifteenth century, with little prestige attached to teaching in the local university, lawyers found the *consilium*—the act of rendering a legal opinion—both their primary professional outlet and a fine economic device. The cost of a *consilium* to the party on whose behalf it was written could be considerable, especially if the jurist enjoyed a significant reputation. Those who purchased the services of a lawyer had interests in a particular case that were substantial enough to justify the expense.[2]

The *consilia* written by Florentine lawyers were published and transmitted among them along with *consilia* originating elsewhere. These *consilia* became the basis for a repository of general norms extracted from individual cases, norms that served the practical requirements of the legal practitioners.[3] At times, these norms were gathered together as a common learned doctrine in statute commentaries and legal glossaries. This commentary literature furnished the legal fraternity with an index to shared or authoritative opinions on various statutes or types of statutes. Within Florence and directed at Florentine law were writings like the commentaries of Alessandro di Salvi di Filippo Bencivenni (1385–1423) and Tommaso di ser Jacopo Salvetti (1390–1472), which have survived in part, and the personal legal glossaries of Antonio di Vanni Strozzi. These commentaries were both used by jurists in preparing their opinions, including cases involving emancipation, and were constructed from the opinions of jurists. They contained, among other things, those principles affecting emancipation that were derived from legal interpretive practice in Florence.

Basically, the Florentine statutes posed two general problems regarding emancipation for the lawyers who practiced there. The first problem was the validity of the registration requirement. Bencivenni, in the commentary he wrote around 1420 to 1423, near the end of his career, concerning the statute redaction of 1415, drew on the norms of Roman law and on opinions rendered in Florence to uphold the registration requirement in all of its details.[4] He maintained that a valid registration with the Mercanzia had to include the relevant information stipulated in the statute and had to take place within the prescribed time limits.[5] Jurisprudential practice did not modify one of the keystones of Florentine legislation regarding emancipation.

Jurisprudential practice was not, however, nearly so kind to Florentine legislation in dealing with the other problem it created for the jurists—the existence and extent of liability between fathers and sons as affected by emancipation. Liability between fathers and sons raised a whole complex of issues that clustered about three distinct statutes: one dealing with the obligations of fathers toward their sons; another covering the liability of sons for bankrupt fathers; the third setting forth the liabilities of heirs for debts incumbent on the estate. With respect to all three, the lawyers set limits to the liability created or defined by the statute.

A father's liability for his unemancipated son was limited by a strict jurisprudential interpretation of the relevant statute. Since the statute hinged such liability on a son's public activities within a guild or shop, it was determined that a father was not responsible for his son's activities outside that guild or shop.[6] The son was, of course, liable for his own actions. His liability was perfectly consonant with that established in the civil law; the father's was not. Therefore, Bencivenni went so far as to construct an interpretation that limited a father's liability to when his unemancipated son was a partner in a firm or master in a guild. If the son were simply an apprentice, the father was not liable (unless the son was doing very badly).[7] Allied to Bencivenni's protective stance toward the father was that taken by Antonio Strozzi, who found in a *consilium* of Alessandro Tartagni the principle that a father was liable for the debts of a son condemned in contumacy only if he had also been cited in the suit brought against the son.[8]

If he were not a member of a guild or active in a shop, the unemancipated son was not liable even for his own acts. Nonprofessional activities could only affect the patrimony, but an unemancipated son was not able to control or dispose of the patrimony. Bencivenni cited a principle enunciated in one of his own *consilia* that the acts of an unemancipated son not "in arte vel mercantia" were of no value or effect.[9] Strozzi added that even if a son falsely claimed to be a *publicus mercator*, his acts carried no weight unless the other party was fully aware of his deceit.[10]

According to the Florentine statutes, the mutual liability of father and son was terminated by emancipation. The Florentine jurists hastened to affirm this principle of emancipatory exemption even as they stretched it to what they must have seen as its legal limit. In principle, any simulated contract, including an emancipation, was fraudulent and inefficacious; it could be revoked by mere conjecture.[11] In the case of emancipation, however, conjecture of simulation had to rest on something more substantial than the fact that the son continued to live with his father and that the son's property was subject, therefore, to certain parental controls. Both Bencivenni and Salvetti espoused the proven maxim that an emancipated son resided with his father by a right of familiarity (*iure familiaritatis*). There was no presumption attached to common residence that made a *familiaris* liable for another's debts or made another person owner of his property. So, an emancipatus who continued to live with his father was but a coresident, and his property remained his own even if his father had usufruct of it in order to meet expenses for the emancipated son and his family. The son's emancipation, naturally, had to be valid otherwise. His liability for any particular paternal debt also depended on whether he had been emancipated for at least six months before the debt was contracted and had likewise had his property for one year.[12]

The statute laying out the obligations of sons for their bankrupt fathers received a loose, as opposed to literal, interpretation, because the lawyers trained in civil law found it utterly repugnant. It ran contrary to what they had been taught, since it made liability collective and not individual, thus harming innocent people. In their terms, it "corrected" the *ius commune* and, therefore, had to be "strictly interpreted."[13] This strict interpretation included, for example, the axiom that the father had to be a true bankrupt and not simply declared one because of his failure to appear in court (which carried a presumption of fraud and amounted to proof of guilt).[14]

Finally, lawyers faced the problem of the liability of heirs; here, also, they were strict constructionists. Bencivenni argued that to be held liable, one had to be heir to the debtor's property. Property that did not come from one's father was not bound for his obligations. The mother's dowry, therefore, even if held until death by one's father devolved free from his debts.[15] If the child were not an heir, he or she was, likewise, free of obligations toward the father. Salvetti affirmed that many times, a grown son who had received property from his father before the estate was encumbered with debts was cleared of liability even though the estate itself had gone to his father's daughter or infant grandson—both categories of people not normally liable for paternal debts—because the son had been left only what had been previously given him (for example, in a *praemium*).[16]

The principles and interpretive strategies developed by Florentine lawyers did not evolve in a vacuum. They were shaped by men who were part of the society they analyzed and described, and they affected activity in that society. The relative prominence of the mother's dowry in fifteenth-century emancipations, for example, may, in part, have been the result of the immunity such property was said to enjoy from the father's debts. Any decrease in the use of emancipation for its blanket effects in terminating liability may also have been the result of restrictions on that liability that lawyers were able to work out in principle through legal practice. These possibilities remain conjectures; they gain a degree of certitude only by looking at the way lawyers shaped the fates of those in whose suits their opinions were crafted. Only then can we also understand how practice raised conceptual problems and what those problems were.

Cases Involving Emancipation

A good share of the *consilia* penned by lawyers in Florence survives in manuscript form; of those dealing with private law, most are concerned with problems involving dowry and inheritance, the two most important, regular legal moments of patrimonial transmission. Relatively few *consilia* deal with emancipation, and the reasons are not hard to find. Emancipation, after all, involved relatively few people; it was, in some sense, temporary (the death of the father ended the categorization of legal abilities due to emancipated status), and much of the law on emancipation was relatively clearcut and unequivocal. Problems, however, did arise, generated by breaches between norm and praxis and between contradictory conceptions of the family. At such points where conceptualization was lacking or unclear, the best legal minds of the city were called upon to resolve the chaos and contradiction.[17] With regard to emancipation specifically, such conceptual problems centered on questions of validity, liability, and rights in property, especially as inheritance, and any or all of these issues could be present in a given case. Logically (and perhaps historically), however, the problem of validity came first, for all else depended on the validity of emancipation.

Sometime before he wrote the commentary just discussed, Bencivenni was asked to give his opinion in a case involving Antonio di ser Jacopo Bruogi.[18] The case concerned the implications of the registration of emancipation. Antonio di ser Jacopo was being sued by Tommaso di Federigo Sassetti for a sum that Antonio had pledged as surety on behalf of Gabriele and Antonio Acciaiuoli. Antonio argued that he could not be held accountable for the surety because "he is a *filiusfamilias* and under the power of his father." In accordance with the statute on the obligations of *filiifamilias*, therefore, the surety itself was not valid. In response, it was argued on Tommaso Sassetti's behalf that the language of the various statutes of the Mercanzia was deliberately vague, that indefinite terms like "whoever" included *filiifamilias*. Since Antonio's status as *filiusfamilias* was not in doubt, Bencivenni had only to determine whether Antonio was liable for the sum he had pledged (for his *fideiussio*, in other words). He noted that according to the statute Antonio had cited in his defense, a *filius* who was not in a guild could not make such a promise. He divined the intent of the legislator in establishing this principle as a desire to preclude *deceptiones* and as a presumption that the *pater* did not consent to the son's act in such a case. Therefore, said Bencivenni, it was incumbent upon the creditor to determine whether or not he was dealing with a *non integra persona*, whether, in other words, the debtor "is free from paternal restraints." The creditor had to protect himself by searching through the emancipation registry, which had been established "so that no one may be in ignorance." The indefinite terminology of the statutes Tommaso had alleged in support of his case did not change matters. Since Antonio had not been emancipated and, thus, was not capable in a legal sense, those statutes did not apply to him, claimed Bencivenni.

Bencivenni had had no choice but to uphold Antonio's immunity from the invalid pledge of surety he had given. The Florentine statute clearly exempted him, although Roman law, as Bencivenni remarked, held a *filiusfamilias* accountable for all obligations and sureties he freely contracted. Bencivenni had, moreover, found that registering emancipations was an institutional extension of the principles by which a *filius* was not capable of entering into such obligations. His assertion that the creditor had to consult the records shows that he saw the emancipation registry as an operative legal institution, not merely another requirement for validating an emancipation.

Bencivenni's *consilium* on the case of Antonio di ser Jacopo Bruogi was probably written in the second decade of the fifteenth century. Strictly speaking, it did not deal with the validity of an emancipation, but it did affirm the emancipation registry as a device that could protect creditors, and it upheld the legal necessity of emancipation before a son could obligate himself outside the normal course of business activities. His *consilium*, furthermore, should be viewed in conjunction with another major opinion, written at the beginning of the next decade, that dealt at greater length with registering emancipations.

The importance attached to this later *consilium* is indicated by the fact that it is really four *consilia*, its authors being Antonio Roselli (1381–1466), Paolo di Castro (1360–1441), Nello da San Gimignano (b. 1373), and Bartolomeo Vulpi (1359–1435).[19] All four were not native Florentines but were professionally active in Florence; they were also the most illustrious and esteemed lawyers in the city at the time. These were men who taught for a time in the leading universities and whose *consilia* and commentaries were prized and collected. Vulpi and Paolo di Castro had been employed by the government of Florence to revise and edit the city's statutes in 1415. All in all, these four lawyers represented an impressive array of legal talent available, in all likelihood, toward the end of 1421 to deliver their carefully coordinated opinions.[20]

At first glance, however, it is difficult to tell what there was about the case at hand that attracted or demanded such collective legal expertise. According to the factual summary (*punctus*) inserted between the second and third opinions as they appear in manuscript, the case was not even Florentine. It was alleged that a certain Guido di Piero of Bologna had emancipated his son Filippo in 1405 and had given him various lands and buildings. The emancipation was registered with the Mercanzia as required by law. Filippo, however, continued to live with his father, who continued to draw the fruits of the possessions given in *praemium* to his son, especially when Filippo ventured off to Rome on business. Eventually, 15 years later, Guido went bankrupt. Anticipating this fact, six months before he formally failed to meet his obligations, he again emancipated Filippo from fear that the prior emancipation was somehow not valid and had the property awarded to him by means of arbitration. At stake in the suit were, therefore, the rights of the creditors versus the rights of Filippo. Were the emancipation and *praemium* valid? Did their validity imply that Filippo and his property were immune from the creditors' claims?

The case would appear to have been simple enough, hardly worth the attention of four such illustrious lawyers, who, furthermore, were in Florence at the time and not Bologna. The arguments presented against the validity of the emancipation were, however, of great political significance; and that significance, moreover, bore an unmistakably Florentine flavor. The political significance was twofold. On the one hand, on behalf of the creditors, it was claimed that the notary did not have the proper authority; and on the other hand, it was charged that the notification of the emancipation was formally deficient because the name of the person giving notification was not included, contrary to the statutory language. The second issue was the less pressing of the two; it required clarification only on what elements were minimally necessary for a valid notification and registration. The first issue, however, was crucial; it raised the whole problem of the competence and authority of notaries, those indispensable scribbling drones who were the backbone of the legal and administrative machinery of the communes.

The significance of these issues for Florence lay in the fact that the Bolognese statutes bearing on the case were almost identical word for word to those of Florence. The rubrics were the same; even the date given for the Bolognese statute that established registration of emancipations with the Mercanzia (15 July 1355) was only five days after the identical legislation of Florence. The disposition of the case could, then, function as a precedent for Florentine law, and denying authority in emancipations to the city's notaries could create legal chaos. The fact that the four lawyers had Florentine law in mind as they wrote their opinions is perhaps best demonstrated by the fact that Roselli allowed an inadvertent slip of the pen to refer to one of the statutes in question as a "lege municipali florentina."[21]

The question of Guido's liability was thoroughly secondary to that of the notaries' status; Paolo di Castro ignored the liability issue, and Nello da San Gimignano treated it only briefly as an afterthought. The competence of notaries was the issue at the heart of each jurist's opinion. They had to grapple with the sometimes variant doctrinal assertions produced by their authoritative predecessors, ranging in time from Azo and Accursius to the recently deceased Baldus, regarding the competence of officials in emancipations. And they had to apply these various positions to the specific situation of notaries in Florence and Bologna.

Roselli's opinion appeared first.[22] He began by reviewing the arguments that maintained that "judges who are called *cartularii* have no jurisdiction from their office as scribes alone unless it is expressly given to them in their privileges."[23] He cited a number of passages from the Justinianic *Corpus* as well as Guillaume de Cunh, Bartolus, and the *Glossa ordinaria*. Since "in lege municipali florentina" (here is his slip of the pen), notaries were not expressly given authority in emancipations but only over the various forms of guardianship (*tutela*, *curatela*, and *mundualdus*), it seemed that the notary did not possess the requisite power and that the emancipation, therefore, was invalid. Roselli scholastically countered with the argument, however, that the notary could have the power, if not by grant of the city, then by grant of the emperor and that he could use this imperial power even in church lands like Bologna. And if he acted in emancipations by custom, then this *habitus* of jurisdiction was valid without reference to person or place when utilized for willing parties. "But it is notorious, as I hear, that in Bologna as in the city of Florence, scribes interpose *decreta* in emancipations; therefore, their interposition is valid because such *facultas* can be given by custom."[24] Roselli then went on to argue that it did not matter if the notary were the only one to give witness to possessing such a customary power and that it did not matter if he acted both as judicial authority and scribe. The notary was a public figure and public servant, and his word and writing were to be accepted because they were not given for his benefit but for the benefit of those for whom the contract was drawn up. Having thus saved the notary, Roselli indulged in a discussion of the difference between voluntary jurisdiction and contentious jurisdiction and of the occasions when a notary might need the testimony of others to support his claims to judicial authority.

Having upheld the powers of the notary and, thereby, the validity of the emancipation itself, Roselli addressed himself to the problem of the validity of its registration. Municipal law required that the name of the one who notified the Mercanzia of the emancipation be included in the written record. Since the name of the notifier did not appear in the registration of Filippo's emancipation, it was claimed that the emancipation was simulated and fraudulent, "even if in truth it was not simulated." Yet, Roselli again argued the contrary position. He presumed that the notification had been made by Guido or by another in his name, because the notary had attested that the notification had been given as required by law.[25]

On the issue of the son's liability, there were two reasons, said Roselli, that Filippo appeared vulnerable to the claims of his father's creditors: (1) since the gift had been given to the son, a person closely related to the giver (*coniunta persona*), "such a gift is presumed to have been made to defraud creditors"; and (2) because the father had possessed the property after the emancipation and *praemium* (having rented it to others), there was a presumption of fraud due to the seemingly fictitious transfer. But Roselli struck down both reasons. He declared that relationship was not of itself sufficient reason for presuming fraud in the transfer of property.[26] There would have been no presumption of fraud, Roselli pointed out, had there not been a pack of creditors to raise the issue. Because some 10 to 15 years had intervened between the time of the emancipation and the suit of the present creditors, there could be no presumption of fraud against those same creditors. Matters would have been different, of course, had there been only a brief time interval between the emancipation and the appearance of the creditors.

As for the assertion that Guido had continued to own the property after the emancipation, Roselli turned to an argument based on the concept of *familiaritatis* that was analogous to that of Bencivenni in his commentary. Roselli compared Guido to a guest, a *hospes* or *familiaris*, in his son's house. Such a person did not own the property he or she used, "for they are not said to possess the goods by which they are entertained, but rather these guests or familiar persons [are said] to be kept and possessed, for it they own those goods, they own them

just as an ass 'owns' his saddle." Roselli was led to conclude, therefore, that "Filippo can defend himself because he was emancipated
and the goods were given to him."[27]

Paolo di Castro entered his opinion after Roselli's, and he took up
only the issue of the validity of the emancipation. He was interested
in the authority of the notary and its basis in the corporate nature
of the urban commune. He first dealt on a very formal level with the
question of the notary's powers. He distinguished two types of power:
iurisdictio, the power given by a municipality or province, and *imperium*, the power granted by the emperor or one who held universal
authority. Paolo noted that there were those who argued that only
one who had *imperium* could officiate at an emancipation. This argument was based on a position taken by Azo, and following him, it was
possible to construct an argument that magistrates and notaries did
not have *imperium*, but only *simplex iurisdictio* and, therefore, were not
competent in emancipations. Having laid out this thesis, Paolo introduced the fact that the *Glossa ordinaria* had maintained that a simple
magistrate lacking *imperium* was still able to officiate at emancipations. He then developed this thesis posited by the *Glossa ordinaria*.

He began on the lofty plane of political jurisprudence. According to
Bartolus, a corporation (*universitas*) that consisted of provinces imparted *imperium* to its officials; one that consisted only of a city gave
its officials only *iurisdictio*. Paolo went on to assert that a corporation
that controlled a territory possessed jurisdiction and imparted this jurisdiction to its magistrates. Again, he relied on Bartolus, claiming
that "interposing authority in emancipations is [an act] of the lowest
mixed sovereignty and in civil matters belongs to the municipal magistrate." From these axioms, he deduced that notaries, duly constituted as *iudices ordinarii*, were "magistrates among those willing and
consenting as much." He concluded, therefore, that the Bolognese
notary did, indeed, have the authority to preside at an emancipation.
He also defended the notary's ability to be witness to his own jurisdiction in emancipations. The notary could also act as both judge and
scribe, since both roles were given to him simultaneously. Indeed, it
was ridiculous that one person should record the deed and another
should have to act as judicial authority.[28]

The registration, in the jurist's opinion, was also valid. The statute,
after all, only allowed notification by the emancipator or by another
in his name, so one could assume that the notification was given by
Guido or by one to whom he had delegated the task. In addition, the
statute was more concerned with effect, "that is, that emancipation be
placed in public and for the information of those wanting to do business with the *emancipatus*," than with the form of the act of notifi-

cation itself.[29] If for no other reason, one could presume from the father's extended silence regarding the emancipation that the notification had been performed, if not by himself, then by one whom he had chosen to do so for him.

Paolo di Castro's views had had the same effect as those expressed by Roselli, namely, to defend the powers of the notary and the validity of the notification of emancipation to the Mercanzia. Di Castro had, however, founded the notary's powers on something more legally and politically substantial than custom. He had defended it in terms of the type of jurisdiction enjoyed by a corporation (*universitas*) and exercised through its officials, including the notary. Nello da San Gimignano was, likewise, very much concerned with elaborating a defense of notaries' authority. He tried to add to the cumulative strength of the defense by exploring avenues left untouched by his predecessors.

The problems, he said, were three: Did the notary have authority; could he act as both judge and scribe; and was the notification valid? Like Roselli and di Castro, he found that the answer to all three questions was yes. A notary who was termed *iudex cartularii* or *iudex ordinarius*, as opposed to *simplices notarii*, had ordinary jurisdiction in voluntary legal matters like emancipation. The fact that the statute in question concerning the powers of notaries spoke only of guardianship institutions like the *mundualdus* did not mean that the statute, therefore, did not want notaries to have authority in emancipations. The proper interpretation of the statute had to involve an appeal to legal practice. The fact of the matter was that notaries constantly officiated at emancipations. The ability of notaries to both officiate at and record contracts was simply confirmed by legal practice (*a comuni stilo*), "which is observed daily in places in which notaries render law, compose, and publish their acts that they perform as judges."[30]

As for the registration, it was valid, according to Nello, because it met the intent of the law. Notification had been given within the required time and had provided the date of emancipation and the names of father, son, and notary. Notification is required, he said, "so that the emancipation might be known and the fraud to creditors might not occur, [and] this effect resulted from these things that have been done, as is evident, and, therefore, the statutory provision is satisfied."[31]

As an afterthought, Nello responded to the question of the son's obligation for the father's debts. He concluded, as had Roselli, that the son had been the true owner of the property, that he was liable neither *in persona* nor *in rebus*, "which is especially true because all pretext of fraud ceases on account of the long space of time from the emancipation to the bankruptcy."[32]

Vulpi came last and found himself with little to do but affirm the others' arguments. In essence, the emancipation was valid because the notary had the requisite *mixtum imperium*. One needed *mixtum imperium* to effect a *tutela*, and this a notary could clearly do according to statute, so by extension, he could act in emancipations. Furthermore, he could be both judge and scribe because he functioned "as a public person for the utility of a third party." In an accidental, as opposed to an essential manner, namely, in the notification, the emancipation was also valid. It had provided all the same necessary information specified by Nello da San Gimignano as meeting the intent of the law. Moreover, the requirement of notification concerned only the effect of the act, not its essence, because it was a solemnity arising only after emancipation. In the case at hand, therefore, even if the notification had been lacking, the statute would no longer apply because the interval of over ten years provided sufficient tacit corroboration of the emancipation. The *praemium* likewise held if for no other reason than that there was no firm proof of intent to defraud future creditors. Adverse fortune was not a proof of intent; creditors had to show that things were already going badly for Guido at the time of the emancipation.[33]

For the historian, the problem remains of delineating the impact of what appears to have been a landmark judicial decision reached by four major jurists of the early Quattrocento. In terms of legal practice, their opinions may have amounted to a weighty precedent. The competence of notaries in emancipation does not appear to have been raised as an issue subsequently. The place of emancipation registrations in the Florentine legal world also appears to have been established. Failure to register an emancipation militated against it, while registration marked validity. However, these four lawyers also clearly placed the essence and truth of emancipation ahead of the form of notification. The locally established notification requirement had a laudable legal reason behind it (which is why the lawyers supported it), but they were loath to let a mere technicality in its observance invalidate a legitimate institution of civil law (unlike Bencivenni in his statute commentary). *Ius familiaritatis* was also firmly implanted as a principle in determining ownership and, hence, liability. Each of the four lawyers had constructed his arguments in his own manner; but each had come to the same conclusion. Each hastened to defend the validity of a duly performed legal act and the authority of a duly empowered notary, whether the defense was based upon abstract logic, civil law, relevant statutes, custom, or the facts of the case.

It may be possible, in addition, to attribute another effect to the decision of the four eminent lawyers. In the absence of concrete evidence due to the silence of the legislative and deliberative records, this attribution must remain in the form of a hypothesis. The hypothesis is that the legal decisions of 1421 (if this dating is accurate) produced a political effect, as well, namely, the legislation of December 1421 that initiated the procedure of registering emancipations with the Signoria. There can be little doubt that the decision was applicable in Florence, and, in all likelihood, it could have been known among members of the ruling class. What was there about the arguments of the four jurists that may have justified and urged the Signoria to enter the registration business?

The justification may have been simple enough. The authority of the notaries, according to the lawyers, was derived from the custom and jurisdiction of the commune as a corporation (*universitas*). Emancipation was a public act. Therefore, the Signoria, as the chief public body of the commune, could look after emancipation with at least as much justification as did the Mercanzia, which was the body with authority to try debtors and determine liability. An additional, and perhaps more immediate political and economic reason, was the fact that the Mercanzia's recordkeeping had been brought into question. Only a few years before (in 1410), the Mercanzia had had to caution its notaries to keep the emancipation registries neat and orderly. The notary who had recorded the emancipation of Filippo di Guido in Bologna had neglected to enter the name of the party registering the emancipation. That omission had been sufficient to raise the issue of validity; and although the jurists had determined that that particular bit of information was not essential, what would have happened if the notary had neglected some more essential piece of information, like Filippo's name or the date of emancipation? Vulpi's *consilium* had also raised the spector of tacit emancipation. What guarantee could be given to creditors in Florence if the mere passage of ten years could militate against their claims? A government as interested in the economic health of the city as was the Signoria that sat in December 1421 may, indeed, have found sufficient cause for alarm in the decision presented by the four jurists. The Signoria may, therefore, have made itself the guarantor of the accuracy and completeness of the emancipation records.

Whereas in the case discussed by Roselli and the others, the registration in question had been performed, in other cases there had been a failure to register an emancipation, and lawyers were called upon to spell out the legal implications of that failure. In one such instance, an anonymous *consilium* dealt with a case that arose in Florentine territory. It struck down a gift to an *emancipatus*, in part, because the emancipation had not been properly registered. The emancipation had taken place in Florence, but the principals were citizens and residents of San Gimignano, a town requiring publication of its residents' emancipations. An anonymous jurist determined that the emancipation was valid by Florentine law, but the desire of the legislators to preclude fraud required the emancipation and the *praemium* both to be publicized in San Gimignano. Otherwise, the jurist said, anyone could emancipate a child in another territory to hide the fact, "which is false and absurd."[34] Other reasons moved him to declare the *praemium* invalid (the grandfather's account books, for example, termed it a loan and not a gift), but the failure to publish the acts, above all, led to the presumption of fraudulent intent. The son of the "emancipatus" was entitled to the portion of his grandfather's estate that his father would have inherited, because his father had never been emancipated (that is, the emancipation was not valid), and the property in the *praemium* had, therefore, never been his. Here, there was a clear question of fraud, because the facts of the emancipation had, for the purpose of deception, never been made public (*insinuata*).

In other cases, failure to register did not necessarily carry a presumption of fraud, but any rights gained by the emancipatus were abrogated, since the emancipation was invalid unless performed again and duly registered.[35]

Another *consilium* found in the Florentine archives, this one by Joachinus de Narnia (?), concerns the disputed validity of an emancipation that arose at Siena. A certain messer Jacopo denied that he had been emancipated and had, at the same time, renounced any share in his father's estate, claiming that he had been in Bologna at the time of the alleged emancipation. He even produced witnesses to back up his claim. He also questioned the validity of the protocol produced as proof of the emancipation and renunciation, both because the two acts appeared in a single document and because the notary had been a Jew. The jurist, however, was not fooled by Jacopo's arguments. He confirmed the validity of the acts, first, because the better witnesses —the herald who had published the act and the instrument itself— proved Jacopo's presence and emancipation; secondly, because there was nothing legally wrong with both acts appearing in one protocol drawn up by a single notary; and thirdly, because religion was of no consequence in secular affairs. Finally, after having earlier questioned the trustworthiness of Jacopo by noting that he had once before produced a false witness in court, the jurist pointed out that Jacopo was contradicting himself. He was both denying that he had been emancipated and seeking absolution from his oath not to seek anything from his father's estate, which oath had been made immediately after emancipation: "Since, therefore, Jacopo confesses that he had sworn in emancipation, therefore, he confesses that he was emancipated. And if accordingly he denies emancipation, he is contrary to himself and variant and must not be allowed to deny what he had before confessed with his own mouth."[36] This final and most damning argument undermined the logic of Jacopo's position and bound him to abide by the true state of legal affairs.

Questions about the validity of an emancipation were raised by parties who sought to escape the consequences of a valid emancipation. The lawyers in such cases turned to the principles of the law as well as to custom to sort out the facts in a case. They hastened to affirm the validity of proper emancipations; they hastened equally to overturn those that were fraudulent or fictitious in their opinion. To the jurists, the cases presented questions of law; to the parties involved, they were questions of property, both of rights to inheritance and liability for debts.

Sometime around 1455, two Florentine lawyers, Otto di Lapo Niccolini (1410–1470) and Benedetto di messer Michele Accolti (1415–1464), were asked to submit an opinion in a case where the validity of an emancipation was questioned. The manuscript copy of the *consilium* does not present the facts in the case, so the situation can be reconstructed only with difficulty from the arguments.[37] The emancipation involved a certain Francesco (Tedaldi?), who had been emancipated *in absentia* by his grandfather.[38] Later, other grandsons had been emancipated, and the *praemium* given to Francesco had been revoked and given to them. Francesco's emancipation was rejected quickly by Niccolini, because Francesco had never gone before a judge to ratify it by giving his consent and because the grandfather had never produced the requisite *rescriptum principis* for emancipation of an *absens*. The considerable *praemium* of 5,000 florins given to Francesco was likewise invalid, both because he was *in potestate* as a result of the nullification of the emancipation and because there had never been a true handing over of possession, meaning that there was no de facto gift that could be confirmed by the death of the giver. In fact, it appears that the grandfather had revoked the gift and given it to his other grandsons, and this second gift was determined to be validly publicized. A subsequent revocation of this second gift to the other grandsons, on the other hand, was invalidated by Niccolini on the grounds that there was no expressed reason for it. Accolti immediately and briefly assented to Niccolini's first two conclusions, namely, that the gift to Francesco had been revoked and publication of the subsequent gift to the others was valid. In regard to the third point, that the second gift could not be revoked, Accolti added an argument that he said had been overlooked. The argument was that the emancipation and gift were valid during the period between their enactment and their registration, when, apparently, the invalid revocation was attempted. Niccolini had merely affirmed that the emancipation of the others was valid; Accolti asserted that it was valid at all times and not suspended and to go into effect only after notification. Had witnesses been produced to verify that the grandsons had not paid the *honera* required of them in the gift, then there would have been a reason for revocation. The mere assertion of the giver that there had been deceit causing him to revoke the gift was not acceptable even if that deceit meant that one son remained bereft.[39] The decision of the two lawyers upset all claims Francesco may have had, because his emancipation had been invalid. The claims of the others, despite the express revocation of the gift made to them, had been upheld, because their emancipation had been valid. With claims to 5,000 florins hanging in the balance, validity of emancipation could, indeed, become very important.

When the validity of an emancipation was not in question, there could still be considerable room for doubt with regard to the effects of the emancipation, and inheritance was one such area where the effects of emancipation could be crucial. Two lawyers, Raffaele Raymundi (Cumanus) (ca. 1380–1427) and Raffaele Fulgosio (1367–1427), wrote a *consilium* on a Florentine case where a father, Antonio di Santi, had given his son Baldassare, whom he had emancipated on the eve of his departure for Hungary, 7,000 florins in one way or another.[40] The presentation of the case hints that the sum in the son's possession did not represent a totally voluntary gift on the father's part: "After emancipation, by various ways and means he got and extracted and had subverted to his control over seven thousand florins from the money and goods of the testator." In his will, the father had stipulated that Baldassare had to collate that sum with his three brothers or receive no more. Baldassare, however, claimed that he did not have the money when Antonio died in 1417; he offered to collate everything that could be said to have been his father's, but he did not have 7,000 florins. Raymundi opined that the testamentary stipulation was valid "because the rigor of the law is usually tempered and departs from common law, so that equality might be preserved among brothers, lest envy arise from inequality."[42] He suggested that Baldassare produce evidence from his father's account books that either he had previously returned the money or had never been given it. After the truth had thus been determined, then one could calculate how much Baldassare had to collate with his brothers. Raymundi and Fulgosio upheld the father's intent of equality among his sons.

The illustrious Milanese lawyer Filippo Decio (1454–1535), while lecturing at Florence in 1495, delivered an opinion in another inheritance case, one that arose at Lucca. Decio maintained in his *consilium* that the estate in question belonged solely to the *agnati*. He ruled out a collateral branch because the deceased's father had been emancipated, and agnation between the two branches had, therefore, been canceled. He struck down arguments against the validity of the emancipation and others in favor of the claims of the collateral branch.[42] Antonio Strozzi later made note of Decio's opinion, which he considered a "beautiful *consilium*," in an entry in one of his legal glossaries. He admired Decio's argument because it followed the principle that children born to an emancipated son after emancipation were not truly *agnati*, although they stood to inherit equally with the *agnati*. Decio, in Strozzi's opinion, had also made a useful distinction between those statutes that were favorable to *agnati emancipati* and those that were unfavorable. Decio declared that *agnati emancipati* were to be legally considered agnate when a favorable statute might apply to them.[43]

Decio also commented on a case involving collation of a gift made to an emancipated son; this was a case on which Domenico Bonsi (1430–1502) and Francesco Gualterroti (1456–1509), Florentine lawyers, had previously written opinions.[44] Giovanni Balducci's father had divided his property between his sons in his will, and he later gave Giovanni a further gift when he found that the division incorporated in the will shortchanged his eldest. After their father's death, the other sons, who had been emancipated, demanded collation of the gift or Giovanni's exclusion from the estate. A judge had decided in their favor, but the three lawyers reviewed the case and overturned the judge's ruling.

The two Florentine lawyers concluded that the gift made to Giovanni did not have to be collated. Decio pointed out in his opinion that the shared wisdom (*communis opinio*) was that gifts to an emancipatus had to be collated; but despite this principle, he adhered to the viewpoint of his colleagues. He concluded that the gift was not subject to collation because the testator-father had given it lest there be inequality among his sons. Decio, in other words, interpreted the father's intention as an attempt to restore the material equality between his sons that had been upset during his life, largely due to *praemia* accompanying their emancipations. The guiding principle to Decio was that of equality between the sons. In his words, "When by not collating sons are rather brought to equality, there should be no collation. . . . So also in a simple gift there should not be collation except when inequality would result."[45] Since collation by Giovanni alone would upset the equality established by his father in giving him the additional gift, Decio, like Bonsi and Gualterotti, decided that there should be no collation. Giovanni would be forced to collate only if his brothers did so too.

Another interesting and involved inheritance case was that of Vincenzo di Giuliano Davanzati and his half brothers. The problem was whether Vincenzo could succeed to his father's estate in equal measure with his four half brothers, Giuliano's sons by his second wife. The case drew opinions from four lawyers: Niccolò Guicciardini (1500–1557), Ormannozzo Deti (b. 1464), Giovanni Buongirolami (1464–1542), and Filippo Decio.[46]

It appears that during his life, Giuliano had given all of his property to the sons of his second wife. Guicciardini, citing Decio's lectures among other doctrinal sources, argued that the gift was invalid "because done by the father without confirmation by oath or preceding merits [on the part of the recipients]." The gift was not validated by death or by emancipation, in Guicciardini's opinion and, therefore, it did not prejudice Vincenzo's rights to inherit. Guicciardini then advanced to the thorny question of Giuliano's testamentary dispositions. He determined that the testament was invalid because it passed over Vincenzo. Vincenzo had been emancipated, so the testament could be valid if he had been neglected for a good reason. A reason, however, was lacking in Guicciardini's estimation, largely because Giuliano's letters to Vincenzo had revealed a change of heart at the end—there had been a reconciliation between the two "because he conversed with him as a son, as witnesses state." Two witnesses of good repute also confirmed that Giuliano had voiced his intent to revoke his will and leave equal shares to all his sons. From all this, said Guicciardini, "One can conclude that Vincenzo should be admitted equally with the other sons, just as they are called equally by law."[47]

Deti argued before the court that a good prince should take the side of equality. The gift to the half brothers was of no legal consequence, he claimed, because there had been neither a true nor a fictive transfer of property, since Giuliano had reserved possession for himself. Deti struck down all arguments supporting the validity of the gift and of the wills and codicil. He noted that the "testator was moved to deprive Vincenzo of his property because in the past Vincenzo had had many expenses and had taken his goods and consumed them during the testator's life."[48] But this reason for promoting material equality between the sons by depriving one was deemed false and erroneous.

Buongirolami also struck down the gift. He declared that Giuliano's last will, expressed orally to his confessors on his deathbed, was the one to be followed by the tribunal, because it was intended to exonerate Giuliano's conscience.

Filippo Decio, too, referred to the question of equality. After establishing the duty of the ruler to promote *equitas*, Decio said that the intention to be followed was the one that led to equal succession for all the sons.[49] Decio's *consilium* was far shorter and less detailed than those of the other three and it duplicated their arguments. Decio's opinion had been sought, it would appear, for the weight of the illustrious jurist's name.

The *praemium*, like inheritance, also raised important issues for Florentine lawyers to resolve. Ormannozzo Deti, in one opinion, decided that the common opinion was that a gift had to be publicized in a notarial charter, especially if it were the result of pure generosity and not motivated by an obligation.[50] But a *praemium* of great value or one that was expressly designated as the emancipatus' legitimate portion of the inheritance could be considered not to be an expression of mere generosity. Here opinions varied. Deti himself decided that the gift with which he was concerned had not been a transfer of property belonging to the emancipatus by right of inheritance and that, therefore, it had to be publicized. Failure to incorporate the terms of the *praemium* in a notarized document invalidated it.

Many years before Deti wrote, Paolo di Castro et alii had examined a case involving a gift.[51] Messer Filippo di Guicciazzo had emancipated his legitimated son Lionello and given him a farm and some *Monte* credits (credits in Florence's funded public debt). Filippo's creditors sought payment from that property. The lawyers began by noting the many good reasons for considering Lionello and his property immune from the creditors' claims, among which was the fact that Lionello had been emancipated.[52] There was also the fact that it had been some time since the gift, and, here as elsewhere, the temporal element militated against presumption of fraud. But all these arguments were quickly dispatched: "For the rest, the aforesaid not withstanding, the contrary is truer in law, the truth of which is evident from the fact that confession or alienation made to the utility of a legally incapable person by his father is presumed to have been made in fraud." The son lacked experience in business and was rather young when the property was nominally transferred to him. Lionello was both illegitimate (*spureus*—and possession of property by *spurei* was deemed suspicious by the law) and incapable before the law (so that any disposition made in his name was assumed to be his father's doing).[53] In addition, it was determined from the father's account books that he had continued to receive the revenue from the property and to treat it as his own. The lawyers, therefore, claimed that the property could not be assumed to have been part of the *peculium*, since Filippo obviously considered it his and not Lionello's. Having thus inferred fraudulent intent, the jurists dismissed Filippo's description of the property as his son's and supported the rights of the creditors.

In many ways, this case was similar to that on which Paolo di Castro had delivered his opinion with those of Roselli, Vulpi, and Nello da San Gimignano. There, too, a son had held title to property, but the father had used it. In that case, however, the son had been older, legitimate, and had some business experience, and it had been decided that the son really did possess the land in question. In the case at hand, however, the son had been a young *spureus*; he had no experience, and he made no decisions affecting the farm or the *Monte* credits he was said to own. Both the principles of civil law and an evaluation of the facts produced a judgment of fraud in the one case, a judgment of legal approval in the other.

Another gift tied to emancipation that came under the scrutiny of a Florentine lawyer was that made by Giovanni Tornabuoni to the sons of his son Lorenzo.[54] Antonio Strozzi and Domenico Bonsi were called upon to make sense of several peculiar features of this gift.[55] Lorenzo had later sold some of his own land, but it was not clear if the property given his sons by his father was obligated in the event the sale did not go through or was contested in court. The doubt arose because there were conditions attached to the gift that seemed to obligate it to any sale or obligation made by Giovanni or Lorenzo. Strozzi asked what would happen if Giovanni had sold him (Strozzi) some land from which he was later evicted in favor of Giovanni's creditor with a prior claim against the property. Ordinarily Strozzi could seek compensation from the rest of Giovanni's property, including the property given to the grandsons as a *praemium* if the gift occurred after the sale to him, but not before. The gift, in other words, was not obligated for the claims of someone who subsequently purchased something from the giver. This particular gift to the grandsons, however, had carried clauses to the effect that the property was, indeed, obligated by any subsequent sales or by other contracts entered into by Giovanni and Lorenzo. Therefore, said Strozzi, with regard to the sale by Lorenzo, it was as if the *praemium* had not been given.[56]

Strozzi, however, pressed on by asking what possible gain Giovanni and Lorenzo might have expected by imposing such a condition on the gift. His response was "that such a gift can have another effect, for which effect it is actually believed the aforesaid gift was made."[57] In other words, Lorenzo had recently been judicially condemned "not only because of marital kinship but also by a tie of great friendship" with Piero de' Medici after the turbulent events of November 1494. Lorenzo had feared confiscation of his property, and Giovanni had maneuvered ownership into Lorenzo's sons' hands, while allowing Lorenzo latitude to use the property, or at least not to be hurt by the gift, by placing the condition upon it. So Strozzi concluded that anyone who engaged in sales with Lorenzo was not harmed by the gift. Bonsi filed his assent in a brief appended statement.

Strozzi also dealt with another emancipation-related property transfer. The issue was whether a son who had purchased property in his own name with his father's money before emancipation owned the property afterwards.[58] Strozzi had no difficulty in defending the validity of the sale itself. He also found ample justification in civil law for the position that the property in question, which had been purchased in the son's name before emancipation, fell to him after emancipation as *bona peculii profectitii*. The argument presented by the father's creditors, who were asking for the legal right to seize the reputed property of the son for his father's debts, rested largely on the fact that the son's emancipation had not been registered. Normally, their case would have been very strong, but in this instance, the son was a religious and, as such, not subject to lay laws according to Strozzi. The lawyer thus protected the son from all contrary arguments and claims.

Whether the question brought before the law was the validity of an emancipation or a *praemium* or the effects of an emancipation on inheritance and property ownership, again and again the issue of liability and the possibility of fraud came up. For a third party, if an adverse legal act could not be struck down on grounds of illegality or procedural deficiencies, the only recourse was to argue intent to defraud. There were, however, considerable problems not only in determining whether fraud existed in a given instance but also in fixing the extent of one's liability for a debt.

One area where liability was very important was restitution of dowries. Antonio Strozzi wrote a *consilium* concerning a suit where Ginevra, wife of the late Luca Capponi, demanded reimbursement of her dowry from her sons as heirs to her husband.[59] The sons claimed that they were not liable for repayment of the dowry because they had, in fact, repudiated the inheritance and given the dotal rights (*iura dotalia*) to their sister Nera and because they had been emancipated on 18 February 1482, before the debt to Ginevra had been contracted, for it had been recorded in the family accounts later, on 5 March 1482.[60] However, said Strozzi, the dotal debt had actually been contracted many years before, when the dowry was established at the time of the wedding of Luca and Ginevra. The sons had also been cited to appear in court on 12 August 1484 as codebtors with their father when he was declared delinquent in meeting his obligation to return the dowry. Strozzi concluded without elaborate argumentation that the sons had not been emancipated at the time the obligation to return the dowry had been contracted and were obligated just like their father. The repudiation of the inheritance and the alienation of the dotal rights were dismissed as obviously simulated and fraudulent, having occurred only two days after the public proclamation of delinquency.

Strozzi also analyzed the liability for restitution of dowry in another case where fraud was not at issue.[61] Bartolomeo d'Antonio Fei had emancipated two sons, Benedetto and Bernardo, who were both married in 1470. The father and both sons all obligated themselves for both dowries. Bernardo's wife later died after having given birth to several children. Bernardo remarried and received a second dowry of 1,000 florins; his father did not, however, expressly obligate himself for this second dowry, although Bernardo and his second wife lived with his father. In 1487, Bartolomeo's other two sons, Andrea and Simone, both emancipated, were married with Bartolomeo obligating himself to return both dowries, as with his first two sons in 1470. Within two years, both Bartolomeo and Bernardo had died. The latter's second wife wanted her dowry returned, but there was some difficulty in retrieving it from her husband's estate. With the complication of legal relations created by emancipation, Strozzi had to sort out liability to determine if Bartolomeo's estate was obligated to return the dowry of Bernardo's second wife.

Abandoning the scholastic *pro-et-contra* argumentation, Strozzi launched into a straightforward defense of the woman's right to restitution from the estate of her father-in-law. One of the reasons alleged in defense was that a father had to give a son's wife a *donatio propter nuptias* equal to the dowry as a guarantee; in places where the *donatio* was not given or could not equal the dowry (as in Florence), the father had to accept the solemn legal obligation to restore the dowry should the occasion arise.[62] Emancipation made no difference: A father had to dower his emancipated daughters, and he had to provide a *donatio propter nuptias* in the name of his emancipated sons. Strozzi then adduced a number of other reasons affirming the father's obligation in this case and denying a priority of rights to the son's first wife's dowry.

A woman who married into a family was creditor of the family's patrimony once her dowry had been transferred to husband and (or) father-in-law. In fact, her dowry rights, said Strozzi, had priority on the estate in the face of any other type of claims that might be produced.

Other types of claims were also produced against the property of various Florentine families. These types of claims also found their advocates among Florentine lawyers. Strozzi again, for example, wrote in defense of the rights of the creditors of the son of Rainaldo Altoviti.

Rainaldo claimed that he had emancipated his son and was not liable for his debts, although the emancipation had not been registered. Strozzi, in opposition, enumerated all the ways that the statute "De obligatione filii familias etc." altered the provisions of the civil law. He then undertook to delineate the consequences of an unregistered emancipation. The statute said that an unregistered emancipation was presumed to have been simulated and fraudulent. Strozzi pointed out, however, that one could not presume fraud on the part of the son; indeed, it was to the creditors' advantage to be able to obligate the son without paternal consent. Rather, one had to assume fraud on the part of the father, because he, henceforth, was not obligated for his son, and "creditors, not having notice of the emancipation, may be defrauded, since they thought they had the father obligated and with that understanding they had confidence in his son."[63] In terms of the logic of the situation, then, the father's failure to register his son's emancipation was suspect; Florentine statutes, unfortunately, seemed to offer little legal basis for pursuing this logic. The problem in interpreting the statute lay in the phrase *quantum ad commodum emancipati* (insofar as [it is] to the convenience of the emancipatus), a phrase that Strozzi labeled obscure. As he saw it, the son gained no *commodum* from emancipation, for thereafter he faced his creditors alone. Nonetheless, the provision of 1421 establishing the communal emancipation registry spoke only of the benefit or harm accruing to emancipati and their creditors. The law said nothing at all about the benefit or harm of fathers. In leaving fathers out of consideration, the statute appeared to give Strozzi no legal way to allow Rainaldo's son's creditors to get at Rainaldo himself.

Strozzi found a way to obligate Rainaldo by once again referring to the logic of the situation. An unregistered emancipation could not result in a loss for the father, he argued, because the father retained his *potestas* and his property. For that reason, the statute had simply not bothered to speak of the benefit and harm to fathers. The statute also accorded fathers full protection from liability for the most minimal registration of emancipation, according to the prevailing opinion among practicing lawyers.[64] Strozzi, however, faced a case where the emancipation had never been registered. He concluded, therefore, that nothing in the statute contravened his initial position that there was a presumption of fraud against a father who failed to register his child's emancipation. Rainaldo Altoviti, he said, was liable for his son's debts.

Where there was no doubt that an emancipation was legitimate and properly registered, on the other hand, the father was no longer vulnerable to his son's creditors. Alessandro Bencivenni put this theory in practice in a *consilium* he wrote on behalf of ser Andrea da Radda. By a number of arguments from both civil law and the city's statutes, Alessandro was able to support ser Andrea's contention that he was not liable for his sons because he had emancipated them. The major argument lay in the very character of emancipation itself—the fact that it changed a child's status to that of *extraneus* (an outsider with respect to his family, as defined by ties of *patria potestas*), and that the father "separated his son from his family by emancipation."[65]

A father's liability for his son was a relatively simple matter to determine. He was obligated if his sons were not validly emancipated; he was not obligated if they were. The obligation of a son for his father was not, however, so simple a matter. If he were emancipated, the timing of the emancipation—as well as its validity—entered the picture. There was also the problem of determining whether rights to property had been really transferred or only fictively. The dowry case involving the widow of Luca Capponi is only one example of the kinds of issues that came into play in determining the legal liabilities of sons for their fathers.

Florentine lawyers faced questions of liability of both emancipated and unemancipated children. The rigor with which they approached these problems in turn determined to what extent emancipation functioned legally to exempt sons from liability for their fathers.

Perhaps one of the first cases to arise in the fifteenth century occupied the attention of three lawyers; Bencivenni, Nello da San Gimignano, and Giovanni Buongirolami da Gubbio (1381–1454). The particulars of the case were the following: In 1382, Giovanni Masini dall'Antella petitioned for bankruptcy. One of his creditors, Rinaldo Rondinelli, asked for his condemnation, which was given in contumacy, because Giovanni failed to appear before the podestà to answer the charges. In 1385, Rondinelli was granted a decree against Giovanni as *cessans*. Giovanni died in 1389 in Castro Santo Stefano, leaving his son Taddeo, a lad of less than ten years of age. Taddeo continued to reside in Florence, unmolested by his father's creditor, so that in the course of events, he became politically active, his name appearing in the electoral purses and being drawn for offices. Now suddenly, many years later, Taddeo's right to hold office was questioned on the grounds that he was the son of a condemned *cessans*. The lawyers agreed that it seemed that Taddeo could lose his right to hold office because he was the unemancipated son of a fugitive bankrupt under the ban of the commune. It was also fitting, they said, that a son suffer for the failings of his father, since "even by divine law the case is strengthened in the passage where it is given fathers have eaten bitter grapes and their sons' teeth are set on edge."[66]

The three jurists, however, quickly reversed their opinion. They declared that it was not just neither by divine nor human nor civil law that a son suffer for the sins of his father. The statement from the Bible was merely a casual remark and not dispositive. The city's statutes, therefore, for all that they were concerned with the public good, ran contrary to divine, natural, and civil law and were to be interpreted restrictively, "especially since they contain an irrational hatred."[67] Among the elements of that strict interpretation was the fact that there was no proof of a true bankruptcy (*vera cessatio*), that contumacy could not harm third parties, and that Taddeo would have been exempt in any case as an *infans* and, thereby, *indefensus* at the time of the bankruptcy.

Taddeo's political rights were thus upheld by a strict reading of the statutes, which, in fact, flew in the face of the intent to hold sons liable for their fathers. It was not that the three jurists could expect favors from Taddeo or his friends the Medici, though it was possible. The three operated on the firm moral and legal basis that Florentine law holding sons liable for fathers judicially condemned as bankrupt was unjust.[68] Their opinion was only one of a number limiting the scope of the Florentine statutes in this regard and for much the same reason.

Another jurist greatly repelled by Florentine law on liability was Luca Corsini (1462–1511). On behalf of Francesco Corsellini, Corsini wrote an opinion where he decided that Francesco was not subject to the statute of Florence obligating sons for the debts of a bankrupt father (*pater cessans*), a statute that Corsini termed "odious and harsh."[69] Francesco had been emancipated at the time of the formal declaration of his father's delinquency in meeting his obligation, but he had not been emancipated at the time when the debt was contracted. By the language of the statute, it would seem that Francesco was clearly responsible for his father's obligations.[70]

His lawyer, however, constructed an argument to release him from the strictures of this "odious" statute. Corsini focused on the difference between two times—the time of the contract and the time of the declaration of debt and delinquency—and elaborated his case on that difference. Until Stefano, the father, had been declared in default by the court of the Mercanzia, said Corsini, he had not been "truly and properly a debtor." To be sure, his son-in-law, the creditor (a fact strongly suggesting that the debt involved a dowry), had described him as his debtor in his accounts, but "from that description alone, without another declaration, he could not demand [satisfaction] from him."[71] The fact that such a declaration was intended to be retroactive to the time of the contract, argued Corsini, could affect only the father. As for the son, it was unjust to subject him to the consequences of that retroaction. To do so would be to transfer the obligation to him from the father. But whereas at the time of the contract, the son was *in potestate*, at the time of the declaration, he was emancipated. Corsini contended that there was a qualitative, or substantive, difference between the two times—the time when Francesco had been *in potestate* and the time when he was emancipatus. In any case, Corsini knew that his position could not be carried by this legal argument; therefore, he also argued that since the son had not been called to court when the declaration of delinquency was rendered, he should not be harmed by the subsequent sentence against his father. He claimed that many Florentine lawyers had maintained that it was necessary to cite the son in court to hold him liable for such a debt. But, above all, he declared, "We should not join these times to induce such odious qualities so that the son bears the iniquity of the father against divine law and against the common law . . . especially since the strict logic of the law will not suffer it."[72]

Corsini argued the case on a very abstract and ethical level: The names and facts of the case were quickly left behind; citations of Roman law or the statutes ceased. He based his position on ethics, and he constructed his argument with persuasive rhetoric and subtle logic more than with law. There was certainly no basis in civil or Florentine law for his logical distinctions between the various times or for the result of those distinctions—exempting a child from liability for a debt incurred before he was emancipated. Unfortunately, there is no way of knowing how Corsini's opinion was received by the court. Corsini himself remained consistent; he presented a similar opinion elsewhere, also intended to extract a son from the consequences of the same odious statute.[73]

Not all cases were decided in the same vein. Domenico di Baldassare Bonsi (1430–1502) in an opinion rejected the argument made on behalf of a young son, Ghinozzo Pazzi, that he was not liable for his father's debts even though he had not been emancipated. Ghinozzo was, says the *consilium*, over eight years of age but under 14. Therefore, it had been argued that he was not subject to the rigor of Florentine statutory law because the civil law stated that he could not be jailed as a minor and because he was *inemancipabilis* (not emancipatable). Bonsi, arguing on behalf of the creditor, Niccolò Capponi, maintained that this was not the case, that the language of the statute did not allow such an interpretation. Since the statute was "made principally for correcting the civil law, it should be understood indiscriminately and generally and indefinitely with respect to everything." The fact that minors could not be jailed under the provisions of the civil law, therefore, did not carry any weight in Florentine law. Similarly, the statute had to be understood to include all unemancipated children regardless of whether or not they were *emancipabiles*. Bonsi's opponents wanted to assert that sons under the age of seven and a half were properly *inemancipabiles* and not merely unemancipated—an argument that he claimed varied greatly from legal truth. Not only that, they wanted to clear even sons over seven and a half who could unequivocally be termed unemancipated. Bonsi reacted to these arguments by shifting the terms of debate. Sons were not being held for their father's deeds, he said; rather, they were themselves guilty as participants. In other words,

> it is not true that sons are held liable for the father, because instead they are presumed to be in crime and fraud along with the father. This reason does not appear written in the statute and cannot, because from this it follows that they should be considered just like elder emancipated sons. But those *in potestate* should be said to participate in fraud rather than *emancipati*, because fraud is limited with respect to sons who are not present [with the father].[74]

Bonsi's arguments took no cognizance, except perhaps obliquely, of opinions concerning the injustice of penalizing a son for his father. He seems not to have been swayed by the ideology of divine and natural law; rather, his arguments were based on another underlying practical and ideological consideration. Fraud, Bonsi noted, was intolerable in a city that lived by trade:

> Moreover, a truer reason may be assigned, because the statute wanted the sons to be bound for the father. Since it is so harmful that merchants become bankrupt in Florence by being defrauded, the legislators indeed considered keeping fathers from so evil an act on account of the penalty inflicted on the sons rather than by the penalty imposed on them. Someone wanting very much to fail his creditors, if he knows he will be held, considers keeping himself [safe] by fleeing or otherwise takes counsel with himself. But when he sees his innocent sons held, he might be kept from so evil an act in Florentine territory, whose greatest utility lies in the abundant traffic or business of its citizens.[75]

Bonsi had divined the intent of the legislators and used it to support the claims of his client, Niccolò Capponi, whose interests were thus assimilated to the common good. Finally, he denied that it was his client's responsibility to produce proof that Ghinozzo had not been emancipated. The burden of proof, he said, lay with the opposition, because one assumed the intrinsic quality of *patria potestas* into which a legitimate son was born, and not the extrinsic quality of emancipation.

We would like to know, of course, if Bonsi's arguments or those of his opponents won the day. It does appear, though, that Bonsi was swimming against the legal tide. Far more prevalent than a defense of

Florentine statutes were the attempts to render a strict and limiting interpretation of them.

There was a limit to the interpretation of the statute. The language clearly obligated sons. Even Luca Corsini's weak, if ingenious, interpretation of the law left no doubt that an elder son who had not been emancipated, neither at the time of the debt nor at that of the declaration, was left at the mercy of the creditors. The law proclaimed that the creditors' interests were legitimate, and it sought to protect their interests. The creditors, after all, were not nameless and faceless; they were fellow citizens, business partners, relatives, and even one's own offspring.

Perhaps the most famous and influential *consilium* dealing with the liability of an unemancipated son was one written by Antonio Strozzi and his friend and teacher, the illustrious Sienese jurist Bartolomeo Sozzini (1436–1507).[76] The son whose liability was at stake was Francesco d'Antonio della Luna, whose father had caused something of a legal and political scandal by his bankruptcy. Antonio and his brother Rinaldo had been hailed before the Signoria as bankrupts (*falliti*) to appear with their account books on 17 June 1467. Their case was such that following the decree ordering their appearance, the Signoria passed a *provvisione* designed to prevent similar fraudulent bankruptcies, which ordered all bankrupts to appear with their books before that body within three days or face condemnation as rebels. Francesco della Luna quite simply sought to get free of any further disabilities caused by the bankruptcy of his father's and uncle's bank on the grounds that he was an *infans* at the time.[77] And Strozzi and Sozzini carefully crafted a long and involved argument to that effect.

They began by defining three types of bankrupts: actual bankrupts (*verus cessans*), those who had been legally declared bankrupt (*cessans declaratus*), and those to whom syndics had been assigned for the purpose of liquidating their assets (*cui fuerunt dati sindici*). They derived these types by examining the language of the statutes. In similar fashion, they concluded that the statutes obligated sons in all three cases and not merely in the last two (it being assumed that actual bankruptcy or insolvency always preceded the legal state of bankruptcy). The statutes were concerned, they said, with the temporal point when the debt was contracted (for those born but not yet emancipated [*nati post debitum contractum*]). The official pronouncement of the debtor's insolvency did not create the son's obligation, they said; it only published the fact of the debt and his liability for it. Thus tacitly—for they did not mention his name—they refuted the position taken by Luca Corsini in the case of Francesco Corsellini.

Then Strozzi and Sozzini turned their attention to the problem of those who had been *infantes* and unemancipated at the time of the debt and to the problem of those who had been unborn and were unemancipated *infantes* at the time of the *cessatio*. As *infantes*, such children were *inemancipabiles* according to Strozzi and Sozzini and were not, therefore, comprehended by the law. To bolster their position, they produced six separate, if similar, arguments. The true reason, in my opinion, came only at the end of the list: "Because the statute is odious and exorbitant, therefore, in so far as it can, it must be restrained so as to alter the common law less."[78] In other words, they were ethically in agreement with Corsini.

There followed the important question of whether such a *cessatio* was one continuous crime or many crimes. Of course, if it were many crimes, then there would be many *tempora cessationis*. Perseverance in *cessatio* would mean that the creditors need only wait until the child was no longer an *infans* to be able to exact their claims from him. Strozzi and Sozzini were well aware of this, and they had just employed their artistry in releasing the *infantes* from the creditors. Quite naturally and logically, they argued that *cessatio* was one continuous crime. They drew the telling argument from Bartolus: There was only one *animus* (one intent to commit a crime), so there was only one crime. Thus, the unemancipated *infans* could not be obligated because his father persisted in his crime. The parallel case was adduced of the heir who, as a minor, was excused from the duty to avenge a murder because of his age and who was not punishable for failure to do so when he reached majority. The lawyers declared that "certainly every interpretation is to be admitted so that sons might not be obligated or punished without their guilt."[79]

To the *consilium* of Strozzi and Sozzini was appended a shorter one by Baldus de' Bartolini (1409–1490) and Pierfilippo da Corneo (1420–1492).[80] This opinion dwelt only on excluding the *infans* from the terms of the Florentine statutes. The problem, said the second two, was that the statute contained many indefinite terms and sought to make liable sons who otherwise were blameless and innocent. Echoing the concluding argument of Strozzi and Sozzini on this matter, they said that the Florentine statutes stood squarely contrary to the civil law, the *ius gentium*, and the *ius divinum*. "Therefore it does not seem absurd nor reprehensible if by some subtle logic of the law, such a statute—both harsh and odious with irrational hatred—is restricted."[81] Bartolus and Baldus, the jurists with greatest *auctoritas*, were also included. The two authors themselves concluded that just as an *infans* was not liable because *inemancipabilis*, so, too, all other *inemancipabiles* (*furiosus*, *absens*, and *ignorans*) were exempted.

In general, this opinion took a middle road between the positions of Luca Corsini and Domenico Bonsi previously outlined. The four lawyers did not attempt to sweep most of the effect of the statute under the courtroom rug as Corsini had. But they were not unsympathetic to his point of departure—the injustice inherent in the statute. They contrived an argument that at least served the infant sons. Bonsi had not allowed such an interpretation, but, then, he had based his position almost entirely on the statute itself, whereas Strozzi and Sozzini had found their ammunition in the conception of equity in the civil-law tradition.

The cumulative effect of this legal practice of restrictively interpreting Florentine legislation concerning debts and bankruptcy may, finally, have had an impact on emancipatory practice in Florence. It is worth hypothesizing, at least, that the evident tendency of the city's lawyers to limit filial liability, a tendency clearly manifested in the fifteenth century, reduced the impetus on the father's part to emancipate sons in order to prevent their liability for paternal debts. Infant sons, like Taddeo dall'Antella and Francesco della Luna, would not be held liable for debts incurred by their fathers during their infancy. And if their fathers fled, so that they were condemned in contumacy and not proven bankrupts, sons could argue exemption on the grounds that the father was not a *verus cessans* and that contumacy could not affect third parties. However, emancipation was still the safest route, for the exemption it effected was expressly sanctioned by statute, and there was still the cultural presupposition that sons and fathers were so closely identified that one should feel the pain of the other.

Reflections

The influence of the legal process in Florence on emancipation and its related issues were twofold. Certain principles were fixed and affirmed; they set the parameters and limited the strategies open to the jurists in constructing their arguments. On the other hand, certain problems remained open, becoming the focus of argumentation and debate. Among the principles that were fixed by legal practice were that: (1) registration was required for the validity of emancipation in Florence and its territory; (2) notaries had competence in emancipations; (3) many rights and claims were dependent on the validity of emancipation; and (4) equality among heirs was to be fostered if at all possible. These principles, among others, served as a language for the lawyers, a language that did not determine behavior but provided the means of justifying and explaining and directing future behavior. These elements of the law amounted to a system of symbols that could be manipulated in order to conceptualize and manage the social world.[82]

This language was, in turn, brought to bear on those problems that remained open, where a distance was apparent between theory and practice or where theories presented contradictions. With regard to emancipation, the element that forever remained open to judicial disposition was the rights of the respective parties. Animating the controversies were differing conceptions of the origin and nature of property rights. On the one hand were the rights and responsibilities of the family member, which were derived from his status with regard to a *casa* and a *patria potestas*. On the other hand were the rights and responsibilities of the legally active adult individual (*homo sui iuris*), which arose from contracts freely entered into. The legal conception of emancipation referred to the rights of this individual.

Because the survival of the *casa* rested in good part on its ability to cut losses due to the misfortune or incompetence of any one member, collective liability could not go unchallenged by the rival notion of individual liability. Appeals, therefore, were made to the validity of emancipation, the operability of the emancipation registry, the timing of emancipation, the ability to be emancipated, *ius familiaritatis*, and to divine and natural law. These conceptual appeals make it clear, moreover, that a legal text cannot be confused with its possible interpretations or even those interpretations attributed to it over time. The jurists called upon to use their expertise to make doctrinal accommodations where contradictions arose were not simply ideologues for a social class and conservators of the social order. They sought to locate the variables presented to them by social praxis within a grid of invariant conceptual elements.[83] Their solutions were not free of constraints. Their creativity was just that, creative, because it operated within constraints established by the legal tradition.[84] The lawyers could justify and explain certain actions, but they could not drive away the many sided problem of the relation between legal theory and social praxis.[85]

The limits to jurisprudential solutions are evident in the *consilia* dealing with the liability of sons for their fathers in Florence. The jurists, who were educated in the principles of the legal culture as found in the universities, generally tried to restrict the principles of the Florentine statutes, which they termed odious and exorbitant. Within the civil law, they found the basis for the concept of the *inemancipabilis*, which enabled them to exempt *infantes* from the rigor of the statutes. Their opinions were left to succeeding generations, who would, in turn, find a meaning or meanings for them. Yet, the lawyers were not free to ignore the statutes or their language. They found an argument that might establish *infantes* as blameless and innocent parties, but older sons, who might be equally blameless, could receive no such relief. There was, after all, a cultural logic behind the extension of liability to sons (a logic elaborated by Domenico Bonsi, for one), and the lawyers were not free to ignore it.

On the other hand, the conceptual constraints lawyers faced did not preclude a range of choice. The lawyers' textualized responses to events were themselves events occupying a political space. That space may have been circumscribed by the rules that justified decisions, but as Sbriccoli has demonstrated, there was still room to maneuver.[86] There was some range of alternatives, and we must look to social factors to determine why a particular choice was selected from among the set of available options.

Florence was a city constantly plagued by the nonpayment of debts, a problem of even greater proportion in moments of economic adversity. For any individual or family, advantage lay in dodging one's own obligations, while enforcing those of others. Lawyers were part of this society and its problems; they, too, incurred obligations and gained rights. They, too, were raised in families and raised families; they, too, were emancipated and in turn emancipated.[87]

As men who at one time had started out in public careers with some degree of wealth and prestige or with the hope of gaining them through their legal expertise; who had moved away from their fathers to pursue careers and to gain their professional education, lawyers as a group were generally more sympathetic to the difficulties of those starting out with an adverse paternal legacy than they were to the needs of the merchant-creditor. Where debts had been incurred in the normal course of the risky and uncertain pursuit of mercantile ventures, lawyers moved to limit the liability of those involved. Valid emancipation or related issues like the ability to be emancipated or the timing of emancipation were invoked, therefore, on the behalf of people like Filippo di Guido of Bologna, Antonio di ser Jacopo Bruogi, ser Andrea da Radda, Taddeo dall'Antella, Francesco Corsellini, and Francesco d'Antonio della Luna. These people had been left vulnerable through no fault of their own. Lawyers were, however, also aware of the vulnerability of the creditors, especially when the creditors' vulnerability was increased either due to supposedly natural weakness or to deception and deceit. As a result, women who were creditors for their dowry (like the widows of Luca Capponi and Bernardo di Bartolomeo Fei) and the creditors of those who failed to register their emancipations or who misused emancipation (men like messer Filippo di Guicciazzo, Rainaldo Altoviti, Ghinozzo Pazzi, and Luca Capponi and his sons) were defended by the lawyers. In analogous fashion, those who through no fault of their own were in danger of receiving less than a fair share of the patrimony (people like the brothers of Baldassare d'Antonio di Santi, Giovanni Balducci, and Vincenzo Davanzati) were defended, while those who did not deserve anything or any more than they already had (Baldassare d'Antonio di Santi, messer Jacopo of Siena, and Francesco Tedaldi) saw their claims denied. For Florentine lawyers, rights and obligations were not accidental, nor were they purely the result of either status or contract; they resulted, instead, from the dialectic between status and contract.

Conclusion

Emancipation was both a legal institution and a mechanism for change and adaptation in the family. Florentines who emancipated children or who were themselves emancipated sought to apply one or more of the legal meanings of emancipation for the benefit of themselves and their families.

As a legal institution, emancipation's meanings were dictated in the first instance by the legal system. Within the law, emancipation carried a dual significance. The civil law (and the Florentine law, by implication of its tacit acceptance of the *patria potestas*) reveals that emancipation endowed a son or daughter subject to it with all the rights and abilities of an independent legal adult (*homo sui iuris*). The emancipatus, thus, became the legal equivalent of the *paterfamilias* who had emancipated him. As a legally enabling act, emancipation conferred on its beneficiary the ability to write a will, to sue in court, to own property directly, and to enter into any type of legal contract. It changed the relationship between father and child from one of status to one of contract. The jurists of the universities, therefore, observed the sweeping powers and rights gained through emancipation and termed the act an *honor* and *beneficium* for the child who received so much when his father relinquished his *potestas* over him.

The second legal significance of emancipation, evident in the civil law but exaggerated in Florentine legislation, was the termination of obligations and liabilities between emancipator and emancipatus. Because emancipation produced a legally independent, contractual relationship between emancipator and emancipatus, most obligations and liabilities were no longer automatically transmitted from one to the other. Because emancipation carried such implications, in order to protect the rights of creditors, the commune of Florence found it expedient to order the registration of emancipations, first with the Mercanzia in 1355 and later with the Signoria in late 1421, as a means of publishing the facts for interested or potentially interested third parties. In this way, both those who used the institution legally and ethically and those who would be harmed by its fraudulent use could hope to see their rights preserved.

The problem of fraud through emancipation arose because the law —both civil law and Florentine statutes—maintained a crucial distinction between being legally *emancipatus* and physically *separatus*. The two conditions were kept conceptually distinct, although they could, in fact, coincide. This conceptual distinction extended to the point that neither emancipation nor separation was a prerequisite for the other: An emancipated child could remain in the house of the *pater emancipans*, and an unemancipated child could have his own residence. Therefore, emancipation did not mean separate residence, and although separate residence might imply (tacit) emancipation, it did so only after a ten-year period of uninterrupted and undisputed separation, so that separation was only one piece of essential evidence in judicially determining tacit emancipation.

Emancipation, then, was only a legal separation, which implied at most a patrimonial separation. This implication is most evident in the Florentine *speculum* legislation. In requiring that fiscal liabilities could be terminated only if there were both emancipation and separate residence, the *speculum* legislation guaranteed that there was a real, as well as a legal, patrimonial separation. No such guarantee, however, graced the Florentine legislation regarding liability for private debts. Emancipation and its merely implied patrimonial separation were alone sufficient to terminate liabilities for private debts, and therein lay the potential for fraud. For one thing, emancipation was not so easily apparent and verifiable as physical separation. This problem was met with the legal instruments of publication and verification. But more fundamentally, the potential for fraudulent manipulation of emancipation remained so long as the law left patrimonial separation implicit and contingent upon emancipation. The Florentine lawyers, moreover, defended this legal state of affairs. Roselli and others who pooled their opinions in the case of Guido of Bologna, for example, rejected the claim that there was no patrimonial separation as long as father and son cohabited. To their way of thinking, patrimonial separation was linked to possessing and exercising the legal abilities of the *paterfamilias* and *homo sui iuris*; and any emancipatus acted legally "ut verus paterfamilias et homo sui iuris."[1]

Yet, the very same factors that made emancipation such a potential for fraud gave it a great capacity for a wide range of uses (and fraud itself was useful to some at least). Emancipation and separation could be effected at different moments, and the addition of property (rights) to give substance to either emancipation or separation could take a variety of forms and occur at yet different times. In addition, there were few legal obstacles to emancipation: Gender was no barrier; age was only a hindrance for the very young; marital status did not matter. If there were some kind of sine qua non for emancipation, it lay in the necessity of a legal father-child (*paterfamilias-filiusfamilias*) relationship, a familial relationship embodied legally in the *patria potestas* and in the possession or potential possession of property or substantive rights that would be transmitted or redefined as a result of emancipation.

As an institution affecting the rights and responsibilities of family members, emancipation was situated in the context of Florentine conceptions of the family. Some of the wealthy and powerful Florentines left a variety of account books and handbooks of advice and proverbial wisdom. These writings reveal that familial wealth and honor were among the most important objects Florentines could own or acquire. The activities of one's life took meaning from the family's traditions and honor; these activities were made possible by the family's wealth and social position; and they were intended to increase or preserve the real and symbolic patrimony. Managing the *casa* and its wealth was entrusted to the father as its head. Among the most important aspect of managing the *casa* was raising the children, especially the sons, who carried on the family name and eventually succeeded the father in controlling the patrimony. The father-son relationship was seen as the point in the family structure where continuity could be guaranteed by transmitting values, habits, and property. But this crucial relationship was also laden with tensions. It was not a relationship of direct mutual understanding so much as an indirect relationship formed in terms of the means and objects in the family's care. One's prestige in the community rested, in good part, on the evaluation of how well one fulfilled his or her role in regard to those means and objects. Sons could not hope to gain a reputation without access to some portion of the patrimony, and their initial position in the community could be greatly prejudiced by paternal incompetence in managing the patrimony, a likely eventuality as fathers aged into weakness and senility. Projected in theory as the point of unity and continuity for the family, the father-son relationship could also, therefore, be marked by competitive tensions, which at times erupted into open conflict. This structural contradiction was managed by a variety of means: Sons could be sent off on business, thereby gaining some degree of independence; if worse came to worse, they could be disinherited and even jailed. But perhaps the chief means of dealing with the structural contradiction was linguistic. Injunctions to sons to treat their fathers with proper regard filled the writings of Florentines and can be seen as attempts to deny the implications of training young men to run families while refusing them the opportunity as long as the father lived.

Emancipation directly affected this central, and sometimes precarious, father-son relationship with all its real and symbolic, legal and extralegal ramifications. As both a positive freedom to do things and as a negative freedom from having to do things (like a father's bidding or paying his debts), emancipation could serve familial interests through the emancipatus' new legal rights and abilities or lack of legal liability for others. The termination of liability protected the patrimony in obvious ways by cutting losses due to any one family member and diversifying risks. On the other hand, the emancipatus' newly acquired legal abilities could be used to acquire or dispose of rights to property. Emancipation could also be used to manage tension between fathers and their children, especially sons. Positively, a son acquired the legal ability to be his own man, and negatively, he gained freedom from liability for an incompetent father (or a father was rid of a headstrong and prodigal son).

The great variety of emancipatory practices in Florence reveals how the practice was adapted to the particular needs and interests of Florentine families. The history of emancipatory practices further reveals that familial strategies were tied to shifting economic and social factors. The availability or lack of economic opportunities played an important part in decisions to emancipate. In the fourteenth century, many young children were emancipated, largely, it seems, to terminate liability. The continued connection of these children to their families was affirmed by symbolic gifts of small amounts of property. In the fifteenth century, fewer children were emancipated and at later ages. Emphasis had shifted to creating and using legal capacities of adult children in familial strategies and to maintaining paternal control over children's property. Women, when emancipated, were almost always the tools of some familial purpose.

Delaying emancipation in the fifteenth century, coupled with increases in household size, as revealed by the research of Herlihy and Klapisch, increased the likelihood of competitive tensions within the *casa* reaching a serious level. In the fifteenth century, men like Alberti and Rucellai advocated a gradual softening of effective, if not legal, paternal control in hopes of defusing this tension. The fifteenth century also saw a greater incidence of paternal retirements formalized by emancipations and related legal mechanisms. Formal patrimonial separations between fathers and sons also resulted through emancipation, often leading to a subsequent arbitration settlement by means of which a son could gain exclusive control over his own earnings, his wife's dowry, and his share of his mother's dowry.

In both the fourteenth and fifteenth centuries, Florentine fathers seem to have avoided turning over to their sons a substantial share of the patrimony before their death (except, of course, for the dowries of their daughters, which passed to the daughters' husbands or to their husbands' families). *Praemia* were rare in the fifteenth century and small in the fourteenth, and transfers of ample holdings before a father's death were often legal maneuvers designed to preclude creditors' claims and not effective changes in control. In general, while emancipation was worked out between fathers and sons, patrimonial separation was left to the siblings to work out after their father's death.[2] Shifts in emancipatory practices in the fifteenth century, which involved older childen, fewer females, utilizing the legal capacities and rights of the emancipatus, giving fewer but more substantial *praemia*, and imposing performative restrictions and conditions on property use, may, however, indicate the desire to exercise more direct and formative paternal control over the transmission and division of property formerly left to one's sons. Fatherly admonitions to live and share together peacefully, to preserve the unity of the family and its *substantia*, were supplemented in some cases by active legal dispositions aimed at preserving the *casa* and its real and symbolic patrimony.

Some form of paternal control over property and rights in the next generation was a constant feature of Florentine society. This control was most often exercised by means of dowry and testamentary inheritance, and emancipation operated within this legal context. The changes in the uses of emancipation around the middle of the fifteenth century were accompanied by corresponding changes in the inheritance mechanisms, most notably in the use of the *fideicommissum*, which became one of the most important means of preserving familial wealth in the sixteenth and seventeenth centuries.[3] It involved entailing land (limiting or forbidding its alienation) and stipulating a line of succession to it. The *fideicommissum* began to appear in Florence and the rest of northern and central Italy in the fifteenth century, usually in the form of a testamentary stipulation, but also, at times, as a stipulation attached to a *praemium*.[4] The *fideicommissum*, in fact, shared several characteristics with emancipation. Like emancipation, it was tied to the perpetual and extensive *patria potestas*; by means of a *fideicommissum*, a father could control property and family members from beyond the grave. Like emancipation, the *fideicommissum*, too, adversely affected the rights of creditors by burdening property with restrictions and prohibitions that prevented it from being claimed by creditors as collateral for unpaid debts.[5] The emphasis of the *fideicom-*

missum on the collective character of the patrimony paralleled using emancipation to involve children actively as consenting legal adults in preserving the patrimony. The very appearance of the *fideicommissum* in the fifteenth century may, therefore, have been both cause of and response to the less frequent or delayed use of emancipation in that century.

However, the *fideicommissum* awaits its historian, and until research is undertaken and completed, we can only speculate on how emancipation was related to it in familial strategies. Because legal institutions like emancipation operated within a shifting complex of social relations, the conclusions reached in this study cannot confidently be extended to other times and places. The questions addressed here require proper treatment by historians of other city-states, such as Venice and Genoa. Comparisons with practices in other places can be valuable in enriching the historical understanding of institutions like emancipation. A comparison, for example, of paternal retirement (the transmission of property and its management before death) in fifteenth-century Florence with the practices of thirteenth-century England, seventeenth-century Germany, or eighteenth-century Provence may serve to highlight the peculiar features of each set of practices.[6] Likewise, further study of emancipation in Florence and elsewhere can reveal how it interacted with other familial strategies in those years—for example, *fideicommissum*, late marriage, marriage of a single heir, birth control.[7]

Mechanisms like emancipation and the *fideicommissum* were the means with which Florentine families could achieve some form of stability and continuity. And a number of Florentine families, especially among the wealthy and powerful, were able to attain a great degree of stability and continuity, for a time at least. Indeed, such families seemed to be harmonious, functional units, moved by an internal logic and a set of rhythms all their own as they passed from generation to generation and handed down property, prestige, and traditions within a nexus of kin relations. But the stability and continuity they achieved did not come to them naturally. Continuity of membership and transmission of wealth were socially defined and consciously pursued. Florentine households, as the basic mechanisms of social reproduction, were involved in relations of production, exchange, and distribution with other households. These relations took the form of marriage alliances, business contracts, and a number of other connections that served to produce the physical and symbolic continuity of the *casa*. And they were established, broken, affirmed, and reaffirmed—manipulated, in other words—in accord with familial interests; they were also limited by, and dependent upon, the material and symbolic capital at the family's disposal. Emancipation was only one mechanism, one opportunity for capitalizing on the resources of the *casa*—its members, its property, and its prestige.

The study of emancipation reveals that the Florentine family was not simply a genetically constituted, coresidential unit of production and consumption. It was a group with practical interests that were validated and mediated by a cultural logic. The family was metaphorically termed the *casa*. As such, the *casa* was more than a residence; it was a monument, a sanctuary, a repository—the expression of desired continuity stretching from ancestors to generations yet unborn. The *casa*, therefore, was also not an organism with a life of its own;[8] it shared an environment with a number of other similar bodies with whom it alternately cooperated and competed. But the organic metaphor is inadequate and even deceptive, for the life force of this organism was not only, or mainly, biological; it was cultural. And the cultural dimension of the *casa* was not epiphenomenal, it was fundamental. The *casa* was not defined solely by genetic descent, nor did it move solely by the rhythms of the domestic developmental cycle. The genealogies kept by Florentines were not genetic records; their *ricordi* and *prioristi* were genealogical pedigrees, symbolic capital presenting claims to power and prestige. The effects of the domestic developmental cycle were shaped by the cultural logic by which Florentines attempted to live their lives. The members of a *casa* had to be marshalled into a smoothly functioning unit (and some potential members might have to be excluded as a result); and the responsible agents within the *casa* had to maintain their control, become adept at accurately assessing the economic and political environment, and adopt strategies to meet the family's needs and aims. Emancipation was just one adaptive mechanism available to Florentines for realigning economic relations, hastening or retarding the developmental cycle, confirming or denying the effects of genetic links.

The *patria potestas* was the legal expression of that profoundly authoritarian "single will" that Florentines believed should rule the *casa*.[9] This *potestas*, as Bellomo (for one) has pointed out, was a strong factor in promoting unity in the *casa* and continuity between generations. Yet, even this central, indeed, essential, paternal power could get in the way of familial goals and thwart individual plans to achieve those goals. Emancipation provided a legal means of adjusting the *patria potestas* to overcome its failings (even when only temporary or limited in scope). It provided a way of manipulating or even ignoring relationships generally defined in the culture; and wealthy and powerful Florentines like Lapo Niccolini were well aware of the occasional need to manipulate or ignore kinship relations.[10] Of course, just as the *patria potestas* did not always prove functional, there was no guarantee that emancipation would have the immediately desired results or might not lead to unforeseen problems later.

As a legally enabling act, emancipation remained a flexible instrument, capable of a wide variety of uses. It was not just a means of dealing with domestic economic crises by cutting off one family member, as Bellomo and Cammarosano have claimed, although this was an important role it could and did play. Nor was it simply part of the cycle of individual growth and maturity, a means of establishing a son in a career or of giving a widowed daughter the legal means to manage her deceased husband's estate, as Herlihy and Klapisch imply. Emancipation was, in fact, an important means of managing domestic tension and of pursuing familial strategies under the direction of the *paterfamilias*.[11] Located at the socially crucial nexus of the father-child relationship, emancipation was multifunctional and polysemous.

The overriding values, ones that Florentines were loath to relinquish, were family, honor, and patrimony. And individuals, relationships, and rights were all subject to manipulation in the interest of attaining and preserving these overriding values. Emancipation, then, was a transaction undertaken in pursuit of valued social resources. It involved the ability to claim respect and support from others and to deny similar claims advanced by others.[12] As such, emancipation was a political act. It asserted a concept of rights, obligations, and concurrent relationships that others, both outside the *casa* and within, were called upon to accept. Emancipation facilitated the arrangement of contractual relations and the transmission of property; it operated, moreover, principally among the ruling class.

The wealthy and powerful were in a position to impose their meanings on the rest of society. To the extent that they were able to make proportionally greater use of emancipation, beginning in the 1420s at least, they were able to utilize emancipation advantageously. The favored wealthy also seem to have been able to limit the availability of emancipation as a financial and legal remedy to those lower in the social hierarchy. The dominance of the wealthy and politically powerful among those involved in emancipation was evident at a time when total emancipatory activity had decreased drastically. Since the third and fourth decades of the fifteenth century were marked by recurrent serious fiscal problems and emancipation was one of the conditions for terminating extended fiscal liabilities, we would expect emancipatory activity to have increased during those years. Instead, increasing tax burdens and the greater frequency of fiscal delinquency were accompanied by a sharp relative decline in emancipatory activity after the passage of the second registration law of 1421. The new registration with the Signoria and the higher price for registration effectively eliminated much of the emancipatory activity of the lower social orders. Largely cut off from the legal remedy of emancipation, their only hope increasingly lay in obtaining a patronage-linked favor to reduce their taxes or cancel their debts. The wealthy, meanwhile, disposed of both emancipation and patronage to sidestep fiscal liabilities. The ability of the wealthy to use emancipation to create opportunities and avoid liabilities was not duplicated among the poor, especially in the *contado*, where to the costs of emancipation was added the expense of traveling to Florence to see to its registration.[13]

The degree of wealth in the hands of relatively few families in Florence is one of the most important historical discoveries of recent years.[14] Emancipation and such other instruments as dowry and inheritance contributed to the erection and maintenance of this economic and social inequality. Emancipation itself could be utilized both to transmit resources and to manage threats, internal and external, to the existence and transmission of resources. The *patria potestas*, too, a strong element of familial cohesion, provided the central and powerful paternal authority and the concomitant, though severely limited, filial patrimonial autonomy that was the hallmark of families with substantial property interests.[15] Together, the various legal instruments and the indispensable *patria potestas* kept valued resources, real and symbolic, largely within the wealthy families and at the disposition of the *padri di famiglia*.

APPENDIXES
NOTES
BIBLIOGRAPHY
INDEX

Appendixes

Appendix One

Notification to the Mercanzia of the Emancipation of Migliorato di Piero Ghori, 24 July 1370.
(SOURCE: ASF, Mercanzia 10819 bis, fol. 123v)

Migliorato di Piero Ghoris, chorazzaio, popolo Sancta Liparata di Firenze, no-
tiffica a voi messer Macchagnino, iudice et officiale dela Merchatantia della città di Fi-
renze et alla vostra corte et officio che nel ano presente mccclxx, indictione octava, dì
xxiii del presente mese di luglio, il dicto Migliorato fu emancepato dal detto Piero suo
padre, in presenza di messer Nicola Lapi, della quale macepagione ser Nicolò Perozzii,
notaio fiorentino, fece carta.

Appendix Two

Notification to the Signoria of the Emancipation of Simeon di Paolo di Berto de' Carnesecchi, 24 January 1422.
(SOURCE: ASF, Notificazioni 1, fol. 1r)

In dei nomine, amen. Anno incarnationis domini nostri Yeshu Christi millesimo
quadringentesimo vigesimo primo, indictione quinta decima, die vigesimo quarto men-
sis januarii. In consilio populi communitatis Florentiae, in palatio populi florentini, in
quo domini priores artium et vexillifer iustitie populi et comunis Florentie moram
trahunt more solito congregati. Et adstantibus sex et ultra de officio dictorum domi-
norum priorum et vexilliferi in consilio predicto, personaliter constitutus Bartholo-
meus dominorum publicus preco et approbator comunis Florentie publice palam et alta
voce, vice et nomine Pauli Berti de Carnesechis, populi Sancte Marie Maioris de Flo-
rentia, notificavit qualiter dictus Paulus emancippavit et a nexibus sue patrie po-
testatis penitus liberavit Simeonem eius filium legitimum et naturalem per instrumen-
tum inde rogatum per ser Benedictum Martini Ghini, notarium Florentie, sub anno
domini mccccxx primo, indictione quinta decima, die quarto decimo mensis januarii.

Qui Bartholomeus preco predictus incontinenti de pecunia predicti Pauli misit in
capsa existenti in sala magna dicti palatii, in qua consiliarii dicti consilii cohadunantur
secundum formam ordinamentorum comunis Florentie, florenum unum auri.

Acta fuerunt omnia et singula predicta in palatio populi Florentie in sala magna
dicti palatii, presentibus Mario Lupiani, ser Juliano Simonis, et Johanhino Anpelini,
civibus Florentie, testibus ad predicta vocatis et habitis.

Appendix Three

Emancipation of Giovanni di Testa di Ruffinaccio, 1 November 1327.
(SOURCE: ASF, Notarile C480 [1324–29], fol. 125r)

Item eodem anno et indictione, die prima mensis novembris. Attum Florentie, presentibus Niccholo Baldi, Fatio Arrighi Paradisi, et Bartholo Orlandini, populi Sancte Trinitatis etc. Pateat omnibus evidenter quod in presentia mei notarii et testium suprascriptorum, accedens ad presentiam sapientis viri domini Nicchole filii domini Falchonis, iudicis legiste de Licingnano, Testa condam Ruffinaccii, civis florentinus populi Sancte Trinitatis de Florentia, coram dicto domino Nicchola iudice et testibus suprascriptis. Et in hoc publico instrumento dixit et exposuit se habere Johannem filium suum unichum et ipsum Johannem legittimum filium suum esse dixit. Asservit eidem domino Nicchole se velle Johannem predictum filium suum emancipare et a sua manu et potestate liberare. Ideoque suplicavit eidem domino Nicchole quatenus emancipatione eiusdem filii sui ibidem presentis et se emancipari velle dicentis decretum et auctoritatem suam et comunis Florentie interponet. Unde dictus dominus Nicchola iudex legista predictus, volens favore iuste petitionis predicti Teste donantis, decretum et auctoritatem se interponere velle dixit. Ideoque dictus Testa dictum Johannem filium suum ibidem presentem et volentem cum auctoritate et decreto dicti iudicis emancipavit et a sua manu et potestate exemit et liberavit. Et capiens eum per manum dextram ipsum dimisit et relaxavit, dicens ego Testa te Johannem filium meum a mea manu et potestate libero et absoluo, et dicens eidem exsto civis romanus et homo tui iuris et in tua potestate. Et tibi do licentiam deinceps omnia faciendi et administrandi ut verus pater familias et homo sui iuris. Cui attui legittimo et omnibus et singulis suprascriptis dictus dominus Nicchola iudex suam et comunis Florentie auctoritatem interposuit et decretum. Rogantes me notarium infrascriptum dictus dominus Nicchola, Testa, et Johannes de suprascriptis omnibus et singulis publicum conficere instrumentum.

Appendix Four

Emancipation of Giovanni di Cristofano di Blando of Impruneta, 12 December 1422.
(SOURCE: ASF, Notarile B522 [1420–28], no pagination)

In dei nomine, amen. Anno domini ab eius incarnatione millesimo ccccxxii, indictione prima, die xii decembris. Actum Florentie in loco residentie consulum Porte Sancte Marie, presentibus testibus Antonio Schiatte Marci populi Sancti Bartoli del Corso, ser Johanne Ciucci populi Sancti Andree de Empoli, comitatus Florentie, testibus ad hec vocatis, habitis, et rogatis, et aliis. Pateat omnibus evidenter quod, constitutus in presentia mei notarii et iudicis ordinarii, matriculati et descripti in arte et matricula artis iudicum et notariorum civitatis Florentie, ser Johannes filius legittimus et naturalis Cristofani quondam Blandi populi Sancte Marie Inprunete, comitatus Florentie, petiit se a dicto patre suo emancippari et a sua patria potestate eximi et liberari. Quare dictus Cristofanus dictum ser Johannem filium suum legittimum et naturalem, maiorem annis decem otto, ibidem presentem et emancippari volentem et petentem, a se emancippavit et a sua manu et patria potestate penitus dimisit, eximit, et liberavit. Ita quod deinceps ipse ser Johannes possit et valeat sine patria potestate obtentu agere, contrahere, pascisci, in iudi⟨ci⟩o esse et stare, testari, codicillari, et omnia et singula alia facere et exercere, tam in iudicio quam extra, que facere et exercere potest quilibet pater familias et homo sui iuris. Et onus et onera remittens dictus Cristofanus dicto ser Johanni filio suo emancipato ibidem presenti et recipienti et stipulanti pro se et suis heredibus, et quibus concesserit omne peculium adventitium et profe⟨cti⟩tium, castrense et seu quasi castrense. Et generaliter undecunque quesitum et querendum et omnem usumfructum sibi competentem quoslibet in quibuscunque bonis profecti⟨ti⟩is et adventitiis et aliis quibuscunque dicti ser Johannis. Qua quidem emancipatione et remissione facta, dictus Cristofanus in premium dicte emancipationis dedit et tradidit dicto ser Johanni filio suo unum petium terre laborate, vineate, et arborate, positum in populo Sancte Marie Impruneta in loco dicto in Quercieto, cui a primo via, a secundo fossa, a iii° Nannis Neri, a iiii° Lodovico Marci, infra predictos confines vel alios signi forent plures aut veriores, cum omni iure et actione sibi ex ea re aut ipse rei modo aliquo pertinente. Constituens se dictam rem predicti ser Johannis nomine possidere usque quo ipsius rei possessionem acceperit corporalem, quam accipiendi sua auctoritate et retinendi deinceps ei licentiam omni modo dedit. Promictens per se suosque heredes dicto eius filio emancipato pro se et suis heredibus, stipulans predictam emancipationem et dationem et omnia et singula suprascripta firma et rata habere atque tenere et non contrafacere vel venire aliqua ratione vel causa, sub obligatione omnium suorum bonorum presentium et futurorum. Quibus omnibus sic peractis, ego Johannes, notarius et iudex predictus et infrascriptus, interposui meam et comunis Florentiae, quibus fungor, auctoritatem et decretum, rogans tam dictus emancippans quam dictus emancipatus me notarium publicum et infrascriptum quod de predictis omnibus publice conficerem instrumentum.

Appendix Five

Emancipation of Dietisalvi and Lotterio di Nerone di Nigi di Nerone Dietisalvi and an Arbitration between Dietisalvi and Nerone, 5 February 1434.
(SOURCE: ASF, Notarile A671 [1431–34], fols. 381v–82r)

Item postea dictis anno, indictione, et die quinto mensis februarii. Actum Florentie in populo Sancte Marie in Campo, presentibus testibus etc. Paulo Marci della Terra Rossa populi Sancti Michaellis de Vicedominis de Florentia et Mactheo Girolami de Ugubio dicti populi Sancte Marie. Nerone olim Nigi Neronis Dietisalvi, civis florentinus, constitutus in presentia egregii legum doctoris domini Johannis Girolami de Ugubio, civis et advocati florentini, et mei notarii matriculati etc., emancippavit etc. Dietisalvium eius filium legitimum et naturalem, maiorem annorum decemotto, presentem et se emancippari petentem etc. Et remisit etc. eidem omne peculium etc.

Item postea dictis anno, indictione, die, loco, et coram prefatis testibus etc. Suprascriptus Nerone olim Nigi, constitutus ut supra etc., emancippavit etc. Locterium eius filium absentem etc. et Bastianum Johannis Loncelli procuratorem et procuratorio nomine dicti Locterii, ut de suo mandato constare dixit et vidit, manu ser Guiglielmi Cardona, notarii, valenti mccccxxxii et die xviiii mensis decembris, presentem et pro dicto Locterio petentem etc. Et remisit etc. eidem omne peculium etc.

Item postea dictis anno, indictione, die, loco, et coram prefatis testibus etc. Su-
prascriptus Nerone, ex parte una, et suprascriptus Dietisalvi filius emancippatus, ex
parte alia, omnes lites etc. compromiserunt in suprascriptum egregium legum doc-
torem dominum Johannem Girolami tamquam in ipsorum arbitrum et arbitratorem
etc. Dantes etc. licentiam etc. laudandi etc. de iure et de facto et de iure tantum etc.
hinc ad duos dies proximos futuros etc. et infra ipsum tempus etc. cum pacto etc. quod
intelligatur litis etc. promictentes etc. stare etc. omni laudo etc. et non appellare etc.
sub pena etc. fraus etc. obligatio etc. Rogantes etc. guarantigiam.

In dei nomine, amen. Nos Johannes doctor et arbitror suprascriptus, visis dicto
compromisso etc. et litibus dictarum partium etc., laudamus etc. reperto etc. etc. quod
dictus Nerone etc. satisfecit etc. et assignavit etc. suprascripto Dietisalvi dotem flo-
renorum auri milletrecentorum domine Margherite uxoris dicti Dietisalvi, et tum in
lecto et pannis et libris et aliis fulamentis tamquam dicti Dietisalvi quam in denariis
existentibus super apoteca dicti Dietisalvi et Neronis artis lane, laudamus etc. quod
dictus Dietisalvi teneatur etc. ad conservandum etc. dictum Neronem a dicta dote in-
dempnem etc. Item laudamus quod dictus Nerone teneatur dare etc. victum etc. dicto
Dietisalvi et uxori dicti Dietisalvi etc. Et quod dictus Dietisalvi, occaxione dicti victus
etc. teneatur dare etc. dicto Neroni, quolibet anno quibus dictus Dietisalvi cum uxore
sua steterit in domo dicti Neronis et dictum victum perceperit etc., florenos auri quin-
quaginta recti ponderis etc. et ad sic dandum etc. et observandum etc. dictas partes
condempnamus etc. Et predicta etc. mandamus etc. a dictis partibus observari etc.
Latum etc. in nobis supra laudum etc. in domo suprascripti arbitratoris, sita in su-
prascripto populo Sancte Marie in Campo etc., presentibus dicto Nerone et Dietisalvi
et quolibet ipsorum, et dictum laudum ratificantibus etc. et promictentibus etc. et fa-
cientibus etc. pro observatione suprascripti laudi etc., et presentibus testibus etc. su-
prascriptis Paulo Marci et Mactheo Girolami etc. sub anno domini ab eius incarnatione
millesimo quadringentesimo trigesimo tertio, indictione duodecima, et die quinto men-
sis februarii.

Appendix Six

Emancipation of Monna Guiglelma di ser Giovanni di Neri da Castrofranco,
wife of Sandro Baroncelli, and Renunciation of Further Claims on Her Mother's
Dowry, 20 May 1412.
(SOURCE: ASF, Notarile G211 [1412–16], fols. 14v–15r)

Item postea dictis anno et indictione et die vigesima prima mensis maii. Actum
Florentie in populo Sancti Petri Scheradii, presentibus testibus ad hec vocatis et rogatis
ser Johanne ser Bartoli Gherardini et ser Bonifatio Bartolomei Bonifatii, notariis flo-
rentinis et aliis. Ser Johannes Neri da Castro Franco, civis et notarius florentinus,
constitutus in presentia mei Francisci, iudicis ordinarii etc., Guiglelmam eius filiam et
uxorem Sandri de Baroncellis, presentem et cum consensu dicti Sandri eius viri, et
quem sibi dedi primo pro eius mundualdo etc., [emancipavit et] a sacris sue patrie po-
testatis nexibus exemit. Et in premium emancippationis donavit eidem dotes suas per
dictum ser Johannem datas dicto Sandro et per dictum Sandrum confessatas etc. Pro-
mictens etc. predictam emancippationem firmam habere etc. sub ypoteca sui et bono-
rum etc. Guarantigia etc. Auctoritatem interposui etc.

Item postea dictis anno et indictione et die et loco, et presentibus dictis testibus ad hec vocatis et rogatis suprascriptis. Prefata domina Guiglelma, filia dicti ser Johannis et uxor dicti Sandri, cum consensu dicti Sandri viri sui et quem sibi primo dedi in mundualdum etc., ut heres hereditario nomine ut dixit se esse et esse velle domine Lise quondam matris sue et uxoris olim dicti ser Johannis, fecit dicto ser Johanni presenti et recipienti etc. finem etc. de dote domine Lise quondam eius matris et uxoris olim dicti ser Johannis et de omni eo quod petere posset occaxione dicte dotis etc. Et hoc quia confessa fuit sibi de dicta dote satisfactione etc. Absolvens etc. promictens etc. non venire contra etc. sub pena florenorum quingentorum etc., que pena tot commictens etc., et refecto dampnorum etc. et obligans bona etc. Rogans etc. Guarantigia etc.

Manuscript Sources and Abbreviations

Archivio di Stato, Florence (ASF)
Acquisti e Doni (AD)
Carte cerchi
Carte strozziane (CS)
Manoscritti
Mercanzia
Notarile antecosimiano (volumes cited by letter and number)
Notificazioni di atti di emancipazione (Notificazioni)
Provvisioni, registri (PR)
Statuti del comune di Firenze 16 (Podestà 1355)
Tratte

Biblioteca Nazionale, Florence
Landau-Finaly
Magliabechiano (Mag.)
Palatino (Pal.)
Panciatichiano (Panc.)
Principale (Princ.)

Biblioteca Apostolica Vaticana
Urb. Lat.
Vat. Lat.

Statuta populi et communis Florentiae, anno salutis mccccxv,
3 vols., Freiburg, 1778–83 (Statuta 1415)

Statuti della repubblica fiorentina, ed. Romolo Caggese, vol. 2:
Statuto del podestà dell'anno 1325, Florence: E. Ariani,
1921 (Podestà 1325)

Notes

INTRODUCTION

1. Certainly social scientists have noted the origins of the concept of emancipation; for example, *Encyclopedia of the Social Sciences*, s.v. "Emancipation," by Leland H. Jenks.

2. Emancipation forms a little known part of American family law, largely in the guise of judicial emancipation roughly equivalent to the medieval tacit emancipation discussed in Chapter 1. Cf. Sanford N. Katz, William A. Schroeder, and Lawrence R. Sidman, "Emancipating Our Children: Coming of Legal Age in America," *Family Law Quarterly*, 7 (1973): 211–241, now reprinted in *Having Children: Philosophical and Legal Reflections on Parenthood*, eds. Onora O'Neill and William Ruddick (New York: Oxford University Press, 1979), pp. 327–350.

3. Medieval Latin knew several meanings for the word. Cf. Charles du Fresne du Cange, ed., *Glossarium mediae et infimae latinitatis*, 12 vols., 3: 250b–252a.

4. *Enciclopedia del diritto*, s.v. "Emancipazione (diritto intermedio)," by Manlio Bellomo, 818 (cited hereafter as Bellomo, "Emancipazione").

5. Cesare Beccaria, *Dei delitti e delle pene*, ed. Gian Domenico Pisapia (Milan: Giuffrè, 1964), pp. 121–122.

6. Ibid., p. 121.

7. Francesco Dalmazzo Vasco, "Note all' *Esprit des loix*" in *Riformatori lombardi, piemontesi e toscani*, ed. Franco Venturi (Milan: Ricciardi, 1958), pp. 848–849, vol. 3, *Illuministi italiani*.

8. Alfonso Longo, "Osservazioni su i fedecommessi," in *Riformatori lombardi, piemontesi e toscani*, ed. Franco Venturi (Milan: Ricciardi, 1958), p. 227, vol. 3, *Illuministi italiani*. On the legal aspects of eighteenth-century reform, see Giuliana d'Amelio, *Illuminismo e scienza del diritto in Italia* (Milan: Giuffrè, 1965).

9. Maxime Lemosse, "L'incapacité juridique comme protection de l'enfant en droit romain," *Recueils de la société Jean Bodin pour l'histoire comparative des institutions*, 35 (1975): 254, argues that emancipation in modern law derives from the Roman *venia aetatis*, a privilege accorded to an underage orphan between 20 and 25 on application to a judge to escape some of the severe effects of the judicial incapacity of a minor.

10. On modern Italian law before 1975, see *Enciclopedia del diritto*, s.v. "Emancipazione (diritto civile)," by Cesare Ruperto.

11. On the Roman law of emancipation, see *Enciclopedia del diritto*, s.v. "Emancipazione (diritto romano)," by Alberto Berruti.

12. Antonio Pertile, *Storia del diritto italiano dalla caduta dell'impero romano alla codificazione*, 2d ed., 3:381–382; Nino Tamassia, *La famiglia italiana nei secoli decimoquinto e decimosesto*, pp. 249–253; Enrico Besta, *La famiglia nella storia del diritto italiano*, pp. 202–205; Pier Silverio Leicht, *Storia del diritto italiano: Il diritto privato*, vol. 1: *Diritto delle persone e di famiglia*, pp. 227–229. For France, see Le Comte J. du Plessis de Grenédan, *Histoire de l'autorité paternelle et de la société familiale en France avant 1789* (Paris: Rousseau, 1900), pp. 486–500.

13. Sergio Mochi Onory, "*Manumittere et emancipare idem est*: Studio sulle origini e sulla struttura della 'persona' nell'età del rinascimento," 497–510; Antonio Marongiu, "Patria podestà ed emancipazione per scapigliatura in alcuni documenti medievali," pp. 719–729.

14. See Introduction, Note 4; also Manlio Bellomo, "Comunità e comune in Italia negli statuti medievali 'super emancipationibus,'" 81–106.

15. Paolo Cammarosano, "Aspetti delle strutture familiari nelle città dell'Italia comunale (secoli xii–xiv)," 417–435; Diane Owen Hughes, "Urban Growth and Family Structure in Medieval Genoa," 1–28, and "Domestic Ideals and Social Behavior: Evidence from Medieval Genoa," pp. 115–143; David Herlihy, "Family and Property in Renaissance Florence," pp. 3–24.

16. This latter opinion is most clearly espoused by Giulio Vismara, *Famiglia e successioni nella storia del diritto*.

17. Manlio Bellomo, *Ricerche sui rapporti patrimoniali tra coniugi* and *Problemi di diritto familiare nell'età dei comuni: Beni paterni e 'pars filii.'*

18. Most notably in his contribution to the *Enciclopedia del diritto*, s.v. "Famiglia (diritto intermedio)," by Manlio Bellomo, 750 (hereafter cited as Bellomo, "Famiglia").

19. Richard A. Goldthwaite, *Private Wealth in Renaissance Florence*. See also his "The Florentine Palace as Domestic Architecture," 977–1012; Marvin Becker, "Individualism in the Early Italian Renaissance: Burden and Blessing," 273–297.

20. Lauro Martines, *The Social World of the Florentine Humanists, 1390–1460*, pp. 50–57; Gene A. Brucker, *Florentine Politics and Society, 1343–1378*, pp. 28–29, and *Renaissance Florence*, p. 90; Christian Bec, *Les marchands écrivains: Affaires et humanisme à Florence, 1375–1434*, pp. 279–286.

21. A useful and illuminating review of the historical literature on the Italian family can be found in Francis William Kent, *Household and Lineage in Renaissance Florence: The Family Life of the Capponi, Ginori, and Rucellai*, pp. 3–15, and in his "A la Recherche du Clan Perdu: Jacques Heers and 'Family Clans' in the Middle Ages," 77–86.

22. Other contributions preparatory or adjunct to the book (in addition to the piece by Herlihy cited in Introduction, Note 15) are: David Herlihy, "Vieillir à Florence au Quattrocento," 1338–1352; "Some Psychological and Social Roots of Violence in the Tuscan Cities," pp. 129–154; "Family Solidarity in Medieval

Italian History," 173–184; *The Family in Renaissance Italy*; "Mapping Households in Medieval Italy," 1–24; Christiane Klapisch, "Household and Family in Tuscany in 1427," pp. 267–281; idem and Michel Demonet, "'A uno pane e uno vino': La famille rurale toscane au début de xvᵉ siècle," 873–901.

23. The most extensive presentation of these results can be found in David Herlihy and Christiane Klapisch, *Les toscans et leurs familles*, pp. 420–522.

24. F. W. Kent, *Household and Lineage*, p. 13.

25. Cf. Julius Kirshner, "Some Problems in the Interpretation of Legal Texts *re* the Italian City-States," 22. An example of the pitfalls of disregarding the law is the assertion of Frank McArdle, *Altopascio: A Study in Tuscan Rural Society, 1587–1784*, p. 136, that emancipation amounted to "autodetermination," a view that study of the law cannot support and that mars an otherwise revealing discussion of parent-child relations in peasant families.

26. Kirshner, "Some Problems," p. 26; and the trenchant comments, albeit with an ideological destination, of Luigi Berlinguer, "Considerazioni su storiografia e diritto," 3–56.

27. Note the comments of E. P. Thompson, "The Grid of Inheritance: A Comment," in *Family and Inheritance: Rural Society in Western Europe, 1200–1800*, eds. Jack Goody, Joan Thirsk, and E. P. Thompson (Cambridge: Cambridge University Press, 1976), pp. 328–360.

28. Herlihy and Klapisch, *Les toscans*, pp. 525–613; Ibid., pp. 604, 617, and 525, where we find the remark that the writers of *ricordi* "ont médité sur le rôle social de la famille" and that these men "ont vécu cette parenté, l'ont reconnue et parfois théorisée."

29. For example, the discussion of patrilineage as a means of keeping the patrimony intact "dont dépendent fortune et statut du lignage" (ibid., p. 533) may seem to be a circular argument without considering the cultural imperatives making preservation of the patrimony a value in society and of practical interest to individuals. Other means of social reproduction may have been equally effective in achieving a goal of patrimonial integrity.

30. Kent's *Household and Lineage* has received a careful appraisal from Anthony Molho, "Visions of the Florentine Family in the Renaissance," 304–311. Kent's theoretical point of departure is the work of the anthropologist Meyer Fortes, which has also been subjected to close scrutiny, most notably by Peter Worsley, "The Kinship System of the Tallensi: A Reevaluation," *Journal of the Royal Anthropological Institute*, 86 (1956): 37–75; and by J. A. Barnes, *Three Styles in the Study of Kinship* (Berkeley and Los Angeles: University of California Press, 1971), pp. 181–189.

31. Kent, *Household and Lineage*, pp. 26–43, 48–54, 300. Cf. Kent's analysis of the separation of certain impoverished branches of the Ginori and Rucellai, "which had never been quite in step with the others from the beginning" (ibid., pp. 162–163). In contrast, there is the evidence presented by Melissa Meriam Bullard, "Marriage Politics and the Family in Florence: The Strozzi-Medici Alliance of 1508," 668–687, that the Medici in exile could find it convenient to establish marriage ties with a formerly hostile lineage; and that the members of that lineage, at least temporarily, could find it useful to dissociate them-

selves from the bridegroom, who was far from poor or merely from a collateral branch out of step with the rest. On these themes, see also my "Honor and Conflict in a Fifteenth-Century Florentine Family," 287–304.

32. Cf. Herlihy and Klapisch, *Les toscans*, pp. 548–549; Cammarosano, "Aspetti delle strutture familiari," 432–435.

33. My approach to the family has been influenced by readings in anthropological works, foremost among them: Marshall Sahlins, *Culture and Practical Reason*; Roy Wagner, *Habu: The Innovation of Meaning in Daribi Religion* (Chicago: University of Chicago Press, 1972); Pierre Bourdieu, *Esquisse d'une théorie de la pratique* and "Les stratégies matrimoniales dans le système de reproduction," 1105–1127.

34. Ibid., pp. 1106–1107.

35. Herlihy and Klapisch, *Les toscans*, pp. 571, 575–576; Cammarosano, "Aspetti delle strutture familiari," pp. 428–429. Bellomo, "Emancipazione," 817; Kent, *Household and Lineage*, p. 64, relative to division of the patrimony among brothers but echoing the statement of Brucker, *Renaissance Florence*, p. 91: "Even after a son was legally emancipated from his father, he was bound to his relatives by many ties."

CHAPTER ONE

1. For a discussion of emancipation in Roman law up to the time of Justinian, see Max Kaser, *Das Römische Privatrecht*, 1:56–71, 1:345–350, 2:149–156; also *Enciclopedia del diritto*, s.v., "Emancipazione (diritto romano)" by Alberto Berruti; Barry Nicholas, *An Introduction to Roman Law* (Oxford: Clarendon Press, 1962), pp. 65–68; Maxime Lemosse, "L'enfant sans famille en droit romain," *Recueils de la société Jean Bodin pour l'histoire comparative des institutions*, 35 (1975): 257–270.

2. On the survival and use of Roman legal concepts by the Lombards, see Francesco Calasso, *Medioevo del diritto,* vol. 1, *Le fonti,* pp. 245–259; Ennio Cortese, "Per la storia del mundio in Italia," 323–474.

3. Manlio Bellomo, "Emancipazione," 809; Antonio Marongiu, "Patria podestà ed emancipazione per scapigliatura in alcuni documenti medievali," p. 721; Pier Silverio Leicht, *Il diritto privato preirneriano*, p. 281.

4. On this form of emancipation, see Bellomo, "Emancipazione," 810; Antonio Pertile, *Storia del diritto italiano dalla caduta dell'impero romano alla codificazione*, 3:381–382; Enrico Besta, *La famiglia nella storia del diritto italiano*, p. 204.

5. The forms of tacit emancipation are enumerated by Pertile, *Storia del diritto italiano*, 3:382–386; and Besta, *La famiglia*, pp. 205–206.

6. Bellomo, "Emancipazione," 810–811; Calasso, *Medioevo del diritto*, p. 256.

7. Bellomo, "Emancipazione," 811–812; idem, *Problemi di diritto familiare nell'età dei comuni: Beni paterni e 'pars filii,'* pp. 2–6; Tamassia, *La famiglia italiana nei secoli decimoquinto e decimosesto*, pp. 248–249. The pseudo-Bartolist *Tractatus de differentia inter ius canonicum et civile*, in Bartolus da Sassoferrato, *Opera omnia*, vol. 10, provides an interesting distinction (fol. 153ra): "Item dif-

ferunt quia iure civile durat patria potestas in omnem etatem filii, sed de iure canonico solvitur patria potestas adveniente adulta etate, quo ad matrimonium carnale et spirituale, et quo ad iuramentum." I can find no corroboration for the assertion of Charles Donahue, Jr., "The Case of the Man Who Fell into the Tiber: The Roman Law of Marriage at the Time of the Glossators," 38, that emancipation was automatic at age 25 in medieval Roman law.

8. Accursius gl. *pupillus* to D. 45.1.141: "etiam sexagenarius . . . in potestate est." Quoted in Bellomo, "Emancipazione," 811.

9. Placentinus to C. 8.48(49), *De emancipationibus liberorum, Summa codicis,* p. 412: "Emancipatio est filii de parentis potestate, vel de filiatione exemptio, iudicis intercedente autoritate."

10. Odofredus to *rubrica* C. 8.48(49), *De emancipationibus liberorum, Lectura super codice,* vol. 2, fol. 175rb; Baldus de Ubaldis to D. 4.4.44, *Non omnia, In primam digesti veteris partem commentaria,* fol. 248rb; Antonio da Budrio to c. xi, *De privilegiis, Decretalium commentaria,* fol. 90rb; Salatiele, *Ars notarie,* 1:34.

11. Sergio Mochi Onory (Introduction, Note 13) examines the language of emancipation from the point of view of legal *persona.*

12. Placentinus to C. 8.48(49), p. 412. For a discussion of the medieval jurists' use of definition and genus/species distinctions as well as other interpretive tools, see Vincenzo Piano Mortari, "Il problema dell'*intepretatio iuris* nei commentatori," 29–109; Gerhard Otte, *Dialektik und Jurisprudenz: Untersuchungen zur Methode der Glossatoren.*

13. All references to the Codex (C.), Digest (D.), Institutes (I.), and Novels (A. or N.) can be found in the *Corpus iuris civilis,* eds. T. H. Mommsen, W. Kroll, P. Krueger, and R. Schoell, 3 vols. (Berlin: Weidmann, 1928–1929).

14. Placentinus to C. 8.48(49), p. 412. See also *Glossa ordinaria,* gl. *a sua manu* to C. 8.48(49).6, *Cum inspeximus, Corpus iuris civilis cum glossis (Glossa ordinaria),* vol. 4, col. 2486.

15. Salatiele, *Ars notarie,* 1:34.

16. Guglielmo Durante, *Speculum iuris,* p. 690b. A similar account is furnished in Rolandino Passaggieri, *Summa totius artis notariae,* fol. 178vb.

17. See Manlio Bellomo, "Comunità e comune in Italia negli statuti medievali 'super emancipationibus,'" 83.

18. *Summa institutionum vindobinensis* to I. 1.12, *Quibus modis ius potestatis solvitur,* p. 15; Azo to C. 8.48(49).1, *Si lex, Lectura ad singulas leges duodecim librorum codicis,* p. 665; *Glossa ordinaria* to C. 8.48(49).3, *Non nudo,* vol. 4, col. 2483; Odofredus to C. 8.48(49).1, *Lectura supra codice,* vol. 2, fol. 175rb–175va; Passaggieri, *Artis notariae,* fol. 178vb; Cino da Pistoia to C. 8.48(49).3, *Non nudo, In codicem et aliquot titulos primi pandectorum commentaria,* vol. 2, fol. 518vb; Bartolus to C. 8.48(49).5, *Iubemus, Opera omnia,* vol. 8, fol. 113va; Angelus de Ubaldis, *cons.* 93, *Consilia,* fols. 36vb–37ra; Baldus de Ubaldis to C. 8.48(49).5, *In vii, viii, ix, x, et xi codicis libros commentaria,* fol. 178rb; Bartolomeo da Saliceto to C. 8.48(49).3, *In vii, viii, et ix codicis libros commentaria,* fol. 149ra.

19. Odofredus to C. 8.48(49).3, *Non nudo, Lectura super codice,* vol. 2, fol. 175va; Baldus to C. 8.48(49).3, *In vii, viii, ix, x, et xi commentaria,* fol. 178rb; Guillaume de Cunh to C. 4.21.11, *Emancipatione, Lectura super codice,* fol. 56vb;

Pietro d'Ancarano, *cons.* 430, *Consilia*, fol. 227rb; Bartolomeo da Saliceto to C. 4.21.11, *In tertium et quartum codicis libros commentaria*, fol. 146va.

20. Bartolus da Sassoferrato to C. 1.1.1, *Cunctos populos, Opera omnia* (Venice, 1615), vol. 7, fols. 3va–7ra. This segment of Bartolus' commentary has been translated by J. A. Clarence Smith, "Bartolo on the Conflict of Laws," *American Journal of Legal History*, 14 (1970): 157–183, 247–275, with the relevant passage on p. 255. Unless otherwise noted, all subsequent references to Bartolus are to the 1570 edition of the *Opera omnia*.

21. Angelus de Ubaldis to C. 8.48(49).3, *Non nudo, Super codice*, fol. 244vb: "Non sufficit nudus consensus paternus ad liberandum filium a patria potestate nisi interveniant iuris solemnia."

22. Cino to C. 8.48(49).3, *In codicem*, vol. 2, fol. 518vb; Baldus to C. 8.48(49).3, *In vii, viii, ix, x, et xi commentaria*, fol. 178ra: "Not. quod in emancipatione filii non requiritur causa."

23. Azo to C. 8.48(49).3, *Lectura*, p. 665.

24. *Glossa ordinaria* to C. 8.48(49).1, vol. 4, col. 2481–2482 and quote from C. 8.48(49).6, *Cum inspeximus*, vol. 4, col. 2486: "Cui sola consuetudo municipalis iurisdictionem dedit emancipandi."

25. Odofredus to C. 8.48(49).1, *Lectura super codice*, vol. 2, fol. 175va. Also Petrus de Bellapertica to C. 8.48(49), *Lectura codicis*, fol. 393ra.

26. Durante, *Speculum iuris*, p. 690b.

27. Cino to C. 8.48(49).1, *In codicem*, vol. 2, fol. 518rb–518vb.

28. Bartolus to C. 8.48(49).1, *Opera omnia*, vol. 8, fol. 113va, and to D. 1.7.36, *Emancipari*, vol. 1, fol. 29vb.

29. The date and place of the *consilium* (note 20 above) are indicated in the signature at the end.

30. Azo to C. 8.48(49).2, *In emancipationibus*, p. 665: "Non tam scriptura quam veritas considerari solet."

31. *Glossa ordinaria* to C. 8.48(49).2, vol. 4, cols. 2482–2483: "In emancipatione an necessaria sit scriptura queritur. Dicitur quod non. Vel si pater filium emancipaverit, et intervenit scriptura, quae amissa est postea, an propterea debeat retractari emancipatio? Dicitur quod non, si veritas possit aliter probari. Vel si ficta erat emancipatio, vel donatio, per scripturam, non tam scriptam quam actus considerandus est." Angelus to C. 8.48(49).2, *Super codice*, fol. 244vb.

32. Cino to C. 8.48(49).2, *In codicem*, vol. 2, fol. 518vb.

33. Bartolus to C. 4.21.11, *Emancipatione, Opera omnia*, vol. 7, fol. 144vb: "Alii dicunt, et ista magis tuta esta opinio, quod hic ab initio scriptura intervenerit."

34. Baldus to C. 4.21.11, *In quartum et quintum codicis libros commentaria*, fol. 60ra.

35. Saliceto to C. 8.48(49).3, *In vii, viii, et ix commentaria*, fol. 149ra: "Scriptura tamen est necessaria, et sic instrumentum fieri debet."

36. That there was general agreement about the features of emancipation can be determined by the fact that later commentators such as Bartolomeo Sozzini, Alessandro Tartagni da Imola, and Paolo di Castro did not comment on the appropriate sections of the law. See Sozzini, *Commentaria ad digestum*

vetus; Alessandro Tartagni, *In primam et secundam codicis partem commentaria;* Paolo di Castro, *In primam digesti partem commentaria* and *In secundam codicis partem commentaria.*

37. Placentinus to C. 8.48(49), *Summa codicis,* p. 412.

38. *Glossa ordinaria* to D. 1.7.3, *Si consul,* vol. 1, col. 66; Bartolus to D. 1.7.3, *Opera omnia,* vol. 1, fol. 25rb.

39. Odofredus to *rubrica* C. 8.48(49), *Lectura super codice,* vol. 2, fol. 175rb.

40. Baldus to D. 1.7.25, *Post mortem, In primam digesti veteris partem commentaria,* fol. 43rb: "Sed quero an filius qui diu vixit seorsum a patte habitando et negociando presumatur emancipatus? Et dic si allegatur emancipatio cum cursu xx an⟨norum⟩ sufficit, C. de prescri. lon. tem. que pro li.l.ii [C.7.33.2] et C. de patria po. l. i [C.8.46(47).1] et hic aut cum cursu decennii; et idem videtur ut hic. . . . Si autem non allegatur emancipatio sed sola quasi possessio libertatis? Tunc requiruntur xx an⟨ni⟩ per dicta iura. Ergo apparet quod aliquid presumitur mixtum ex actibus et tempore." Implied here is the ability of a *filiusfamilias* to set up a separate residence, a subject discussed by Bartolus to D. 50.1.4, *Placet, Opera omnia* (Venice, 1615), vol. 6, fol. 218rb.

41. Baldus to I. 1.12,1, *cum autem,* and to I. 1.12,4, *filiusfamilias, Super institutionibus commentum,* fol. 9va; and to C. 2.26(27).2, *Si cum pater, In primum, secundum, et tertium codicis libros commentaria,* fol. 159va.

42. See Besta, *La famiglia,* pp. 202–205.

43. Filippo Decio to D. 50.17.2, *Foeminae, In tit. ff. de regulis iuris,* p. 32a–32b: "Et verissima conclusio videtur quod filia nupta gaudeat privilegio dato patri suo et filiabus: quia licet mulier nupta sit, remanet tamen in potestate patris, ut no. per glos. insti. ad Turtul. § i in versi. parentes [I. 3.3,2], et no Bald. in l. si uxorem in princ. C. de cond. inser. [C. 6.46.5]." See also my "Women, Marriage, and *Patria Potestas* in Late Medieval Florence," *Tijdschrift voor Rechtsgeschiedenis* (in press).

44. *Glossa ordinaria* to C. 8.48(49).4, *Nec avus,* vol. 4, cols. 2483–2484: "Sic ergo nota absentem non emancipari invitum, vel ignorantem, quod est hodie generale." See also Odofredus to C. 8.48(49).4, *Lectura super codice,* vol. 2, fol. 175vb; Baldus to C. 8.48(49).5, *Iubemus, In vii, viii, ix, x, et xi commentaria,* fol. 178rb.

45. Angelus, *cons.* 44, *Consilia,* fols. 17vb–18ra. The introductory "pater quidam" seems to indicate that this opinion was held largely in theory.

46. Alberico da Rosciate to D. 1.7.25,1, *Post mortem § neque adoptare, In primam ff. vet. partem commentaria,* fols. 59vb–60ra: "Sed emancipatio non videtur consistere in administratione patrimonii, et ideo per curatorem vel procuratorem expediri posse non videtur, ut infra de manu. l. servus furiosi [D. 40.1.13]."

47. See Kaser, *Römische Privatrecht,* 1:275–276. Durante, *Speculum iuris,* p. 690a, confirms that age seven marked the end of infancy and the point at which a child could be emancipated in the regular manner: "Hoc cum filius maior est septennio, quia minor septennio emancipari non potest, nisi imperialis interveniat autoritas." On ages in medieval civil law, see *Enciclopedia del diritto,* s.v. "Età (diritto intermedio)," by Ugo Gualazzini, 16:80–85 (Milan: Giuffrè, 1967).

48. C. 8.48(49).5: "Nisi infantes sint, qui et sine consensu etiam hoc modo sui iuris efficiuntur." See Bartolus to C. 8.48(49).5, *Opera omnia*, vol. 8, fol. 113va.

49. Placentinus to C. 8.48(49), *Summa codicis*, p. 412.

50. *Glossa odinaria*, gl. *iniuriam* to C. 8.48(49).4, *Nec avus*, vol. 4, col. 2483.

51. Odofredus to C. 8.48(49).4, *Lectura super codice*, vol. 2, fol. 175vb; Durante, *Speculum iuris*, p. 690a; Bartolus to I. 1.12, *Opera omnia*, vol. 9, fol. 68rb; Paolo di Castro, 2 *cons*. 142, *Consilia*, fol. 61vb; Bartolomeo da Saliceto to C. 8.48(49).4, *In vii, viii, et ix commentaria*, fol. 149ra; Antonio da Budrio to C. 8, *De restitutione in integrum, Decretalium commentaria*, fol. 132rb.

52. *Glossa ordinaria* to C. 8.48(49).4, vol. 4, col. 2483: "Sed quaeritur an ex iisdem causis quibus pater compellitur emancipare, compellitur econtra filius recipere emancipationem? Rspon. non . . . Item quia non est eadem aequitas."

53. Jacopo d'Arena to D. 45.1.132, *Quidam cum filium, Super iure civili*, fol. 203va: "Filius invitus ex causa potest a patria potestate dimitti."

54. Bartolus to I. 1.12,8, *Opera omnia*, vol. 9, fol. 68rb–68va: "Sed tunc quaeritur utrum in iisdem casibus, si filius male tractet patrem, vel patri imponat necessitatem peccandi an filius cogetur emancipari, quia sicut invitus non emancipatur . . . sic nec invitus emancipat. Dicendum quod non, et ratio quare cogitur pater emancipare in praedictis casibus est illa: quia non expedit filio quod sit in potestate patris, sed pater non esset in potestate filii, unde de similibus ad similia non est procedendum. Item poena est patris emancipare, quia amittit ius patrie potestatis. Idem propter delictum cogitur emancipare: sed emancipari non est filio poena, sed libertas; ideo non cogitur emancipari propter delictum suum: quia hoc esset sibi commodum, et quia non debet consequi commodum de eo de quo poenam meretur. . . . Unde propter delictum non meretur emancipari, immo si esset emancipatus propter delictum suum reduceretur in patria pote⟨state⟩."

55. Baldus de Ubaldis to I. 1.5,1, *multis autem, In quatuor institutionum libros*, fol. 7vb; Paolo di Castro, 2 *cons*. 142, *Consilia*, fol. 61vb.

56. Bartolomeo da Saliceto to C. 8.48(49).4, *In vii, viii, et ix commentaria*, fol. 149ra.

57. Azo to C. 8.49(50).1, *Filios et filias, Lectura*, p. 666.

58. *Glossa ordinaria* to C. 8.49(50).1, vol. 4, col. 2486. The Novel is 115 § *causas* (A. 8.2,3 in c.). The reasons were: (1) hitting a parent, (2) "gravem et inhonestam iniuriam," (3) accusing parents of a crime, (4) committing crimes against parents, (5) marrying one's stepmother or father's concubine, (6) informing on a parent, (7) refusal to *fideiubere* for a parent, (8) prohibiting parents from making a will, (9) associating with actors and other riffraff, (10) wanton lifestyle, (11) not caring for a *parens furiosus*, (12) failure to try to ransom a captive parent, (13) heresy.

59. Baldus to C. 8.53(54).17, *Sive emancipatus, In vii, viii, ix, x, et xi commenaria*, fol. 183va.

60. Ibid.; Bartolus to C. 8.53(54).17, *Opera omnia*, vol. 8, fol. 116va; *Glossa ordinaria* to C. 8.53(54).11, vol. 4, col. 2509; Passaggieri, *Artis notariae*, fols. 180va, 181ra.

61. Cino to C. 6.20.17, *Ut liberis, In codicem*, vol. 2, fol. 360rb–360va.

62. Bartolus to C. 6.20.17, *Opera omnia*, vol. 8, fol. 13rb.

63. Baldus de Ubaldis to C. 6.20.17, *In sextum codicis librum commentaria*, fol. 52va.

64. Tartagni, 2 *cons.* 142, *Consilia*, fol. 112ra.

65. Bartolus to I. 3.1,12, *eadem haec observantur, Opera omnia*, vol. 9, fol. 87va: "Donatio in filium emancipatum a patre facta ultra quantitatem legitimam sine insinuatione non valebit."

66. Dino del Mugello, *cons.* 20, *Consilia*, fols. 19vb–20ra.

67. On the Roman law of *peculia*, see Kaser, *Römische Privatrecht*, 1:344, 2:152–154. Baldus provides an interesting insight into the nature of the *praemium* and the *peculium* in 3 *cons.* 394, *Consilia*, fol. 111vb: "Quod si quidem filius non est emancipatus, sed in potestate patris, videtur ei pater concedere in peculium. . . . Si autem nomine filii emancipati pater talia faceret, praesumetur donatio."

68. See Bellomo, *Problemi di diritto familiare*, pp. 11 n. 4, 25, 116–134; idem, "Famiglia (diritto intermedio)," pp. 753–756. Idem, *Problemi di diritto familiare*, pp. 131–134. Ibid., pp. 116–131.

69. Jacopo d'Arena to D. 39.5.31,1, *Donationes* § *pater qui filie, Super iure civili*, fol. 156rb: "Qui erat in potestate patris et habuerat libros ab eo, ut se faceret emancipari, si vellet illos libros precipuos habere, nisi pater sibi expresse adimeret in emancipatione, videtur donare si non adimit, ut dicitur in hac lege, et idem in armis et equis et similibus." Cino to C. 6.61.6, *Cum oportet, In codicem*, vol. 2, fol. 435va: "Nam postea in eo peculio filius potest contrahere sine patris consensu, et dicitur patrimonium filii, et ideo si pater tempore emancipationis non auferat expresse, videtur concedere propter precedentem voluntatem."

70. Pietro Torelli, *Lezioni di storia del diritto italiano: Diritto privato: La famiglia*, p. 59.

71. *Summa institutionum vindobinensis* to I. 1.12, p. 15: "Pretio emancipationis, si volunt, retento, id est dimidia ususfructus." See also *Glossa ordinaria* to C. 6.61.6, *Cum oportet*, vol. 4, col. 977; Baldus to C. 6.61.6, *In sextum codicis*, fol. 201ra.

72. Paolo di Castro to D. 18.1.6, *Qui in potestate, In primam infortiati partem commentaria*, fol. 46va: "Item an possit pater emancipare filium, quantum ad hunc actum solum, ut possit testari? Bar⟨tolus⟩ videtur tenere quod sic in l. i § in filii ff. ad treb. [D. 36.1.1,6]. Bal⟨dus⟩ contra in l. senium quia patria potestas est indivisibilis, unde emancipatio non potest fieri quantum ad unum actum sicut nec manumissio . . . sicut nec legitimatio."

73. Gian Savino Pene Vidari, *Ricerche sul diritto agli alimenti: L'obbligo 'ex lege' dei familiari nel periodo della Glossa e del commento*, esp. pp. 93–97, 152–153, 173–175, 288, 297–299. For an example of the use of natural law in obligations between father and son, see Ennio Cortese, *La norma giuridica*, 1:60.

74. Salatiele, *Ars notarie*, 1:34.

75. Gigliola Villata di Renzo, *La tutela: Indagini sulla scuola dei glossatori*, pp. 29–30. She notes that guardianship of an emancipatus was a rare topic in the doctrinal sources (p. 148, n. 26).

76. Ibid., pp. 255, 271–284, 345–352, 360–374.

77. Jason del Maino, 3 *cons*. 10, *Consilia*, fol. 64va: "Pater et filius censentur una et eadem persona. . . . Item pater et filius una caro probantur." Andrea Romano, ed., *Le sostituzioni ereditarie nell'inedita 'Repetitio de substitutionibus' di Raniero Arsendi*, p. LV; AD 203/1 (a fragment of a commentary on the Institutes) to I. 1.9, *De patria potestate*, fol. 167r: "Inter patrem et filium non potest esse obligatio civilis quia sibi ipsi obligatus esset."

78. Torelli, *La famiglia*, pp. 52–53.

79. Cino to C. 5.4.18, *Viduae, In codicem*, vol. 2, fol. 293va: "Nam filia emancipata, sine patre, et sine iudice, potest nubere cui vult."

80. *Glossa ordinaria* to D. 37.12.4, *Patri*, vol. 3, col. 2151.

81. Baldus de Ubaldis to D. 24.3.24, *Si constante, In primam et secundam infortiati partem commentaria*, fol. 73ra: Saliceto to C. 3.36.2, *In tertium et quartum codicis libros commentaria*, fol. 68va; Alessandro Tartagni to D. 24.3.22,12, *Si cum dotem* § *transgrediamur, Super primam infortiati partem commentaria*, fol. 40ra. Tartagni observes, however, that a son who simply lives apart from his father can compel him to hand over his wife's dowry only if "sive filius habitet seorsum a patre propter patris servitiam sive ob aliam iustam causam."

82. Azo to C. 6.20.9, *Si emancipati, Lectura*, p. 423: "Nullum enim dicit acquiri hodie patri per emancipatum liberum." *Glossa ordinaria* to C. 7.15.1, *Sancimus*, vol. 4, col. 2000; Oldradus da Ponte, *cons*. 214, *Consilia*, fol. 111va–111vb.

83. Jacopo d'Arena to I. 4.6,12, *penales quoque, Super iure civili*, fol. 287va.

84. Dino del Mugello, *cons*. 7, *Consilia*, fols. 13rb–13vb.

85. Guido Rossi, *Consilium sapientis iudiciale*, pp. 287–288, mentions a *consilium* of 1248 that declared that a father's *estimo* should be reduced by the amount of the *praemium* given to a son who no longer lived at home. Baldus dealt with a similar case, 1 *cons*. 138 and 139, *Consilia*, fols. 41rb–41vb.

86. *Glossa ordinaria* to C. 4.13.1, *Neque*, vol. 4, col. 888: "Si cum filio sui iuris effecto contraxisti, pecuniam ei mutuando, patrem nisi specialiter se obligaverit, pro filio non habes obligatum, et hoc in prima. Si vero filiofam⟨ilias⟩ in potestate existenti sine iussu patris mutuasti, quatenus est in peculio, vel quatenus in rem patris versum est, patrem habebis obligatum."

87. Odofredus to C. 4.13.1, *Lectura super codice*, vol. 1, fol. 203vb: "Pater non tenetur ex contractu filii emancipati sed ex contractu filii in potestate constituti." Azo to C. 4.13.1, *Lectura*, pp. 274–275; Cino to C. 4.26.2, *Eius nomine, In codicem*, vol. 2, fol. 230ra–230rb; Bartolus to C. 4.26.(8)9, *Si ex alio, Opera omnia*, vol. 7, fol. 149va; Bartolomeo da Saliceto to D. 14.5.2, *Ait praetor, In secundam digesti veteris partem commentaria*, fol. 72ra. See also Bellomo, *Problemi di diritto familiare*, pp. 98–102.

88. Cino to C. 4.26.2, *In codicem*, vol. 2, fol. 230ra–230rb; Saliceto to D. 14.5.2, *In secundam digesti veteris partem commentaria*, fol. 72ra.

89. Cf. Calasso, *Medioevo del diritto*, 1:595–596.

90. Bartolus to D. 37.6.1, *Hic titulus, Opera omnia*, vol. 4, fol. 168ra. Idem, to C. 7.75.1, *Si haeres, Opera omnia*, vol. 8, fol. 89vb.

91. Baldus to *rubrica* C. 7.75, *De revocandis his quae in fraudem, In vii, viii, ix, x, et xi commentaria*, fol. 127va: "Quaero, pone cum concepissem in animo

meo exercere artem cambii, mittendo pecuniam ultra mare, et timendo de periculis maris, emancipavi filium meum, et secrete donavi sibi omnia bona mea. . . . Deinde caepi facere dictam mercantiam, et omnia mobilia perdidi in mari, quomodo potest subveniri illis, qui habent me obligatum ex cambio? Et videtur quod non subvenitur eis, quia adversus creditores futuros potest excogitari fraus. . . . In contrarium videtur, quia dolus dedit causam huic contractui, et quod malo more gestum est, debet rescindi. Nec est aequum in lucro morari filium, et creditores damnum sentire. . . . Et ego dico quod haec praesumuntur facta non solum in fraudem, sed simulate, quae simulatio nullis creditoribus nocet . . . secus si futuri creditores essent creditores ex causa lucrativa."

92. Baldus to C. 7.71.3, *Si pater tuus*, ibid., fol. 118rb: "Filius emancipatus pro patre damnari non debet . . . No. quod filius emancipatus bona sibi donata a patre potest defendere a creditoribus paternis, quod intellige, nisi emancipatio esset facta in fraudem creditorum, quia simulata emancipatio non valet."

93. The opinions of Bartolus and of Baldus formed the core of the later opinion of Pietro da Petrosancta in his *Singularia seu notabilia ex utroque iure collecta* (Lyons, 1560), p. 569a–569b, which was written in 1506 (p. 575b).

94. Pietro d'Ancarano, *cons.* 430, *Consilia*, fols. 227rb–227va. His conclusion is as follows: "Concludo igitur primo quod si non fuerint observata solemnia dicta emancipatio in fraudem venientium ab intestato ipsi filie, et subsequenter etiam successorum ipsi infanti sit nullius momenti. Fraus autem ex his quae incontinenti subsecuta sunt praesumitur." There is no indication in this edited version of where and when the *consilium* was written.

95. Giovanni d'Anagni, *cons.* 23, *Consilia*, p. 13a: "Licet prima facie dici posset quod emancipatio tenet que facta videtur contracta fiducia . . . nihilominus ex duplici causa potest dici in fraudem factam et sic invalida quo ad effectum iuris, de quo queritur. Et primo istud colligitur ex brevitate temporis quo emancipatio et testamentum facta fuerunt. Nam ex his que incontinenti fiunt presumi potest et colligitur qualis fuerit mens et intentio circa preterita."

96. Ibid., p. 13a–13b.

97. For example, Odofredus to D. 37.4.7, *Si retentus*, *Lectura super digesto novo*, fol. 103rb.

98. Sir Henry Maine, *Ancient Law* (1861; reprint ed., Oxford: Oxford University Press, 1931), p. 123.

99. On succession law, see Kaser, *Römische Privatrecht*, 2:334–340; Nicholas, *Introduction to Roman Law*, pp. 238–250; A. Berger, *Encyclopedic Dictionary of Roman Law, Transactions of the American Philosophical Society*, vol. 43, pt. 2 (Philadelphia, 1953), pp. 375, 395.

100. For an introduction to the whole field of succession law in the Middle Ages, see *Enciclopedia del diritto*, s.v. "Erede e eredità (diritto intermedio)," by Manlio Bellomo; Enrico Besta, *Le successioni nella storia del diritto italiano*.

101. *Glossa ordinaria* to D. 37.4.1, *In contra tabulas*, vol. 3, col. 2029; Odofredus to *rubrica* C. 6.28 *De liberis praeteritis*, *Lectura super codice*, vol. 2, fol. 49vb, and to C. 6.42.31, *Quidam filium suum*, ibid., fol. 72rb; Bartolus to I. 3.1,12, *Opera omnia*, vol. 9, fol. 87ra; Baldus to D. 28.2.29, *In primam et secun-*

dam infortiati partem commentaria, fol. 66va; Alessandro Tartagni to C. 6.12.2, *Postumo, In primam et secundam codicis*, fols. 78va–79va.

102. *Summa institutionum vindobinensis* to I. 3.5, *De successione cognatorum*, p. 99.

103. *Glossa ordinaria* to D. 1.7.26, *Quem filius meus*, vol. 1, col. 75.

104. Cino to C. 6.14.3, *Qui se patris, In codicem*, vol. 2, fol. 355rb.

105. Bartolus to I. 3.2,8, *ad legitimam, Opera omnia*, vol. 9, fol. 87va–87vb, and to I. 3.4,2, *sciendum autem est*, ibid., 88vb: "Agnatus, si emancipetur, desinit esse agnatus."

106. Baldus to D. 1.7.26, *Quem filius, In primam digesti veteris*, fol. 43va. And to C. 5.30.4, *Frater emancipatus, In quartum et quintum codicis*, fol. 203va: "Dic quod emancipatio solvit iura agnationis passive, sed non active."

107. Paolo di Castro to *C. 6.55.12, *In successione, In secundam codicis partem*, fol. 132ra: "Dicit enim Bal⟨dus⟩ hic quod per emancipationem non tollitur agnatio quantum ad materiam feudorum . . . quia dicit ipse quod agnatio sumitur potius pro generatione paterna quam pro impetratione iuris communis."

108. Cf. Tartagni to C. 6.14.3, *Qui se patris, In primam et secundam codicis partem*, fol. 84va. With agnation terminated by emancipation, the father's right to inherit from his emancipated son was said to rest on the fact that emancipation was performed *contracta fiducia*, meaning that the father reserved his inheritance rights in the emancipation. See Giulio Vismara, "I patti successori nella dottrina di Paolo di Castro," *Studia et documenta historiae et iuris* 36 (1970): 281–282.

109. Odofredus to C. 6.20.9, *Si emancipati, Lectura super codice*, vol. 2, fol. 34vb; Baldus to *rubrica* C. 6.20, *De collationibus, In sextum codicis*, fol. 47ra; Tartagni to *C. 6.20.1, *Ex testamento, In primam et secundam codicis*, fol. 92rb.

110. Azo to C. 6.20.9, *Lectura*, p. 473; Odofredus to C. 6.20.9, *Lectura super codice*, vol. 2, fol. 34vb; Cino to C. 6.20.9, *In codicem*, vol. 2, fol. 360ra; Bartolus to C. 6.20.9, *Opera omnia*, vol. 8, fol. 13va; Baldus to C. 6.20.9, *In sextum codicis*, fols. 50vb–51rb.

111. Rogerius to C. 6.20, *De collationibus, Summa codicis*, p. 155.

112. Azo to C. 6.20.9, *Lectura*, p. 473.

113. *Glossa ordinaria*, gl. *datorum* to C. 6.20.1, *Emancipatos*, vol. 4, cols. 1609–1610.

114. Cino to C. 3.28.36, *Scimus, In codicem*, vol. 2, fol. 157vb and to C. 6.20.6, *Ea demum*, Ibid., fol. 359vb.

115. Bartolus to C. 6.20.17, *Ut liberis, Opera omnia*, vol. 8, fol. 13rb; Baldus to *C. 6.20.1, *Ex testamento, In sextum codicis*, fol. 48ra; Paolo di Castro to *rubrica* C. 6.20, *De collationibus, In secundam codicis*, fol. 38ra; Tartagni to C. 6.14.3, *In primam et secundam codicis*, fol. 84va.

116. Bellomo, "Emancipazione," 816.

117. Ibid.

118. Tamassia, *La famiglia italiana*, pp. 249–262.

119. Besta, *La famiglia*, pp. 201–202.

120. Onory, "*Manumittere et emancipare idem est*," 500.

121. *Glossa ordinaria*, gl. *si pater* to D. 1.7.41, *Si pater*, vol. 1, col. 79: "Respon. quia quasi liberatus fuit hic nepos a patris sui potestate, eo scilicet patre emancipato, id est hoc consecutus est, quod non debeat avo mortuo eius recidere in potestatem: et qui liberatus est, postea reverti non potest, nisi per adoptionem, vel nisi ingratus existat."

122. Bartolus to I. 1.12,8, *sed et si pater*, *Opera omnia*, vol. 9, fol. 68rb–68va: "Emancipari non est filio poena, sed libertas." And see Chapter 1, Note 54.

123. Baldus to D. 4.4.44, *Non omnia*, *In primam digesti veteris*, fol. 248rb–248va, and to C. 6.61.6, *Cum oportet*, *In sextum codicis*, fol. 201ra–201rb: "No. hic in tex. per emancipationem liberentur, quod emancipatio est quaedam libertas et ideo dicit Cyn⟨us⟩ quod minor non restituitur contra emancipationem paternam."

124. Odofredus to D. 45.1.132, *Quidam cum filium*, *Lectura super digesto novo*, fol. 136ra.

125. *Statuti di Bologna dell'anno 1288*, 2 vols., eds. Gina Fasoli and Pietro Sella (Vatican City, 1939), 2:68.

126. Jacopo d'Arena to D. 45.1.132, *Super iure civili*, fol. 203va: "Sed obiicitur; sed nonne emancipari est honor emancipato. . . . Ad hoc respondeo: si intelligas de adoptivo indubitanter est pena. . . . In legitimo vero sine dubio in aliquo est honor, videlicet quia a modo ut paterfamilias omnia faceret, nec que faciet retractabuntur: nam retractare omnia facta iniuria quedam mihi est . . . et in hoc est honor."

127. Bartolus to D. 45.1.132, *Opera omnia*, vol. 6, fol. 55ra: "Opp. quod emancipatio non sit poena, sed honor. . . . Responsio, et sunt verba Jac⟨opi⟩ de Are⟨na⟩ fateor, quod emancipatio quo ad quid est honor, quia solvitur patria potestas, quo ad quid est poena, cum filius adoptivus emancipatus privetur totaliter successione. . . . Item in naturali secundum ista tempora erat poena, quia amittebat ius agnationis."

128. Angelo to C. 8.48(49).5, *Iubemus*, *Super codice*, fol. 244vb: "No. quod cum pater emancipat filium liberalitatem in eum exercet quia facit hominem sui iuris: tribuit ei potestatem testandi et ceteros actus similes faciendi et sibi acquiretur non solum adventitia immo etiam profectitia. Nam filio emancipato pater donare potest: quia ergo liberalitatem exercet. Non expedit patri in premium emancipationis filio donare sed ita moris est addere liberalitatem liberalitati."

129. Torelli, *La famiglia*, p. 46; Bellomo, *Problemi di diritto familiare*, p. 5, n. 13.

130. Filippo Decio to D. 50.17.106, *De regulis iuris*, p. 295b: "Libertas inaestimabilis res est. . . . Eodem modo inaestimabilis est patria potestas."

131. Baldus to D. 1.7.25, *Post mortem*, *In primam digesti veteris*, fol. 43ra: "An magis mereatur pater emancipando quam filius consentiendo, dic de verb. ob., l. quidam cum filium per Jac⟨opum⟩ de Are⟨na⟩ [D. 45.1.132], et C. de col., l. ut liberis per Cyn⟨um⟩ [C. 6.20.17], et formam instrumenti emancip⟨ationis⟩, vide in Spe⟨culo⟩ in tit. de natis ex libero ven. , . . . Sed quare in emancipatione requiritur decretum . . . primo quia emancipatio in se est in-

aestimabilis donatio, secundo quia patria potestas est sacra, et ideo est de iure publico." Idem, 2 *cons.* 452, fol. 121ra.

132. Passaggieri, *Artis notariae,* fol. 178vb: "Et quod dicitur hic in tex. et a sacris suis patriis, eum penitus relaxavit, expones, id est a sua patria potestate, dicitur sacra quantum ad ipsum filium que ideo dicitur sacra: quia persona patris semper debet videri filio honesta, sacra, et sancta etiam si non sic sit, et liberto persona patroni, sic et discipulo magistri." And Chapter 1, Note 148.

133. Paolo di Castro to D. 45.1.141,1, *Si servus aut filius* § *extranei, Commentaria in digesti novi partem secundam,* fol. 56vb: "Dic quod patria potestas non fuit inventa ad supplendum defectum aetatis quia si hoc esset, cessante defectu aetatis cessaret patria potestas, sicut cessat potestas tutoris, tamen contrarium est, quia etiam sexagenarius potest esse in patria potestate: fuit ergo inventa favore ipsius patris, ut per filium sibi acquiratur et ut possit eam exercere circa personam filii in ipsius patris favorem." Note how this statement contrasts with the opinion of Torelli, among others, who claims the *patria potestas* came to be exercised for the benefit of the children and not the father (*La famiglia,* p. 85).

134. Passaggieri, *Artis notariae,* fol. 126rb–126va. Also see Chapter 1, Note 80.

135. Bartolus, *Opera omnia,* vol. 10, *Tractatus ad reprimendum,* fol. 97va: "Alia est fidelitas, que debetur patri, quem quis etiam tenetur defendere verbo et opere, et detur patri iudicare que cognoscat contra eum . . . detur etiam reverentiam. . . . Non autem reperio quod quis teneatur patrem defendere facto, scilicet opponendo se, vel simili modo."

136. Baldus, 1 *cons.* 62, *Consilia,* fol. 21vb. The case arose at Cortona from actions occurring in 1371.

137. Baldus to *C. 6.20.1, *Ex testamento, In sextum codicis,* fol. 48rb: "Lucrum filius familias non tenetur conferre, videlicet industriale, ideo etiam si negotiatur cum pecuniis patris, medietatem lucri non tenetur conferre." On the legal capacities of a *filiusfamilias* with respect to property, see Bellomo, *Problemi di diritto familiare,* pp. 96–205.

138. Bartolus to D. 31.[1].69, *Peto, Opera omnia,* vol. 4, fol. 42ra: "Emancipatus non est de familia"; and to D. 30.[1].114, *Filiusfamilias,* ibid., fol. 27vb: "Quod emancipatus non potest petere, cum desinat esse de familia."

139. Baldus, 1 *cons.* 138, *Consilia,* fol. 41va: "Nam post emancipationem duae familiae sunt, quia duo patresfa⟨milias⟩, sed si filius esset in potestate una familia est."

140. My notion of legal fiction owes much to Lon L. Fuller, *Legal Fictions,* esp. pp. 51–54.

141. Baldus, 1 *cons.* 139, ibid., fol. 41vb: "Nec certe aliquid facit emancipatio, quia per eam non tollitur ius publicum, sed sola paterna potestas, nec per eam solvitur origo, vel domicilium." Also interesting is his comment to *C. 6.20.1, *In sextum codicis,* fol. 48ra: "Quia nec sui nec emancipati magis participant de natura extraneorum, qui sunt a collatione remoti, quam emancipatus, in quo adhuc remanent reliquae precedentis potestatis."

142. Le Comte J. de Plessis de Grenédan, *Histoire de l'autorité paternelle et de la société familiale en France avant 1789* (Paris: Rousseau, 1900), pp. 486–500; John Gilissen, "Puissance paternelle et majorité émancipatrice dans l'ancien droit de la Belgique et du Nord de la France," *Revue historique de droit français et étranger*, 4th ser., 38 (1960): 5–57.

143. Leicht, *Diritto privato*, 1:229.

144. The *additio* to Baldus's commentary to D. 1.7.25, *Post mortem, In primam digesti veteris partem*, fol. 43rb, reads in part "Emancipatio non solemniter facta lon⟨gi⟩ tem⟨poris⟩ silentio confirmatur et contra factum proprium ab initio nullum, sed postea confirmatum quis venire non potest, hoc dicit. Baldus." H. F. Jolowicz, *Roman Foundations of Modern Law*, p. 202, in speaking of emancipation, declares that "there is no general rule that emancipation can be implied by conduct, but there are texts according to which a father who has let his rights lie dormant for a long time is, so to speak, estopped from asserting them." His emphasis on the father's inactivity is echoed by Torelli, *La famiglia*, p. 47.

145. Baldus to C. 2.26(27).2, *Si cum pater, In primum, secundum, et tertium codicis libros commentaria*, fols. 159rb–159va: "Tertio no. quod pater venire potest contra factum suum tam agendo quam replicando de nullitate, quia factum quod est nullum nunquam parit reo defensionem. Quarto no. quod sententia lata contra emancipationem redigit filium in patriam potestatem, quod apparet hic quia est necessaria in inte⟨grum⟩ rest⟨itutionis⟩ decretum. . . . Iuxta hoc quaero, quando filiusfam⟨ilias⟩ gerit se pro emancipato sciente et patiente patre, valent contractus celebrati cum eo, ac si esset emancipatus, ut ff. ad Mace. l. iiii [D. 14.6.4]. Modo revoco in dubium quanto tempore oportet quod filius gesserit se pro emancipato? Ex praedictis videtur dicendum quod aut nulla praecessit emancipatio, et requiruntur xx anni, aut praecessit invalida, et sufficiunt x anni. Veritas est quod non requiruntur xx anni, quia illud est ad praescribendum se in libertate non quo ad actus validandos, qui celebrantur secum tanquam cum emancipato: sed lex quarta praeal⟨legata⟩ praesupponit patriam potestatem, et nihilominus dicitur actus valere. Dico ergo sine dubio quod sufficit decennium, quia per tantum spatium inducitur consuetudo sic agendi et sic contrahendi."

146. Alberico da Rosciate to D. 1.7.25, *Post mortem, In primam ff. vet. partem commentaria*, fols. 59ra–59vb: "Contra factum proprium venire non licet ubi est cursu temporis roboratum, licet ab initio tenuerit ipso iure, hoc dixit. Ibi, vixerat, et sic praescripserat libertatem seu essentiam sui iuris, . . . Si ergo quaeratur specialiter an liceat patri venire contra emancipationem, dic quod hic quatuor obstabant patri, scilicet factum suum, temporis causa, mors filiae, et favor existentiae sui iuris. . . . Sed contra predictam distinctionem videtur, quia favor publicus videtur quod filii remaneant in potestate parentum, et tamen contra emancipationes non potest venire pater, ut hic. Sed dic quod pater bene possit convenire si emancipatio non esset solemnis, nisi alia, quae supra dixi, sibi obstarent, et maxime cursu temporis, C. si adver. rem iudi. l. 2[C. 2.26(27).2]."

147. My intent here is overtly anthropological. I am indebted to the ideas

of the following scholars on the nature of gift giving: Raymond Firth, "Symbolism in Giving and Getting," in his *Symbols: Public and Private* (Ithaca: Cornell University Press, 1973), pp. 368–402; Marshall Sahlins, *Stone Age Economics* (Chicago: Aldine, 1972); Maurice Godelier, *Rationality and Irrationality in Economics*, trans. Brian Pearce (New York: Monthly Review Press, 1972); Scott Cook, "'Structural Substantivism': A Critique of Marshall Sahlins' *Stone Age Economics*," *Comparative Studies in Society and History*, 16 (1974): 355–379. See also the recent article of Annette B. Weiner, "Reproduction: A Replacement for Reciprocity," *American Ethnologist*, 7 (1980): 71–85.

148. CS, 3rd ser., 41/16, fol. 196v: "Filius magis est obligatus patri, quia sit emancipatus, quam si erit in potestate." Passaggieri, *Artis notariae*, fol. 179ra: "Pater emancipans non tenetur aliquid de suo, filio dare . . . immo econtra tenetur filius praemium dare patri, qui sibi honorem facit faciendo eum sui iuris. . . . Et etiam l⟨ex⟩ cavetur quod emancipatus filius in honore et reverentia plus debet patri servire, quam si esset in potestate."

149. Status and contract are, of course, the terms used by Maine to summarize legal history and development. He used them with Roman legal history in mind as an example, and I believe that the distinction is still useful in the present context. On Maine, see Robert Redfield, "Maine's *Ancient Law* in the Light of Primitive Societies," *Western Political Quarterly*, 3 (1950): 586.

CHAPTER TWO

1. Francesco Calasso, *Medioevo del diritto*, 1:425–426; Julius Kirshner, "*Ars imitatur naturam: A Consilium* of Baldus on Naturalization in Florence," 318; Lauro Martines, *Lawyers and Statecraft in Renaissance Florence*, p. 186.

2. For a complete list of Florentine legislative sources, see Demetrio Marzi, *La cancelleria della repubblica fiorentina*. A revision and redaction of Florentine statutes was undertaken in 1409; however, this redaction was soon superseded by that undertaken in 1415.

3. Martines, *Lawyers*, pp. 238, 419.

4. Ibid., p. 92.

5. Santi Calleri, *L'arte dei giudici e notai di Firenze nell'età comunale e nel suo statuto del 1344*, p. 29.

6. Manlio Bellomo, "Comunità e comune in Italia negli statuti medievali 'super emancipationibus,'" 84–94.

7. Calleri, *L'arte dei giudici e notai*, p. 60. Testaments, *curatela*, *tutela*, and inventories were the other legal instruments that also carried a five *soldi* fee.

8. Manlio Bellomo, "Emancipazione (diritto intermedio)," p. 813, n. 41; Enrico Besta, *La famiglia nella storia del diritto italiano*, p. 205; Pertile, *Storia del diritto italiano dalla caduta dell'impero romano alla codificazione*, 4:385, n. 53.

9. Podestà 1325, liber 2, rubrica 70, quod conservetur in successione et de mundualdis et etate legittima, pp. 141–142; Statuta 1415, liber 2, rubrica 112, de aetate legitima, de obligatione minorum decem et octo annorum. . . . 1:206–207. Age of majority at Pisa was 20 (*Constituta legis et usus Pisanae civitatis*, ed. Francesco Bonaini [Florence: G. P. Vieusseux, 1870], constitutum 38, p. 780), at Pistoia age of majority was 19 (*Statutum potestatis comunis Pistorii*

anni MCCLXXXXVI, ed. Lodovico Zdekauer [Milan: Hoepli, 1888], liber 2, rubrica 18, p. 41), at Arezzo 25 (*Statuto di Arezzo (1327),* ed. Giulia Marri Camerani [Florence, 1946], liber 3, rubrica 65, p. 174), and at Siena 25 (*Il constituto del comune di Siena dell'anno 1262,* ed. Lodovico Zdekauer [Milan: Hoepli, 1897], distinctio 2, rubrica 114, p. 256).

10. Albertus Gandinus, *Quaestiones statutorum,* 3:198, commented on a Florentine statute, which has not survived in any redaction, that released the father from his alimentary obligation to a son of 18. The statute in question seems to have considered the age of majority as somewhat emancipatory in this case. Gandinus, however, opined against the statute because it contravened natural law, which may be the reason it did not survive in later redactions.

11. See Bellomo, "Comunità e comune," 100.

12. *Statuti di Bologna,* liber 7, rubrica 14, De instrumentis emancipationis et sollempnitatibus in eis servandis, pp. 67–68. Other examples are Viterbo (*Statuti della provincia romana,* eds. R. Morghen et al. [Rome: Istituto Storico Italiano, 1930], p. 192) and Ascoli Piceno (*Statuti di Ascoli Piceno dell'anno MCCCLXXVII,* ed. L. Zdekauer and P. Sella [Rome: Istituto Storico Italiano, 1910], liber 2, rubrica 37, p. 42). See also Bellomo, "Comunità e comune," 97–100.

13. On the duties of heralds in Florence, see Anthony M. Christopher Mooney, "The Legal Ban in Florentine Statutory Law and the *De Bannitis* of Nello da San Gimignano (1373–1430)" (Ph.D. dissertation, University of California at Los Angeles, 1976), pp. 11–12; Kirshner, "*Ars,*" 317.

14. Bellomo, "Comunità e comune," 105; Podestà 1325, lib. 2, rub. 44, De obligatione filii emancipati, p. 119.

15. Podestà 1355, lib. 2, rub. 26, De obligatione filii familias et qualiter pater pro filio convenitur, fol. 78v–79v, and lib. 2, rub. 28, De obligatione filii emancipati, fol. 80r; Statuta 1415, lib. 2, rub. 1, De modo procedendi in civilibus, 1:113.

16. Bellomo, "Comunità e comune," 102–105. He mentions registration statutes at Como in 1206 and 1335, Lodi in 1224, Bergamo in 1242, and Bologna in 1265.

17. *Il constituto del comune di Siena,* dist. 2, rub. 72, [of 7 September 1254], p. 226.

18. PR 42, fol. 88r–88v (10 July 1355).

19. On the Mercanzia, see Guido Bonolis, *La giurisdizione della Mercanzia in Firenze nel secolo xiv.* The language of the *provvisione* of 10 July 1355 was incorporated into the new redaction of the city's statutes of the same year (Podestà 1355, lib. 2, rub. 26, fol. 79r–79v) and appeared again in the 1415 version (Statuta 1415, lib. 2, rub. 110, De obligatione filii familias, et qualiter pater pro filio conveniatur, 1:202–203).

20. Mercanzia 5, (Statuti 1393 with additions covering 1405–1473), fol. 48v (December 1410): "Item, considerato l'ordine che parla che i notai dell'ufficiale forestiere sieno tenuti a mettere tutte le emanceppationi, e moltissime volte si truovano degli errori et inconvenienti non piccholi, che'l cancelliere della decta università sia tenuto et debba mettere al libro tutte le decte

emanceppationi nel modo et forma che metteva prima il decto notaio dell'ufficiale. Et similemente debba mettere al libro tutte le sopradette divisioni de'frategli sinceramente che'l decto concelliere possa, e allui sia liato torre per la decta scriptura per insino in soldi cinqua per ogni emanceppato et diviso, et non più."

21. PR 111, fols. 238r–239r (22 December 1421). See also Chapter 2, Note 27.

22. Bonolis, *Mercanzia*, pp. 128–129, notes that the government tended to take over more and more of the powers and prerogatives of the Mercanzia. PR 185, fol. 12v (22 December 1494), contains the ratification of the emancipation registration by the Savonarolan government. PR 202, fols. 58r–59r (21 February 1516), allows a special extension for the registration of emancipations made necessary by the fact that the councils of the republican government were not meeting regularly in this period of Medici rule. On the internal politics of Florence from 1512 to 1527, see Antonio Anzilotti, *La crisi costituzionale della repubblica fiorentina* (Florence, 1912; reprint ed., Rome: Multigrafica, 1969), pp. 55–69 and Rudolf von Albertini, *Firenze dalla repubblica al principato*, trans. Cesare Cristofolini (Turin, Italy: Einaudi, 1970), pp. 20–44.

23. Unfortunately, the pertinent legislative consular records (the *Consulte e pratiche* and the *Signori e collegi, diliberazioni*) either do not survive or make no mention of the discussion surrounding the enactment of the emancipation registration provision of 22 December 1421. In the absence of such records, it is impossible to divine the intention of the legislators, other than that contained in the preamble to the law; namely, the desire to preclude the use of emancipation for fraudulent purposes. It should be pointed out, however, that decreased use of emancipation would, indeed, have been one way to prevent the institution's use as a means of fraud and deception, so such an intent is not beyond the realm of possibility.

24. See Aliberto Benigno Falsini, "Firenze dopo il 1348: Le conseguenze della peste nera," 481–482.

25. PR 42, fols. 88r–88v. The legislation states that the priors acted "multorum fraudibus occur⟨r⟩ere cupientes" and that unless an emancipation were properly registered, "presumatur fictitia et simulata et in fraudem creditorum facta, et nullius sit efficacie vel momenti."

26. The petitions appear in ibid., fols. 70r–76v (19 June 1355). On the judicial role of the Mercanzia with regard to fraud, see Bonolis, *Mercanzia*, p. 34; and *Enciclopedia del diritto*, s.v. "Fallimento (storia)," by C. Pecorella and U. Gualazzini, 16:221–222 (Milan: Giuffrè, 1967).

27. PR 111, fol. 238r: "Ut infrascriptorum maior notitia habeatur viaque ad fraudes difficilior fiat." The presumption in the case of nonregistration was once again fraudulent intent, though the consequences were spelled out in different terms from those of the law of 1355: "Alias talis emancippatio fictitia et simulata et in fraude⟨m⟩ creditorum facta presumatur et nullius sit efficacie vel momenti quoad favorem aut commodum ipsius emancippati. Et ipsi emancippato in nullo prosit emancippatio antedicta, sed redundet in damnum et gravamen tantum emancippati predicti et favorem et commodum

suorum creditorum vel cum eo contrahentium seu mercantium, trafficantium, vel aliud facientium."

28. Gene A. Brucker, *The Civic World of Early Renaissance Florence*, p. 430, and his incisive account of the political concern with economic problems in the period from 1414 to 1422, pp. 406–447.

29. Unfortunately the deliberative records are silent about the creation of the Sea Consuls, just as they offer no insight into the emancipation law. Chapter 5 discusses the legal context of the emancipation law. In addition to Brucker's and Molho's excellent studies of this period, an incisive commentary is offered by David Herlihy and Christiane Klapisch, *Les toscans et leurs familles*, esp. pp. 28–30, 45–46.

30. Cf. Giovanni Cherubini, *Signori, contadini, borghesi: Ricerche sulla società italiana del basso medioevo*, pp. 48–49; and Gino Corti, ed., "Consigli sulla mercatura d'un anonimo trecentista," 114–119.

31. Gene A. Brucker, *Renaissance Florence*, pp. 75–76.

32. Francesco Guicciardini, *Ricordi*, pp. 114–115. On this same theme, with regard to Guicciardini's famous contemporary, Niccolò Machiavelli, see Martin Fleischer, "Trust and Deceit in Machiavelli's Comedies," *Journal of the History of Ideas*, 27 (1966): 365–380.

33. To Leon Battista Alberti, "tutto il mondo si truova pieno di fizioni" (Alberti, *I libri della famiglia*, p. 309). Similarly Matteo Palmieri recognized that "alle volte essere utile quello che non è onesto, et essere onesto quello che non è utile" (Palmieri, *Della vita civile*, pp. 127–128).

34. Julian Pitt-Rivers, "Honour and Social Status," in *Honour and Shame: The Values of Mediterranean Society*, p. 58. Also in the same collection of papers, J. K. Campbell, "Honour and the Devil," pp. 151–159, 167–169; Julio Caro Baroja, "Honour and Shame," pp. 88–89.

35. Brucker, *Renaissance Florence*, p. 106.

36. Pitt-Rivers, "Honour and Social Status," pp. 58–59.

37. Cf. the use of *fraus* by Leonardo Bruni, *Laudatio florentinae urbis*, in Hans Baron, ed., *From Petrarch to Leonardo Bruni: Studies in Humanistic and Political Literature* (Chicago: University of Chicago Press, 1968), p. 248.

38. PR 97, fols. 137r–138v (30 November 1408).

39. PR 150, fols. 1r–1v. The law's intent is clearly contained in the initial observation "quod compromissa que pro longiori tempore fiunt, si nota non fuerunt, commictende fraudis occasione cum danno multorum prebere possunt." I was unable to locate any such registry in the Florentine archives; however, I did find a lone example of a *compromissum* registration among the emancipation records in Notificazioni 15, fol. 182v. This *provvisione* and others, as well as relevant legal opinions on the problem of fraud, are discussed in my "'Multorum Fraudibus Occurrere': Legislation and Jurisprudential Interpretation Concerning Fraud and Liability in Quattrocento Florence," *Studi senesi* (in press).

40. In CS, 3rd ser., 41/14, fols. 577r–589r, survive two *consilia* dealing with some of the problems raised by this *provvisione*.

41. PR 168, fols. 4v–5v: "Desiderando i magnifici et excellentissimi sig-

nori . . . provedere a molte fraude, le quali si commettono per fare occulti molti contracti, pe' quali e beni immobili di qualche cittadino sono alienati o obligati o in modo legati che non se ne può disporre liberamente, et nondimeno per esse così occulti sono tali cittadini giudicati etc. di tali beni et a loro creditto buone somme. Ma quando viene il caso de' pagamenti et loro non gli faccino, cercandosi d'entrare in tenuta et pigliare la possessione di tali beni per satisfactione del credito, esce fuori qualchuno che prima gli à a se obligati, o qualche figliuolo o sorella o altro coniuncto con qualche donagione, o vero alla morte di quel tale e figliuoli o altri a quali s'appartenessi la heredità ab intestato o altrimenti quella rinuntiano et per via di qualche fideicomisso o altro obligo pigliono la tenuta e possessione di tali beni. Et per tal via resta deluso et ingannato chi ha creduto o contractato con alcuno tale di poi morto, credendo i beni che teneva essere suoi liberi, et le fanciulle ne perdono molte volte le loro dote per essere per tal via obligati tutti i beni su quali erano sodate le loro dote. Et per questo molti si ritraggono dal trafficare; molti anchora per tal sospecto non comperano de' beni di chi in vero gli potrebbe vendere, dubitando di tali fraudi, et lui per satisfare alle sue necessità è constrecto spesse volte far contracti assai dannosi, poi che non truova chi e suoi beni realmente comperi. Et perchè tali fraudi sono molto dannose et per tanto si giudica non solo honesto ma necessario porne conveniente rimedio." As far as I could determine, no such registry survives.

42. On the Florentine economy in the fifteenth century, see Enrico Fiumi, "Fioritura e decadenza dell'economia fiorentina," pt. 3: "Politica economica e classi sociali," 117: 427–502; Brucker, *Renaissance Florence*, pp. 74–76, 82; Raymond de Roover, *The Rise and Decline of the Medici Bank, 1397–1494*, pp. 373–375.

43. Bellomo, "Emancipazione," 815–816 (mentioning Como, Parma, Brescia, Moncalieri, and Cremona). The registration enacted at Siena was also established to preclude fraud (*Il constituto del comune di Siena*, p. 226). Similar expressions of concern about fraud were found in the *Statuti di Bologna*, pp. 67–68, and the *usus* of Pisa (*Constituta legis et usus Pisanae*, p. 877).

44. Podestà 1325, lib. 2, rub. 23, pp. 102–104; Statuta 1415, lib. 2, rub. 110, 1:201–203. The text indicates that the relevant sections of the statute hail from 1252 and 1275.

45. The relevant statute on women is Statuta 1415, lib. 2, rub. 113, 1:205. Those covering men are cited in Chapter 2, Notes 44, 48, and 50–52.

46. *Statuti della repubblica fiorentina*, vol. 1: *Statuto del capitano del popolo degli anni 1322–1325*, lib. 2, rub. 25, pp. 108–111; rub. 32, pp. 115–116; rub. 38 and 39, pp. 117–118.

47. Marvin Becker, "Changing Patterns of Violence and Justice in Fourteenth- and Fifteenth-Century Florence," 281–296, has argued that at least in criminal matters, there was a movement in the course of the fourteenth century from a system of corporate liability to one of individual liability. Such was not the case with debtors' laws, for group liability remained in effect.

48. *Enciclopedia del diritto*, s.v. "Fallimento (storia)", by C. Pecorella and U. Gualazzini, 16:230.

49. Ibid., 16:225–231; also Pier Silverio Leicht, *Storia del diritto italiano: Il diritto privato*, vol. 3, *Le obbligazioni*, pp. 86–87; Desiderio Cavalca, *Il bando nella prassi e nella dottrina giuridica medievale*, pp. 159–252, esp. pp. 115, 166–168. On the related problem of extending penalties for heresy to the heretic's sons and appealing to emancipation as limiting liability, see Kenneth Pennington, "'Pro Peccatis Patrum Puniri': A Moral and Legal Problem of the Inquisition," 137–154.

50. ASF, Mercanzia 5, fols. 29v–30r, 32r–32v, 35r–35v.

51. Statuti 10, Statuti del capitano del 1355, fols. 82v–83v, 85v–86v; Podestà 1355, fols. 78v–79v.

52. Statuta 1415, lib. 3, rub. 2, De filiis et aliis descendentibus . . . et qualiter pro eis teneantur, 1:520–521.

53. PR 168, fol. 12v (29 March 1477): "In primis, quia in secundo volumine statutorum civitatis Florentie, sub rubrica de obligatione filii familias, dubitatur an filius familias se obligans cum consensu patris in rem sive utilitatem, que sit aut dici possit esse patris, valeat se iure obligare, et an valeat facta obligatio, cupientes tali dubitationi occurrere et eam declarare prepartim, quoniam ex decreto varie sententiatum est in civitate Florentie, propterea providetur quod deinceps filii familias etatis annorum vigintiquinque completorum possint in rem et utilitatem patris se obligare, interveniente consensu patris, et cum tali consensu obligatio per eos facta ut supra teneat et subsistat." Discordant *sententiae* indicate that perplexed lawyers had asked for clarification of the law.

54. Manlio Bellomo, *Problemi di diritto familiare nell'età dei comuni: Beni paterni e 'pars filii'*, pp. 98–105.

55. A copy of the initial law of 20 September 1402 is found in Tratte 1099, fol. 8v, and reads in part: "Eo etiam proviso e declarato quod, quandocumque aliquis esset descriptus in quocumque speculo, et posset seu deberet cedula sue executionis pro officio laniari. Intelligatur et observetur et observari possit et debeat deinceps omni vice et omni tempore. ⟨Et⟩quod quandocumque aliquis eius filius extraheretur ad aliquod officium, existente patre in speculo lanietur et reiciatur, et laniari et reici debeat, cedula nominis filii, et extractio fit inanis prout esset de patre, posito etiam quod in libris prestantiarum non esset aliquo modo descriptus ipse filius." The text of this law does not appear, however, among the *provvisioni* (specifically not in PR 91, nor in the appropriate volumes of protocols and duplicates), nor does any record survive of deliberation and discussion of this law. It was later reaffirmed on 2 December 1406 as retroactive to 1390 according to the same page in Tratte 1099 (again I found no other records, although PR 95 contains a law of 6 December setting stiff penalties on those not meeting their *onera*). The text of the law of 1402 also appears in a statute of 1415.

Tratte 1099, fols. 8v–9r: "Adtendentes ad quod plures querelas eis factas per nonnullos cives civitatis Florentie, continentes in effectu quod vigore quorumdam ordinamentorum dicti comunis filius gravetur in civitate Florentie pro prestantiis patris, et etiam pro dictis prestantiis in libro speculi dicti comunis describitur, non obstante quod dictus talis filius sit emancippatus et habitet de per se separatus a patre et etiam separatus a dicto patre suo sit prestantiatus, quod quidem est contra ius et iustitiam et contra omnem humanitatem et debitum rationis. Pro inde volentes providere predictis . . . providerunt, ordinaverunt, et deliberaverunt quod de cetero nullus prestantiatus in civitate Florentie possit in dicta civitate vel eius comitatu seu districtu pro prestantiis vel aliis similibus oneribus inductis patri suo capi, detineri, integiri, gravari, vel modo aliquo molestari personaliter vel in bonis. . . . Nec etiam per aliquem in libro speculi poni vel quomodolibet describi eo filio existente emancippato et habitante separato et de per se, ac etiam prestantiato de per se separatim a patre suo.

"Et similiter e converso nullus prestantiatus in civitate Florentie possit in dicta civitate vel eius comitatu seu districtu pro prestantiis vel aliis similibus oneribus inductis filio suo capi, detineri, integiri, gravari, vel modo aliquo molestari personaliter vel in bonis . . . nec etiam per aliquem in libro speculi poni vel quomodolibet describi, eo patre habitante separato et de per se et existente prestantiato de per se separatim a filio, et ipso suo filio existente emancippato." Statuta 1415, tractatus 1, lib. v., rub.: Filius lanietur patre existente in speculo, 3:807, reproduces the Tratte text of 1402 with the following addition: "Dictum etiam ordinamentum habeat locum, et observari possit, et debeat pro omnibus et singulis praestantiis, residuis, nominationibus, praestantionibus et placentibus impositis et imponendis quandocumque et pro omnibus aliis oneribus, et sic observetur et executioni mandetur, salvo quod predicta locum non habeant in aliquo filio suo nomine et separatim praestantiato et seorsum a patre habitante." It is impossible to determine if the omission of emancipation here was deliberate or not; in any case, emancipation was not itself sufficient to terminate liability for taxes. The law looked here perhaps more pointedly for patrimonial and fiscal separation.

On the *speculum* in Florence, see Marzi, *Cancelleria*, pp. 169–172; and on the effectiveness of the speculum, see Anthony Molho, *Florentine Public Finances in the Early Renaissance, 1400–1433*, pp. 104–105, n. 61.

56. Podestà 1325, lib. 3, rub. 64, De filio vel nepote faciente maleficium, p. 226.

57. Bellomo, *Problemi di diritto familiare*, pp. 206–221.

58. Walter Ullmann, "Baldus's Conception of Law," 394, explains that "natural law, according to Baldus, was nothing else but the application to human conduct of the principles in the working of Nature and their transformation into rules for actions which were envisaged by him as 'natural' and 'instinctive' functions." He cites as an example Baldus's opinion on *alimenta* (p. 395). Also on natural law in relation to civil law, see Ennio Cortese, *La norma giuridica*, 1:36–96. For a solid analysis of the concept of *aequitas* and the types of law in Baldus' thought and in the legal tradition, see Norbert Horn, *'Aequitas' in den Lehren des Baldus*, esp. pp. 62–88.

59. Podestà 1325, p. 103; Podestà 1355, fol. 79v–80r; Statuta 1415, 1: 191–192.

60. Podestà 1325, p. 103, does not indicate the meaning of emancipatory

status, although the passage follows immediately on that mentioning pro-digality, which did indicate that emancipatory status was not relevant. *Statuta 1415*, lib. 2, rub. 32, De alimentis, 1:135, does mention emancipation as not relevant to the *alimenta* law.

61. For a discussion of inheritance laws found in statutes of a number of Italian cities, see Franco Nicolai, *La formazione del diritto successorio negli statuti comunali del territorio lombardo-tosco*. Nicolai's discussion, however, suffers from a lack of consideration of the civil and canon law in conjunction with the statutes, which is apparent in his discussion of emancipation and related problems.

62. This opinion runs counter to that widely shared by legal historians that the *patria potestas* was progressively limited and circumscribed, made less rigid and awesome. This argument rests largely on evidence of supposedly new legal capacities of sons to live apart from their fathers and run their own affairs and on statutes that are said to prove the existence of an emancipatory age of majority, at least in some cities. Representative are Nino Tamassia, *La famiglia italiana nei secoli decimoquinto e decimosesto*, pp. 248–249, and Pietro To-relli, *Lezioni di storia del diritto italiano: Diritto privato: La famiglia*, pp. 60–74.

63. See Chapter 2, Note 10.

64. Enrico Fiumi, *Storia economica e sociale di San Gimignano*, p. 229, notes that large family fortunes lasted only a few generations.

65. This institutional manner was defined as standing "in mercantia, arte, vel tabula, seu cambium nummorum . . . sicuti magister, vel sotius, sciente patre . . . et non contradicente" (*Statuta 1415*, lib. 2, rub. 110, 1:201). See also Chapter 2, Note 67.

66. The relevant passage is: "Verum nullo modo possit conveniri, vel gra-vari in persona, vel rebus . . . filiusfamilias . . . qui non steterit in aliqua mer-cantia, vel arte occasione alicuius promissionis, obligationis, aut fideiussionis . . . sine consensu patris . . . sed ipsa obligatio, fideiussio, vel promissio ipso iure sit nulla" (ibid., p. 202).

67. Here I differ from opinions of historians like Torelli, who says that "l'essere o non essere soggetti alla patria potestà appare per tutto il periodo intermedio così indissolubilmente connesso col vivere insieme al padre o vi-vere separati" (*La famiglia*, p. 79). He cites in support a statute of Parma of 1255 that said that an emancipatus who lived with his father was not emanci-pated. However, as he himself notes, not only was this statute badly drafted, but it was concerned with fraud. The statute was clumsily saying that con-tinued coresidence was a condition presumptive of fraud. Florentine law more fully disassociated emancipation and residence (seen most clearly in the *speculum* laws), but it, too, voided emancipations on grounds of fraudulent intent in the registration laws. Coresidence was not cited there as presump-tive of fraud, but it was sometimes considered as such (see Chapter 5). What mattered, however, in both Parma and Florence was not coresidence itself but what it was taken to signify—who really controlled the son's patrimony.

68. Bellomo, *Problemi di diritto familiare*, p. 207.

CHAPTER THREE

1. Robert Davidsohn, *Storia di Firenze*, vol. 4, pt. 3, *Il mondo della chiesa, spiritualità e arte, vita pubblica e privata*, pp. 695–696.

2. Diane Owen Hughes, "Urban Growth and Family Structure in Medieval Genoa," 17–18.

3. Richard Freemantle, "Some New Masolino Documents," 659.

4. Hughes, "Domestic Ideals and Social Behavior," p. 134; see also Ginevra Niccolini di Camugliano, *The Chronicles of a Florentine Family, 1200–1470*, p. 150.

5. David Herlihy and Christiane Klapisch, *Les toscans et leurs familles*, pp. 571–576. Generally, they interpret registering emancipations with the Mercanzia as enrolling one's son in the community of merchants and artisans (ibid., p. 576; Herlihy, "Family and Property in Renaissance Florence," 17). However, as the previous chapter indicated, guild matriculation would seem to have fulfilled that function, while registering emancipations was intended to avoid fraud in cases where the extended-liability principle in Florentine law could be applied. See also Cinzio Violante, "Quelques caractéristiques des structures familiales en Lombardie, Émilie, et Toscane aux xie et xiie siècles," 115–116; Herlihy and Klapisch, *Les toscans*, pp. 487–491; also Christiane Klapisch and Michel Demonet, "'A uno pane e uno vino': La famille rurale toscane au début de xve siècle," 877; and Klapisch, "L'enfance en Toscane au début du xve siècle," 102. Klapisch's earlier articles reveal that most men could not expect to be heads of families until their forties, and she argues that prior to acquiring their economic autonomy, men were not adults but children still subject to *patria potestas*. This functional definition of infancy, adolescence, and adulthood, insightful as it is, ignores legal emancipation and does not always correspond to the Florentine meanings of terms like *adultus*. *Adultus* meant a person over eighteen, although I have discovered one instance where the term was applied to someone designated as over fourteen but less than eighteen (PR 95, fol. 102v).

6. Gina Fasoli, "La vita quotidiana nel medioevo," p. 475. She places herself squarely in opposition to those who see emancipation as a ritual of maturity, declaring that neither age of majority nor the establishment of a separate household removed a child from the father's power.

7. Richard Trexler, "Ritual in Florence: Adolescence and Salvation in the Renaissance," p. 214.

8. Paolo Cammarosano, "Aspetti delle strutture familiari nelle città dell' Italia comunale (secoli xii–xiv)," 423–430.

9. Giovanni Rucellai, *Zibaldone quaresimale*, p. 2. The emancipations of the Rucellai boys appear in Notificazioni 7, fol. 45v (23 September 1458), and Notificazioni 8, fol. 58v (18 March 1465). Buonaccorso Pitti, *Cronica*, says nothing about the emancipations of Roberto (Notificazioni 2, fol. 2v [25 February 1429]) and Luca (Mercanzia 10820 bis, fol. 20r [22 November 1418]). Notice of the emancipation of Bandescha di Goro Dati is found in Mercanzia 10820 bis, fol. 61r (3 August 1420), but no mention is found in Goro di Stagio Dati, *Il libro segreto*. The emancipations of Bernardo and Girolamo di Goro Dati are in

Notificazioni 2, fol. 55r (28 June 1431), and that of Antonio di Goro in ibid., fol. 88r (29 August 1433). Also Giovanni Morelli, *Ricordi*, and the emancipation of Jacopo di Giovanni Morelli in Notificazioni 1, fol. 70r (19 July 1426).

10. For example, CS, 4th ser., 353 (Libro giornale de' debitori e creditori di Marco del Giovanni di Jacopo Strozzi, 1486–1525), fol. 139v: "Richordo, questo dì viiii d'aprile 1507, chom'io ò mancepato Ubertino mio figluolo, roghato ser Bernardo di Piero di ser Giovanni da San Miniato al Todesco, notaio e cittadino fiorentino." AD 11/1 (Ricordanze A di ser Antonio di ser Battista d'Antonio Bartolomei), fol. 30r; CS, 5th ser., 16, fol. 1v; Manoscritti 76 (Memoriale di Francesco e Alessio di Borghino Baldovinetti del 1314), fol. 2v; CS, 5th ser., 1751 (Ricordi di Bartolomeo di Tommaso di Federigo Sassetti, 1471–1477), fol. 157r; *Il libro di ricordanze dei Corsini*, pp. 66–67, 68–69, 70–71, 73–75, 130.

11. Cf. the advice given by Paolo da Certaldo, *Il libro di buoni costumi*, pp. 103–104.

12. The unusually expressive notarial charter is transcribed in Appendix 3. Another one like it is M112, fol. 50r (4 January 1357). A more typical formulaic presentation of emancipation is Appendix 4. Evidence of holding and releasing the son's hand comes from V298, 8 August 1463: "Qui Antonius, auditus predictas, capitus manum dictum Tommasium filium suum ita genuflexum, et ita petentem eundem Tommasium emancipavit." Ibid., B522, 12 December 1422, transcribed in the Appendix.

13. Frequently, the language of the emancipation instruments invoked the terminology of the *donatio* as laid out in the notarial formularies. Hence, in Notarile N2 (1474–1476), fol. 165r (22 May 1476), the father is said to be giving "sponte" and "dedit et donavit pure, mere, libere, simpliciter et irrevocabiliter inter vivos."

14. My discussion of the emancipation ritual owes a great deal to Clifford Geertz, "Deep Play: Notes on the Balinese Cockfight," in *The Interpretation of Cultures* (New York: Basic Books, 1973), pp. 412–453.

15. Ad 190/3, fols. 3v and 17r; Lapo di Giovanni Niccolini, *Il libro degli affari proprii di casa di Lapo di Giovanni Niccolini de' Sirigatti*, pp. 58, 80, 110, 81, 115; Manoscritti 77 (Vari di casa Curiani), fols. 31v and 40v; CS, 2nd ser., 16 (Libro I di ricordanze di Francesco di Tommaso di Francesco Giovanni), fol. 6r; Manoscritti 85 (Libro di Dietisalvi di Nerone di Nigi), fol. 101r; and Notarile A671, fol. 381v.

16. CS, 5th ser., 1751, fol. 182r; Manoscritti 76, fols. 4v and 5v. The emancipation of Lorenzo di Niccolò was registered in Mercanzia 10820, fol. 111r (14 July 1405). Other examples of separate residence occur in Chapter 4. The fact that marriage and emancipation from paternal authority did not coincide is contrary to the rule in other societies. Cf. Oscar Lewis, *Life in a Mexican Village: Tepoztlán Restudied* (Urbana: University of Illinois Press, 1963), pp. 52–53; Charlotte Gower Chapman, *Milocca: A Sicilian Village*, p. 35.

17. The findings of the anthropologist Sydel Silverman, *Three Bells of Civilization: The Life of an Italian Hill Town*, p. 209, seem to indicate that maturity and legal capacity are still quite separate. Chapman, *Milocca*, p. 48, makes a similar observation.

18. Manoscritti 77, fol. 5v: "Manceppai e liberai." 1329 was the year that

Valorino's father died and he and his brother Barna had repudiated their father's debt-ridden estate. On the Curiani and their problems, see P. J. Jones, "Florentine Families and Florentine Diaries in the Fourteenth Century," 190–191.

19. CS, 2nd ser., 17 bis, fols. 115r, 124r: "Emancipai et della mia patria potestà liberai." Ibid., 16, fol. 6r: "Ricordo che a dì xxi d'aprile 1433 io, Francesco di Tomaso Giovanni, liberai e manceppai Giovantomaso mio figliuolo d'ogni legame e obligo paterno." Bartolomeo Masi, *Ricordanze di Bartolomeo Masi calderaio fiorentino, 1478–1526*, p. 148. The Masi brothers were aged 37 and 35. Their birthdates are in Piero's *ricordi*, Manoscritti 88, fol. 141r.

20. Niccolini, *Libro di casa Niccolini*, p. 58.

21. Ibid., p. 110. Lapo was clearly concerned by his son's actions, for he removed himself from any obligations arising therefrom by means of emancipation. In his words: "E questo feci a magiore cautela, non obstante che elgli è vera cosa che, a dì vij di settembre 1409, io avea mandato la grida per tutti i conventi che, da indi innanzi, io non voleva essere tenuto per lui a niuna cosa, né elgli fusse tenuto per me." Lapo later mentioned Niccolaio's prodigality when recording his death (pp. 136–137), and an example of his misadventures is given on p. 125.

22. Ibid., pp. 110–111, reveals several deals in which Lapo used Niccolaio as an agent. The emancipation of Giovanni is recorded in ibid., pp. 115–116.

23. As Gene A. Brucker, *Renaissance Florence*, p. 91, notes: "Even after a son was legally emancipated from his father, he was bound to his relatives by many ties."

24. Francis William Kent, *Household and Lineage in Renaissance Florence: The Family Life of the Capponi, Ginori, and Rucellai*, pp. 5, 44–45.

25. Julius Kirshner, *Pursuing Honor While Avoiding Sin: The 'Monte delle doti' of Florence*, p. 6.

26. These various meanings and metaphoric extensions of *casa* are all accessible in the excellent article by Francis William Kent, " 'Più superba de quella de Lorenzo': Courtly and Family Interest in the Building of Filippo Strozzi's Palace," esp. pp. 320 and 323.

27. Leon Battista Alberti, *De iciarchia*, in *Opere volgari*, 2:266–268.

28. In the law, this meant all those subject to a single *patria potestas*. See Chapter 1, Notes 138–139. On the theme of family unity, see Kent's elegant discussion in *Household and Lineage*, Chapter 2.

29. Alberti, *De iciarchia*, in *Opere volgari*, 2: 279–280.

30. Recognition of the connection between public prestige and proper performance of domestic duties has become commonplace among historians and anthropologists. Among the former, see Gene A. Brucker, *The Civic World of Early Renaissance Florence*, p. 35; Herlihy and Klapisch, *Les toscans*, pp. 595–599; Charles M. de la Roncière, "Une famille florentine au xive siècle: Les Velluti," p. 242. Among the latter, see J. Davis, *Land and Family in Pisticci*, p. 71, and his *People of the Mediterranean*, p. 77; Jeremy Boissevain, "Patronage in Sicily," 18–33; Jane and Peter Schneider, *Culture and Political Economy in Western Sicily*, p. 89.

31. Leon Battista Alberti, *I libri della famiglia*, p. 233 (translation from *The Family in Renaissance Florence*, trans. Renee Neu Watkins, pp. 185–186). In this regard, we note the observation of Rudolph M. Bell, *Fate and Honor, Family and Village: Demographic and Cultural Change in Rural Italy since 1800*, p. 44, that what lay behind comments such as Alberti's was not only an appreciation of numbers but also an implicit estimation of the honor of a man with tangible long-term interests, as represented by his sons and other kin. For a discussion of Alberti's dialogues, see David Marsh, *The Quattrocento Dialogue: Classical Tradition and Humanist Innovation* (Cambridge, Mass.: Harvard University Press, 1980), pp. 78–99.

32. Alberti, *De iciarchia*, in *Opere volgari*, p. 271.

33. Pal. 789, fol. 31v: "Crediamo per più nostra consolatione per vedervi in mezzo padre di tutti circundato, amato, rivherito padrone da tutti et amaestrare la gioventù, la quale cosa è avechi somma letitia imperò che e' figliuoli virtuosi porgano al padre molto subsidio, molto honore, et loda. Nella sollecitudine de' padri sta la virtù de' figliuoli. I sollesciti et officiosi padri ringentilischono le famiglie." Alberti used the same terminology, *I libri della famiglia*, p. 232, and his work was the source for the Pseudo-Pandolfini. On the various *rifacimenti* of Alberti's third book ascribed to Agnolo Pandolfini, see Judith Ravenscroft, "The Third Book of Alberti's *Della Famiglia* and its Two *Rifacimenti*," *Italian Studies*, 29 (1974): 45–53. She assigns Palatino 789 to the second *rifacimento*.

34. Pal. 678 (Compendio dello zibaldone di Antonio Pucci), fol. 4r–4v.

35. Alberti, *Cena familiaris*, in *Opere volgari*, 1:350. It is very difficult to pin down the meaning of a term like respect. Davis, *Land and Family in Pisticci*, p. 50, finds that "respect means that children should be obedient and submissive." Yet, he also finds that respect is extremely plastic: "Words like 'respect' turn out to have no hard core of generally accepted meaning, but are used for forensic justification in particular situations" (p. 51).

36. Marsilio Ficino, "Epistola ad fratres vulgaris," in *Supplementum ficinianum*, pp. 115–119.

37. Lapo da Castiglionchio, *Epistola*, p. 131.

38. On this theme, see Kent, *Household and Lineage*, p. 46, who, among other things, notes that Palla di Bernardo Rucellai named his son Bernardo, declaring that "habbiamo rifacto nostro padre." See also Juliet Du Boulay, *Portrait of a Greek Mountain Village*, pp. 21 and 40.

39. CS, 5th ser., 16, fol. 1r: "Ricordanza amme a dì xiiii° di settembre 1459 mi nacque uno figliuolo maschio in sugli nome Carlo, et viva per Charlo nostro padre."

40. On the obligations of sons in a culture of honor, see Pitt-Rivers, "Honour and Social Status," in J. G. Peristiany, ed., *Honour and Shame, The Values of Mediterranean Society*, pp. 35–36; Pierre Bourdieu, "The Sentiment of Honour in Kabyle Society," in ibid., 191–241; Ernestine Friedl, *Vasilika: A Village in Modern Greece*, p. 80; Silverman, *Three Bells*, p. 206.

41. Morelli, *Ricordi*, pp. 202–221, 232–235. Especially instructive is the statement: "E come è chiaro e aperto vedi, è baratta la volontà d'uno a quella di molti, è baratta l'amore e carità del padre verso il figliuolo, che è infinita"

(p. 219). Richard Trexler, "In Search of Father: The Experience of Abandonment in the Recollections of Giovanni di Pagolo Morelli," 226, interprets such assessments of orphanhood in highly personal, psychological terms, as a seeking for the love and knowledge of a father Morelli had never known. Trexler ignores the implications of such exhortations—a cultural commonplace—for sons who had a father. Lewis, *Mexican Village*, pp. 296–297, 330, has pointed out that the fate of orphans in a society where the family is the primary social unit is a hard one and that this fate is often used to cultivate children's respect for their parents. For a different view of Morelli, see Leonida Pandimiglio, "Giovanni di Pagolo Morelli e le strutture familiari," 3–88.

42. Rucellai, *Zibaldone*, pp. 2–19. Note also the Pseudo-Pandolfini's remarks in Pal. 789, fol. 1r: "Io voglio con voi conferire et communicare quello ho letto e conpreso da altri et provato in questa mia lunga vita. Perchè voi con questi documenti et per vostro studio possiate essere migliori. Non pur debbono i buoni padri essere utili a figliuoli in richezze quanto in fama, in gratia, et in consiglio."

43. Matteo Palmieri, *Della vita civile*, p. 19. Note also Pal. 789, fol. 64r: "Quando la famiglia da te non harà buono exemplo, s'ella ti sarà pocho ubbidiente et meno rivherente. La rivherentia si rende alle persone degne, i costumi danno dignità a chi sa observare la dignità et che sa farsi ubbidire sa farsi rivherire."

44. Alberti, *I libri della famiglia*, pp. 22, 62.

45. Ficino, "Epistola ad fratres vulgaris" in *Supplementum ficinianum*, pp. 113, 120–121.

46. Pasquale Villari, *I primi due secoli della storia di Firenze*, rev. ed. (Florence: Sansoni, 1905), p. 369. His observation has been echoed by F. W. Kent, *Household and Lineage*, p. 45.

47. Franco Sacchetti, *Il trecentonovelle*, pp. 272–273.

48. Alberti, *I libri della famiglia*, pp. 129–130; from *Family in Renaissance Florence*, p. 113; idem, *De iciarchia*, in *Opere volgari*, p. 252. Translation is from *Family in Renaissance Florence*, p. 41. Davis notes a similar sentiment in *Land and Family in Pisticci*, p. 51.

49. Ficino, "Epistola ad fratres vulgaris" in *Supplementum ficinianum*, pp. 114, 116.

50. Giovanni Cavalcanti, *The "Trattato Politico-Morale" of Giovanni Cavalcanti (1381–ca. 1451)*, p. 160.

51. Morelli, *Ricordi*, pp. 457, 475–476. Trexler, "In Search of Father," pp. 227–228, interprets Morelli's grief as the acknowledgment of paternal failures. In fact, it seems that Morelli was proud of the boy and of the way he had raised him. Morelli was mourning the loss of the "best thing that you ever seemed to have, a lad of intelligence, loving toward me his father and toward his mother" (ibid., pp. 245–248). Morelli, *Ricordi*, p. 542. On how Florentines dealt with the deaths of their children, see Herlihy and Klapisch, *Les toscans*, pp. 558–570. For further examples, see Ginevra Niccolini di Camugliano, *Chronicles of a Florentine Family, 1200–1470*, p. 60; and CS, 3rd ser., 111, fol. 50r.

52. Manoscritti 77, fol. 38r, where a father records the death of a fifty-four-year-old son. The father simply concluded "Idio gli abbia ricevuto a suoi piedi chome buono, honesto, e devoto huomo, e guardici gli altri."

53. Du Boulay, *Greek Village*, p. 38.

54. Julius Kirshner and Anthony Molho, "The Dowry Fund and the Marriage Market in Early *Quattrocento* Florence," 435, and the literature there cited.

55. Jacopo d'Arena (quoted by Andrea Romano in his introduction to the edition of Arsendi [see Chapter 1, Note 77], pp. 9–10, n. 5): "Ut familiarum et agnationum dignitas et memoria conservatur . . . que conservatur per divitias, et per inopiam minuitur." The result of this belief was that poor branches of some lineages were deemed spurious on account of their poverty, as was the case in Niccolò Machiavelli's family (see Roberto Ridolfi, *The Life of Niccolò Machiavelli*, trans. Cecil Grayson [Chicago: University of Chicago Press, 1963], p. 2). F. W. Kent runs across several down-and-out branches of the three patrician lineages he studies. Despite the evidence that they were often ignored by the wealthier branches or seen as an embarassment, in accord with his whole approach to the family, he stoutly refuses to entertain the notion that these branches were effectively no longer part of the lineage. See Kent, *Household and Lineage*, pp. 149–163.

56. Davis, *People of the Mediterranean*, pp. 77–101. See also Jane Schneider, "Of Vigilance and Virgins: Honor, Shame, and Access to Resources in Mediterranean Societies," pp. 1–2.

57. Lauro Martines, *The Social World of the Florentine Humanists, 1390–1460*, pp. 25–27; Armando Sapori, "La famiglia e le compagnie degli Alberti del Giudice" in *Studi di storia economica (secoli xiii–xiv–xv)*, 2:975–1012. The interconnection, even equation, of wealth and honor can be seen in the Florentine lawyer Benedetto Accolti's assessment of the legislative intent of an inheritance statute that sought "excludere feminas propter masculos ut honor familie conservetur" (Biblioteca Apostolica Vaticana, Vat. Lat. 8067/1, fol. 25v).

58. Rucellai, *Zibaldone*, p. 5.

59. Paolo da Certaldo, *Il libro di buoni costumi*, p. 85.

60. Ruggiero Romano, "Introduzione," in *I libri della famiglia*, pp. xviii–xxiii (reprinted as "I libri della famiglia di Leon Battista Alberti," in *Tra due crisi: L'Italia del rinascimento*, pp. 137–168).

61. Ibid., pp. xvii–xviii.

62. da Certaldo, *Il libro*, p. 61: "Molto è bella chosa e grande sapere guadangniare il danaio, ma più bella chosa e magiore è saperlo spendere chon misura e dove si conviene. E sapere ritenere e guardare quello che t'è lasciato dal tuo patrimonio o dai altri parenti è sopra le dette virtudi, però che quello che l'uomo non guadangnia è più agievole a spendere che quello che guadangna con sua faticha e con suo sudore e solecitudine."

63. Rucellai, *Zibaldone*, p. 19.

64. Ibid., p. 16; also Pal. 789, fols. 4v–5r. The terms *masserizia* and *massaio* had an important range of meaning in the culture. On the one hand, they referred to the domestic head and to household furnishings and implements.

On the other, they included the ability to gather and use such goods moderately and wisely. On *masserizia*, see Romano, *Tra due crisi*, pp. 143–148.

65. Rucellai, *Zibaldone*, pp. 15–16.

66. Palmieri, *Della vita civile*, p. 149.

67. Rucellai, *Zibaldone*, pp. 12–13, 16–17.

68. Alberti, *I libri della famiglia*, pp. 312–313.

69. Rucellai, *Zibaldone*, p. 16; Pal. 789, fol. 5r.

70. Notarile L130 (testamenti), 13 December 1465.

71. On the *fideicommissum* and Giovanni Rucellai's will, see Kent, *Household and Lineage*, pp. 136–144; on the law of *fideicommissum*, see *Enciclopedia del diritto*, s.v. "Fedecommesso (storia)," by M. Caravale.

72. For examples, see Chapter 4.

73. Rucellai, *Zibaldone*, pp. 10–13.

74. On the nature of patronage, see J. K. Campbell, *Honour, Family, and Patronage*, pp. 229–259; and Boissevain, "Patronage," passim.

75. Alberti, *I libri della famiglia*, p. 3.

76. Ibid., pp. 11–12. On the theme of the precariousness of families as expressed in Florentine *ricordi*, see the incisive remarks of Herlihy and Klapisch, *Les toscans*, pp. 548–549; and note also the comments of Bell, *Fate and Honor*, p. 72.

77. Sacchetti, *Le novelle*, 2:273: "In questa vita non si può stare troppo avvisato, perocchè d'ogni parte sono tesi gli inganni e' tradimenti, per fare dell'altrui suo."

78. "Lettera a Raimondo," in *Prosatori minori del Trecento: I scrittori di religione*, ed. G. de Luca (Milan: Ricciardi, 1954), p. 819.

79. Sacchetti, *Le novelle*, 2:271.

80. Giovanni Sercambi, *Novelle*, 1:132.

81. Alberti, *I libri della famiglia*, p. 51.

82. Idem, *De iciarchia*, in *Opere volgari*, p. 274.

83. Idem, *I libri della famiglia*, p. 69 (translation from *Family in Renaissance Florence*, p. 71).

84. Ibid., p. 20.

85. Ibid., pp. 93–94 (translation from *Family in Renaissance Florence*, p. 88).

86. See Kent, *Household and Lineage*, pp. 57–59. On Pucci, see Iris Origo, *The Merchant of Prato* (Middlesex, Eng.: Penguin, 1957), pp. 363–364, n. 25; and Paul G. Ruggiers's *Florence in the Age of Dante* (Norman: University of Oklahoma Press, 1964), p. 97.

87. Alberti, *I libri della famiglia*, p. 95.

88. Cavalcanti, *"Trattato Politico-Morale,"* pp. 142–143.

89. Kent, *Household and Lineage*, p. 57, n. 138; pp. 71–72.

90. Sacchetti, *Le novelle*, 1:342, praises a man who did not want children: "E fu molto savio; perocchè, delle sei volte, le cinque l'uomo ha volontà d'aver figliuoli, li quali son poi suoi nimici, desiderando la morte del padre per esser liberi."

91. "Lettera a Raimondo," p. 823.

92. Palmieri, *Della vita civile*, p. 135.

93. Paolo da Certaldo, *Il libro*, p. 157.

94. Ibid., p. 165: "Il filgliuolo sta al padre sogietto e sottomesso e umile in fino a tanto che'l padre tiene la singnoria de la chasa e de l'avere suo; e quando il padre à data la singnoria al filgliuolo di ghovernare il suo avere, elgli soprastà al padre e àlo ⟨in odio⟩, e pargli mille anni il dì che si muoia per non vederlosi inanzi: e d'amicho ch'era prima è diventato tuo nimicho per la fidanza che ai presa di lui." Sercambi's fifty-eighth story is an interesting tale of an old man and his daughters that illustrates Paolo's point.

95. On this, see Constance Cronin, *The Sting of Change: Sicilians in Sicily and Australia*, pp. 81, 106–107.

96. Alberti, *Cena familiaris*, in *Opere volgari*, p. 347.

97. Idem, *I libri della famiglia*, pp. 149–150.

98. Cf. Susan Tax Freeman, *Neighbors: The Social Contract in a Castilian Hamlet* (Chicago: University of Chicago Press, 1970), p. 57.

99. An interesting example occurs in PR 150, fols. 60r–61r.

100. Armando Sapori, ed., *I libri di commercio dei Peruzzi* (Milan: Treves, 1934), p. 524.

101. See Richard Trexler, "The Magi Enter Florence: The Ubriachi of Florence and Venice," *Studies in Medieval and Renaissance History*, n. s. 1 (1978): 167, 201–202.

102. The letter of Remigio to his brother Orsino, dated 23 September 1405, which describes the whole incident, is found in Princ., II, v, 7, fols. 137r–138v, and is partially translated in Gene Brucker, ed., *The Society of Renaissance Florence: A Documentary Study* (New York: Harper & Row, 1971), pp. 64–66. On the Lanfredini quarrel and the problem of familial discord, see my "Honor and Conflict in a Fifteenth-Century Florentine Family," 287–304.

103. Herlihy and Klapisch, *Les toscans*, p. 606. See also Herlihy, "The Generation in Medieval History," 360.

104. On this theme, see Davis, *People of the Mediterranean*, pp. 179–181.

105. On some of the problems involving women, see Kirshner, *Pursuing Honor*, pp. 7–15.

106. My perception of the status issue in generational conflicts has been greatly aided by the following: Marvin Davis, "The Politics of Family Life in Rural West Bengal," *Ethnology*, 15 (1976): 189–200; Jose Cutileiro, *A Portuguese Rural Society* (Oxford: Clarendon Press, 1971), pp. 117–119; J. Davis, *People of the Mediterranean*, p. 181; Du Boulay, *Greek Mountain Village*, p. 126.

107. Interesting evidence on this score comes from the Lanfredini family. A year before his quarrel with his father, Remigio left his uncle's shop to make his own way in the world. However, a Florentine who was his innkeeper in Forlì told him that no merchant would dare offer him a job: "In però dicie quando uno mercatante vede uno gharzone di buona aparenzia pensa dibato abia fatto a casa sua qualque male, e mai s'arischiano a torne veruno." Faced with a lack of prospects, Remigio wrote home begging forgiveness: "E che gli piacia volere ch'io torni a vivere e morire cole charni e cole sanghui mia in prometendovi di stare con lui o con chui fuse di vostro piaciere e di fare bene, lasciando stare ongni vizio e ongni male che per lo pasato fuse stato. E prometovi per la fede donde sono cristiano di mai partire da niuna vostra dis-

ubidenza. E farò ragione mentre ch'io viverò d'esere schiavo di te e simile di Giovanni, e come padre amendumi v'obiderò e farò bene, sì solicitamente quello arò fare dunch'io starò, vi parà non sia più quello Romigi sono stato insino a ora. . . . E s'io torno io farò sì arai tanto onore di me quanto ai auto verghongna."

108. On the relationship between economic opportunities and filial autonomy, see Cutileiro, *Portuguese Rural Society*, p. 119; Jan Brögger, *Montevarese: A Study of Peasant Society and Culture in Southern Italy* (Oslo: Universitetsforlaget, 1971), pp. 100–101; and Philip J. Greven, Jr., *Four Generations: Population, Land, and Family in Colonial Andover, Massachusetts* (Ithaca: Cornell University Press, 1970), esp. pp. 123–158.

109. David Herlihy, "Deaths, Marriages, Births, and the Tuscan Economy (ca. 1300–1550)," in *Population Patterns in the Past*, pp. 147–148, 158; Herlihy and Klapisch, *Les toscans*, pp. 211–214, 489, 508–509.

110. Alberti, *Cena familiaris*, p. 348. Idem, *De iciarchia*, p. 277.

111. Ibid., p. 275.

112. Note especially Alberti's sacral terminology in the following passage: "Questo apparecchio e lautizie della mensa ha in sé venerazione, e quasi possiamo dire che la mensa sia come ara sacrata alla umanità, e che 'l convito sia in parte spezie di sacrificio e religiosa comunione a confederarsi con fermissima carità. E per questo dire' io che ne' conviti de' giovani e' vecchi vi bisognassero in luogo del sacerdote, come per altro, sì *etiam* per ornamento del convito" (ibid., pp. 257–258). Of course, it was entirely appropriate for the father, whose position (as defined by *patria potestas* and the image of the second god) was sacred, to act as the priest at this communion. If he left the status of father behind before coming to the meal, his position was, in fact, only enhanced by participating in it.

113. Herlihy and Klapisch, *Les toscans*, p. 550.

114. For an excellent discussion of the establishment, cultivation, and use of various ties of kinship, friendship, marriage, and neighborhood in Florence, see Christiane Klapisch, "'Parenti, amici, e vicini': Il territorio urbano d'una famiglia mercantile nel xv secolo," 953–982. See also the comments of Bell, *Fate and Honor*, pp. 73–77, on the meaning of *famiglia*.

115. In this regard, note the remarks and supportive evidence of Dale Kent, *The Rise of the Medici: Faction in Florence*, pp. 19–28, 193–196.

116. Davis, *Land and Family in Pisticci*, p. 22.

117. Manoscritti 85, fol. 101r: "E più detto dì facemo chompromesso noi, Nerone di Nigi di Nerone et Dietisalvi suo figliuolo, in messer Giovanni sopradetto, et lodò et sentenziò che che [sic] Nerone sopradetto m'assagneria la mie dota, cioè fiorini 1300 d'oro in sulla bottegha, cioè che ogni chosa che fosse in detta bottegha s'intendessi essere mio, eccepto che fiorini cento d'oro che voleva ne fossono suoi, et tutte chose di mia chamera et panni di dosso di me et della mia donna, et tutti i libri me truovo nel mio, et avenché che tutte queste chose non agiugnessono alla somma sopradetta, niente di meno fui chontento per uscire de' noia, et renunzai et chonfesessai avere ricevuto tutta la quantità sopradetta. E più m'obligai che stando in chasa con Nerone io darei ogn'anno a detto Nerone per le spese di me et della mia donna fiorini

cinquanta d'oro per ciaschuno anno et ad altro non volevo essere tenuto." The emancipation and arbitration are preserved in Notarile A671, fol. 381v (5 February 1434). Dietisalvi's brother Lotterio was also emancipated, but since he was not present, his emancipation took place through the offices of a *procurator*, Bastiano di Giovanni di Loncello. The arbitrator was the lawyer Giovanni di Girolamo Buongirolami.

118. Bernardo Masi housed his brother-in-law under terms similar to those undertaken by Dietisalvi Neroni. Manoscritti 88, fol. 143r.

119. The emancipation of Piero and Bartolomeo Masi, for instance, also led to an arrangement of rights and obligations between the sons and their father, affecting both shop and home. Cf. Masi, *Ricordanze*, pp. 148–149.

120. Manoscritti 85, fol. 101v.

121. Niccolini di Camugliano, *Chronicles of a Florentine Family*, pp. 154–156. Especially interesting is her translation of the entry in Paolo's *ricordi*: "'A record that my son Lodovico intended, with my good will and consent, to live separately from me and from my other sons and the rest of the family. As it is a natural thing that every one should fervently seek to have liberty, and because it appeared to me that the said Lodovico knows how to behave himself and to manage his own affairs in every contingency I have not objected, for the said reasons, though it is not possible that a separation of the kind should not grieve one, especially when sons are obedient, and without vices.'" Record of the emancipation appears in Notificazioni 8, fol. 120 (29 November 1466).

122. See Chapter 3, Note 22. Referring specifically to Lapo's use of the term, Christian Bec (*Les marchands écrivains: Affaires et humanisme à Florence, 1375–1434*, p. 326) determines that *cautela* carried a negative connotation in the sense of caution and cutting risk.

123. CS, 2nd ser., 2 (Ricordanze di Nicolò di ser Ventura Monachi), fol. 69v: "Trovossi che il dì che Consiglo, Jacopo, et Niccolò confesserono la dota della decta Margherita, il decto Consiglo vendè alla mogle, cioè a monna Ermellina, la metà per non diviso del podere da Macia per iiiiᶜ fiorini d'oro, cioè nel decto anno di febraio. Onde poi a chiare et instantia di me Nicolò, per istornare lo'nganno, Consiglo manceppò i decti suoi figluoli, et monna Ermellina donò loro la decta metà per non divisa sichè'l decto podere è nell'obligo della dota."

124. Herlihy, "Family and Property," p. 17, views these emancipations as dismantling the patrimony to launch the young men's careers. This view, however, overlooks the sad state of Matteo's finances as seen in his accounts and cannot explain the emancipation of his daughter. See *Il libro di ricordanze dei Corsini*, pp. 65–75, 89–93.

125. CS, 2nd ser., 9 (Ricordanze di Luca di Matteo da Panzano), fol. 3v: "Richordo chome detto dì Tolto d'Antonio di messer Lucha rifiutò l'eredità di monna Maria, figliuola fu di Nofri Busini e donna fu d'Antonio sopradetto. E di poi sentì anche da Tolto detto che Antonio di messer Lucha l'aveva manceppato. . . . E a dì Antonio mancieppò la Mea et detto dì la Mea prese l'eredità di monna Maria sua madre. . . . Richordo chome a dì xi di dicembre, 1414 la Mea, figliuola d'Antonio di messer Lucha da Panzano, emanceppata et non è

maritata, o maritata non n'era ita a marito, prese l'eredità di monna Maria sua madre, non istante vivento Antonio suo padre. E questo si fe' in verità per difendere i beni d'Antonio suo padre perchè fatti del suo bancho istavano male."

126. Panc. 134, fols. 1v–2r. These events took place in 1369 and 1371. Since he records his birthdate as 7 May 1354 (fol. 1r), Bartolomeo was only fifteen at emancipation but had reached the age of majority when he acted on behalf of his father and his family in 1372.

127. AD 190/3, fol. 26v: "A dì 4 di maggio 1471 maciepai messer Nicholò mio figliuolo e à chonsetigli la donagione ⟨che⟩ fecie monna Nanna mia madre 1453. Fu roghato della maciepagione ser Domenicho di ser Santi nottaio al podestà, per piatire chontro Arrighieri Charnccii merzaio per torno. E volla fare e chosì s'è fatto per salvare la roba a me e a mie figliuoli della forza e inghanni." This manuscript contains both the *ricordi* of Guido and his son Giovanni. Ibid., fols. 28v–29r. The actions of Giovanni and Piero are described as follows: "E più sodò detto Giovanni e Piero mio figliuolo fiorini 44 di di [sic] paglie, e fiorini 102 sa⟨ra⟩nno avere dal bancho di Bono di detta dotta per paghargli in chomune per levarmi da spechio. Tocha a paghare alla chasa per eratta. Non ano vuoluto sentire nulla di sodare se no, e sopradetti per lla intengione frodolente chontro a me e lla dona il Dio gli meritti sechondo el dovere o ragluagliargli." Domenico was emancipated 12 December 1482 (ibid., fol. 35r). The dispositions of 1488 are found in Giovanni's *ricordi* (ibid., fols. 12r–12v).

128. PR 176, fols. 47v–48r (17 June 1485). Niccolò had, in fact, been emancipated for some time—since 1470, when, according to the registration, he was already 22 (Notificazioni 9, fol. 21v [27 February 1470]).

129. Information on the Pollini is contained in Herlihy and Klapisch, *Les toscans*, pp. 608–609 and the appurtenant notes.

CHAPTER FOUR

1. The volumes of the two registries utilized are the following: Mercanzia 10819 bis (9 August 1355–24 July 1381); 10819 bis² (31 July 1381–10 May 1399); 10820 (15 May 1399–22 May 1416); 10820 bis (22 December 1417–); Notificazioni 1 (24 January 1422–31 December 1428); 2 (4 February 1429–7 March 1436); 3 (4 April 1436–23 February 1443); 4 (28 March 1443–22 April 1444); 5 (20 June 1444–28 January 1451); 6 (11 February 1451–13 January 1457); 7 (22 January 1457–4 August 1463); 8 (18 August 1463–14 July 1469); 9 (15 July 1469–24 April 1476); 10 (27 April 1476–7 February 1482); 11 (8 February 1482–20 December 1487); 12 (21 December 1487–25 October 1494); 13 (3 January 1495–26 March 1501); 14 (31 March 1501–14 October 1506); 15 (23 October 1506–17 August 1512); 16 (19 September 1512–23 March 1518); 17 (14 April 1518–20 February 1534). The dates I have given for the volumes of the communal registry differ from those given by Demetrio Marzi, *La cancelleria della repubblica fiorentina*, p. 524. He did not notice that from volume 3 on, the registry ends not with notifications of emancipation but with notifications *causarum inopie*. I have given the inclusive dates for emancipations only.

2. Most of the emancipations (around 75 percent) entered in only one of

the two registries involve parties not resident in Florence itself. Not surprisingly, the first year of concurrent operation of both registries saw a fairly substantial proportion of single registrations: five of 33 in the commune's registry and eight of 36 in the Mercanzia's books. Of the total 41 emancipations for 1422, then, eight (19.5 percent) were invalid legally and would not have been detected without crosschecking the Mercanzia registry. A check of the data for 1431 reveals six of 27 Mercanzia-recorded emancipations not found in the communal register (six of 29 in total being 20.7 percent), but the percentage has fallen quite low by 1443, when only 7.8 percent (four of 51) are recorded solely with the Mercanzia.

3. Valorino di Barna Curiani emancipated three of four sons on 29 January 1397, but, he noted, "la detta manceppagio non valse perchè non si portò alla merchantantia secondo gli ordini del comune di Firenze" (Manoscritti 77, fol. 26v). Another example is in AD 190/3 (Ricordanze di Giovanni di Guido Baldovinetti), fol. 29r.

4. Some examples of duplication are: Notificazioni 3, fols. 63r and 64v (12 and 26 August 1439); Mercanzia 10819 bis, fols. 162r and 162v (22 March and 4 April 1373). The most outstanding example of a long-term duplication is the emancipation of Cosimo and Lorenzo di Giovanni de' Medici. The first emancipation was 22 February 1404 (Mercanzia 10820, fol. 88v [29 February]), the second 23 August 1413 (ibid., fol. 251v [1 September]).

5. Notarile N4 (1492–1494), fol. 34r (7 July 1492). In the sixteen books of the notary ser Andrea di Cristofano Nacchianti (N1–N4) (1466–1509) that I consulted, I found 61 unregistered emancipations; only 17 of the 61 involved emancipation alone (at least as revealed in Nacchianti's pages).

6. Nello's emancipation (when he was 30) is recorded in Mercanzia 10820, fol. 76r (12 May 1403). The others (in order) are found in: Mercanzia 10819 bis², fol. 178r (17 September 1392); Notificazioni 1, fol. 52r (24 August 1425); ibid., fol. 15r (19 August 1422).

7. An example involving a member of the Panciatichi can be found in Notificazioni 4, fol. 27r (7 April 1444).

8. To pick two years when there were few emancipations, the city parishes of Ognissanti, San Felice, Santa Reparata, San Pier Maggiore, San Frediano, Santa Trinita, San Simone, Santi Apostoli, San Jacopo were represented in 1358. Rural locales included Monteficalli, Quintole, Martignana, San Lorenzo di Piano, San Quirico da Capalle, Monte Marciano, Quinto, and Settimo. In 1425, urban emancipations came from Santa Maria Novella, San Pancrazio, Ognissanti, San Michele Bisdomini, Santa Lucia de' Magnoli, San Felice, San Pier Maggiore, Santa Felicita, San Lorenzo, Santa Maria Maggiore, Santa Reparata, Santa Maria Sopr'Arno, San Simone. Rural areas were Borgo San Lorenzo, Borgo San Piero a Buggiano, Chianti, Terra Nuova, Rasoio, San Lorenzo Acona, Impruneta, Pistoia, San Miniato, and Gambassio.

9. See David Herlihy and Christiane Klapisch, *Les toscans et leurs familles*, on life expectancies (pp. 200–201), ages at marriage (pp. 205–206, 404), proportion of children in the population (pp. 370–378), and on some crucial differences between getting a start in the city and in the country (pp. 411–414).

10. On the recovery from the plague, see Alberto Benigno Falsini, "Fi-

renze dopo il 1348: Le conseguenze della peste nera," 486–503.

11. Herlihy and Klapisch, *Les toscans*, p. 191, give a list of plague years in Florence.

12. On the early history of the dowry fund, see Julius Kirshner and Anthony Molho, "Dowry Fund and the Marriage Market in Early *Quattrocento* Florence." Herlihy and Klapisch, *Les toscans*, pp. 43–45, 97–99, discuss a variety of evasionary tactics that presented problems in utilizing the *catasto* data.

13. Population trends in Florence and Tuscany are studied by Herlihy and Klapisch, ibid., pp. 165–188, and their findings have been utilized here and throughout.

14. Examples are: Mercanzia 10819 bis, fol. 4r (4 November 1355 Zanobi di messer Jacopo di Amiere emancipated Piera, 8 November his brother Filippo emancipated monna Gheta), fol. 6r (20 January 1356 Filippo emancipated Symone); Notificazioni 5, fols. 34v–35r (4 and 23 December 1445); Notificazioni 7, fols. 110v, 111v, 112r (19 and 24 September 1460).

15. Herlihy and Klapisch, *Les toscans*, pp. 354–369, discusss the problem of rounding off ages in the *catasto* and the variations in numerical exactitude by social position, sex, and residence. All of these problems apply to the ages given by Florentines at emancipations, with the added factor of the legal significance of the ages. As a result, the age data has been treated only with reference to the legally significant age intervals. Some ages were rendered precisely, but generally ages carried only a legal meaning. To say a child was seven was to say he or she could be emancipated. To say he or she was over 18 was to say that all legal capacities were available without recourse to guardianship. Designations as *adultum* or *adultam* have been interpreted as meaning over 18; *etatis legitime* and similar phrases have been ignored because they are too vague. Female marital status has not been considered indicative of age.

16. This source is briefly described in Herlihy and Klapisch, *Les toscans*, pp. 357–358. The data has been computerized, and I owe a debt of gratitude to Professor Herlihy for sending me a copy of the printout. The data in Table 5 is derived from a comparison of this printout with the emancipation registries.

17. In fact, there is a nice increase in the average age across the years in question. For those emancipati that I could locate in the printout, in 1416, average age was 15.9; in 1418, 18.8; in 1419, 17.1; in 1420, 19.9; in 1421, 21.2; in 1422, 20.9; in 1423, 18.0; in 1424, 21.1; in 1425, 23.3; in 1426, 24.3; in 1427, 28.9; in 1428, 22.6; in 1429, 22.3.

18. David Herlihy, "Deaths, Marriages, Births, and the Tuscan Economy (ca. 1300–1550)," p. 152. Age of males in the city was 30.0 in 1427, in the *contado* 25.5. The age in the city rose to 30.5 in 1458 and to 31.4 in 1480.

19. The last decade's figures in Table 1 reflect the fact that the recording notary suppressed all extraneous information. I have taken the titles *monna* and *domina* used there as designating a married woman.

Legal and social historians have often maintained that a woman was emancipated at marriage. Emancipation of married and widowed daughters, if nothing else, shows that such was not the case. Marriage placed the woman in the *manus* of her husband, according to the civil law, but with respect to her family of origin, she remained agnate and *in potestate*. See my "Women, Marriage, and *Patria Potestas* in Late Medieval Florence," *Tijdschrift voor Rechtsgeschiedenis* (in press).

20. The legal norms governing the restitution of dowries were, quite simply, that the husband kept the dowry if the wife predeceased him and there were no children. If he died first, the dowry had to be returned to her. The dowry passed to the children, if any, but the wife took it with her if she remarried. If the woman were not emancipated, her father was able to gain some measure of direct control over the dowry. Cf. Manlio Bellomo, *Ricerche sui rapporti patrimoniali tra coniugi: Contributo alla storia della famiglia medievale*, pp. 180–220. On female mortality in Florence, see Alan S. Morrison, Julius Kirshner, and Anthony Molho, "Life-Cycle Events in Fifteenth-Century Florence: Records of the Monte delle doti," 487–492.

21. Examples: Mercanzia 10819 bis, fol. 16r (23 August 1358, father at San Piero a Quintole, son at San Andrea a Rovenzano); ibid., fol. 83v (27 October 1366, father at San Miniato al Tedesco, son in San Michele Bisdomini of Florence); Mercanzia 10819 bis², fol. 108²v (1 December 1388, Ognissanti and San Lorenzo); Mercanzia 10820, fol. 148r (22 October 1407, Laterino and San Lorenzo of Florence); Notificazioni 1, fol. 7r (10 March 1422, Santa Maria di Coverciano and San Piero a Quintole); Notificazioni 9, fol. 268r (24 April 1476, Fiesole and San Pier Maggiore).

22. Some few notifications to the Mercanzia in the first 30 or so years do show what the *praemium* was. See Mercanzia 10819 bis, fols. 21r (7 November 1359), 24r (11 March 1360), 62r (21 February 1364), 133v (7 May 1371), 252v (4 February 1380); Mercanzia 10819 bis², fols. 41v (14 May 1384), 78r (11 October 1386).

23. Examples: G212 (1430–1433), fol. 23v (7 August 1430); N4 (1492–1494), fol. 57v (11 October 1492); B1238 (1300–1338), 4 March 1338; C479 (1374–1377), fols. 137r–137v (15 June 1375); G330 (1416–1417), fol. 266r (25 April 1417).

24. B1186 (1468–1471), 14 March 1470. In the same chartulary, we find an emancipation by Tanai di Francesco de' Nerli (28 July 1470) that similarly brought no *praemium* to his two sons.

25. An example of a later donation is the gift of 300 florins given by Tanai di Francesco de' Nerli to Benedetto (B1185 [1465–1468], fol. 341r [16 October 1467]). There were also gifts by Ghino di Manetti di Ghino Buondelmonti (A374 [1447–1460], fols. 316r–318r), by Dino di Cambio di Mono (P392 [1326–1330], 11 January 1327), and by Norfri di Palla Strozzi (G321 [1379–1380], fols. 211v–214v).

26. *Il libro di ricordanze dei Corsini*, pp. 66–67.

27. This remark is based on statements like the following: "Omnia et singula superlectilia, masseritias, et peculium existentia penes dictos filios suos" (L268 [1365–1369], fol. 202r–202v) and "omnia et singulas masseritias et superlectilia ac peculium" (ibid., fol. 206r–206v).

28. Any indications that the *lucrum* of a son became his at his emancipation generally hail from the fourteenth century, like the following example where the charter declares that the father gave his son "totum suum mobile et

pecunias, peculium, denarios, pannas, et res omnes, peculium et lucrum quod, quos, et quas habet ipse vel alter pro eo seu in antea acquisiturus erit" (B1344 [1323–1327], fol. 130v (15 March 1327]). Similar indications for the fifteenth century are found in arbitrations awarding sons their earnings, examples of which follow.

29. L268 (1369–1372), fol. 145v (10 September 1371), one piece of farm land. Examples of small monetary gifts are: 5 *lire* (B2768 [1311–1327], fol. 201v [15 August 1324]); 20 *soldi* (U36 [1348–1353], fol. 29v [8 July 1349]); 2 *lire* (M492, fol. 98r [19 August 1339]); 10 *lire* (C430 [1397–1400], fol. 115v [17 July 1399]).

30. To give some idea of the value of money, a *staioro* of grain sold for 17 *soldi* in 1319, for 21 in 1340, and for 30 *soldi* in the famine year of 1346. See Giuliano Pinto, "Firenze e la carestia del 1346–47," 5–6.

31. See Bellomo, *Ricerche sui rapporti patrimoniali tra coniugi*, pp. 15–16.

32. One indication that the gift was considered normal is the fact that Ciliacio di Simone of Borgo San Lorenzo was given ten *lire* as his *praemium* and a house as a *donatio* (made "considerans impensata servitia sibi per infrascriptum Ciliacium filium suum emancipatum facta") (M506 [1372–1386], 10 October 1382). The fact that both gifts were not lumped under the same heading shows that the monetary *praemium* held a character of its own. Other notarial instruments similarly separated the *praemium* from a *donatio* although made to the emancipatus on the same day.

33. J. Davis, *Land and Family in Pisticci*, p. 73. Manlio Bellomo, "Emancipazione (diritto intermedio)," p. 815, ultimately recognizes that not all *praemia* were substantial and that when they were not, they served "a conservare e a perpetuare nei figli tutta la dignità e tutto il prestigio dei quali godeva la famiglia d'origine."

34. See Anthony Molho, *Florentine Public Finances in the Early Renaissance, 1400–1433*, pp. 153–161, who discusses what he terms a "crippling lack of liquid capital" in the 1420s and 1430s.

35. Calculating the correlation coefficient of percentage of *praemia* and average minimum male age at emancipation (from Table 4) through the decades from 1360 to 1499 yields a $-.8785$. This correlation is stronger than that for age and sex, which computes to $-.5654$ for females in the same decades.

36. The most illuminating discussion of the urban/rural relationship is found in Herlihy and Klapisch, *Les toscans*, pp. 109–136, 241–300. See also the remarks of Kirshner and Molho, "Dowry Fund and the Marriage Market," pp. 436–438.

37. The names were taken from the appendix to Lauro Martines, *The Social World of the Florentine Humanists, 1390–1460*. The 308 households were those assessed 10 *lire* or more. Martines' list gives 351 male names (some deceased in 1403). The list does not form a complete roster of the wealthy males, but it is an excellent sample.

38. On the relationship between the age of the head of household and his wealth, see Herlihy and Klapisch, *Les toscans*, pp. 491–499.

39. Again, the names are taken from Martines' lists, and, again, some of

the male names are missing for these households. These lists also present not the actual 600 highest assessments, but the 150 highest of each *quartiere*.

40. Using Herlihy and Klapisch's figures of 9,780 households in Florence and 26,691 in the territory.

41. The 1403 group's activity increased at a rate of .0554, that of 1427 at .2285.

42. Cf. Herlihy and Klapisch, *Les toscans*, p. 45, whose figures show a great increase in *speculum* names in 1432 and 1434.

43. This is by no means to imply that wealth and political power were fully consonant. On the relationship between wealth and political power, see the incisive remarks of Dale Kent, "The Florentine *Reggimento* in the Fifteenth Century," 581–582.

44. A mitigating factor here is the unknown relative extent gauged against the male population as a whole of the politically eligible class and its variation relative to total population over time.

45. G355 (1343–1356), 4 February 1345. G355 (1339–1343), 11 November 1339.

46. N143 (1338–1355), fols. 92r–93r (1 March 1344).

47. G355 (1339–1343), 25 December 1342.

48. F529 (1335–1338), 22 September 1337.

49. U39 (1364–1366), 23 January 1365.

50. C430 (1379–1384), fols. 56r–56v (22 January and 3 February 1382).

51. D78 (1372–1377), fol. 209r (17 June 1376). Other examples are: D83 (1319–1327), fols. 6v–7r (23 August 1319); B765 (1421), fols. 67r–67v (14 July 1421); F486 (1350–1362), fols. 19v–20r (10 November 1351).

52. As one example, Antonio di Lenzoni di Simone gave two sons each 10 *lire* (M332 [1452–1457], fols. 43r–43v [27 May 1454]).

53. A374 (1447–1460), fols. 315r–316r (10 December 1455). Ibid., fols. 398v–400r (1 February 1457). On Poggio's wealth, see Martines, *Social World*, pp. 123–127.

54. A great deal of information on Poggio is readily available, thanks to the documentation gathered by Ernst Walser, *Poggius Florentinus: Leben und Werke* (Berlin: Teubner, 1914), pp. 338–427.

55. See Chapter 4, Note 32.

56. N3 (1487–1489), fols. 151v–152r (5 February 1489): "In eius necessitatibus subvenerunt et cum eorum industria et sudore lucrati sunt pro maiori parte omnium masseritiarum et bonorum mobilium et textorum in domo." Matteo's other son, Francesco, received nothing because 15 years before "recessit de domo dicti Mattei et ipse Matteus eidem Francisco consignavit tot tantumque ius, mobilia, et masseritias adscendentia ad multum maiori de legitima, que fuerunt dos matris dicti Francisci."

57. As in the case of Antonio d'Angelo di Marco of Vactugo, who emancipated his son Andrea in 1497 and gave him his share of the patrimony in view of the fact that Andrea "habitasse seorsum et pro diviso a dicto eius patre pro anno in preterito vel circa et absque bonis vel de bonis dicti Antonii" (G429 [1496–1497], fol. 174r (3 April 1497]). Another example is B832 (1476–1481), fols. 196r–196v (18 April 1479).

58. J. Davis, *People of the Mediterranean: An Essay in Comparative Social Anthropology*, p. 187, attributes such a function to the conditions attached by parents to property given their children.

59. R208 (1387–1389), fol. 143v (18 November 1380). R208 (1379–1383), fols. 423v–425v (2 June 1383).

60. L297 (1373–1377), fols. 149r–149v (28 February 1377).

61. G355 (1334–1339), 6 December 1338: "Hoc pacto quod dicto Bonaventure liceat stare et habitare in dicta domo toto tempore sue vite absque molestia et contradictione dicti Spinellis."

62. N2 (1478–1481), fol. 22v (3 February 1478).

63. B831 (1472–1475), fol. 7r (2 October 1472): "Ipse Vierus donator tempore vite sue possit et sibi liceat exigere ab eius debitoribus et de dictis creditis facere velle suum ac si ipsius donatoris facta non constituit presentem donationem." And ibid., fol. 178v (1 February 1475): "Idem Antonius donatarius teneatur ipsam retinere in dicta domo prout consuetum est fratribus retinere sororem in casu viduetatis."

64. Cf. the obligations placed by Stefano Buontalenti on his son Domenico (N4 [1492–1494], fols. 81r–82r [2 January 1493]) and those placed on Alessandro di Jacopo Alessandri with regard to his mother and sister (M562 [1466–1475], fols. 163r–163v [12 May 1470]).

65. S689 (1438–1440), 1 October 1439.

66. N2 (1474–1476), fols. 129r–129v (6 February 1476).

67. CS, 4th ser., 353, fol. 142v: "Ricordo questo dì iii d'aprile 1499 chome io Marcho di Giovanni di Jacopo d'Ubertino Strozzi ò mancepato Giovanmaria mio figliuolo. . . . E a dì detto detto Giovanmaria à rinunziato a ongni ragione e utile gli potesi pervenire dela mia redità per qualunche modo. E tutto quello à donato Alesandro e Ubertino mia figliuoli e frategli di detto Giovanmaria. E più à rinunziato ale dote de monna Lena sua madre e al presentia mia dona; e di quello gli potese pervenire di tutto à fatto donagione al detto Alesandro e Ubertino suoi frategli e mia figluoli, chome di tutto pienamente apare. . . . E tutta contravantia dele chose facte di mia volontà e licenza e in mia presenza e simile di licenza di monna Lena mia donna, e detto Giovanmaria giurò d'oservare a quanto s'era usi chauto.

"E questo sì fatto, per amore detto Giovanmaria andò fino a dì 7 d'aprile 1498 [sic] nella badia di Settimo a farsi frate." The son later returned and in 1506 entered a wool shop (fol. 140r). Another example is found in A382 (1489–1497), fols. 22r–23v (28 December 1489 and 5 January 1490).

68. N4 (1494–1497), fols. 184r–185r (27 March 1497): "Et considerans qualiter dictus Bartholomeus [Bellandini] pater suus quamplurima substinuit onera in gubernatione dicti sui filii et qualiter non habet in bonis nisi dictam dotem, et est in etate senili constitutus, et volens dicto suo patri subvenire, ut decet, et aliis iustis de causis motus. . . ."

69. N75 (1340–1346), fols. 10v–11r (29 September 1340), provides a fourteenth-century example of a father carefully spelling out the division of the house between his two sons.

70. G694 (1450–1455), fols. 175v–177r (1 August 1455). Note also N4 (1494–1497), fols. 133r–133v (4 November 1496): "Ita volentibus et rogantibus

desiderans, ut decet, litibus que oriri possent inter eos filios obviare et veritati locum esse. Considerans qualiter a nonnullis annis proxime preteritis et citra ipse Angelus una cum prefato Zenobio . . . et Bartholomeo, Antonio, et Francisco aliis filiis legitimis et naturalibus dicti Antonii exercuit artem calzolarii et galigarii et concie ex dicta Sancta Croce de Florentia; et qualiter Zenobius ipse et cum suo patre et fratribus predictis se separavit, dicens nolle cum eis in dicta traffica et exercitio esse vel participare in aliis sed divisim et separatim et de per se trafficare et negotiare. Et ulterius considerans qualiter in dicta traffica seu et debitis et creditis que plurimi in quibus etiam haberet ipse Zenobius participare pro ratha et participando res naturales potius debitor quam creditor, et tantum cum ipse Zenobius et alii sui filii predicti desiderare pro eorum maiori pace dividi et separari etc. Zenobio ad evitanda scandola et non unus pro altero de cetero teneatur. . . . et qualiter Zenobius ipse est ut supra liberatus a debitis dicte traffice et in aliis coequatus, et ita volente et consentiente ipso Zenobio, et dicens alias suorum filiorum et pro maiori pace eorum declaravit quod ipse Zenobius per decem annos proxime futuros non possit pro se vel familia sua vel alius pro eo esse vel habitare in dicta domo vel in possessionibus dicte domus, dictos alios suos fratres molestare."

71. See Francis William Kent, *Household and Lineage: The Family Life of the Capponi, Ginori, and Rucellai*, pp. 132–133.

72. R208 (1379–1383), fols. 120r–122r (17 September 1380).

73. In U43 (1376–1380), 17 and 23 January 1378, we find an arbitration following emancipation, where two emancipati were awarded *praemia* because they received nothing at emancipation and because "conveniens est quod ipsi aliquid habeant de bonis paternis."

74. M534 (1406–1409), fols. 226v–227r, 256r–259r (18 June and 17 August 1408); C187 (1417–1418), fols. 137r–140r (16 December 1417).

75. C187 (1409–1410), fols. 164v–166v (29 October 1410). The arbitrator is described as "volentes amorem paternalem in filium conservare." Another case is that of Felice di Matteo Benedetti, who was adjudged various pieces of land owned by his father in partial compensation for his mother's estate. Felice was given the property because of the need "se alimentandi extra familiam dicti sui patris" (G212 [1422–1429], fols. 25v–28r [25 and 26 June 1422]).

76. P130 (1466–1469), fols. 61r–61v, 63r–64v (25 September and 4 October 1466).

77. R208 (1374–1376), fols. 191v–193r (15 October 1375).

78. G427 (1485–1486), fols. 77r, 87r–87v (12 and 29 December 1485): "Fuisse et esse propriam ipsius Sandri et pro eo ex sua industria ⟨ac⟩quisitam et ad eum pertinet et expectat ut peculium quasi castrense." G212 (1422–1429), fols. 265v–267r (1, 2, and 4 January 1427), records the case of Leonardo di Ridolfo di Taddeo Bardi, who went to arbitration to get possession of a farm actually acquired "ex sua propria pecunia et sua propria industria" but that "pro quadam sui cautela censeri fecit in dictam dominam Paulam eius matrem."

79. Davis, *Land and Family in Pisticci*, p. 43, remarks that "a family may also be a property-holding unit; and—against strangers—the property owned by any individual member is regarded as family property." The implication is that claims to ownership vary with context.

80. A995 (1347–1349), 9 August 1348.

81. Three examples, all involving the estates of mothers or grandmothers, are in C478 (1343–1348), fols. 6v–7v (17 December 1343), 14v–15v (29 February 1344), 24v–25r (14 June 1344). The fact that these three occur in the chartulary of a single notary, ser Francesco Ciai, suggests that he may have acted as an adviser, pointing out this legal maneuver to his clients.

82. See Gigliola Villata di Renzo, *La tutela: Indagini sulla scuola dei glossatori*, pp. 247, 271–272, 303–304, 314–316, 318, 382–383. A study of the social and economic dynamics of the *tutela* is greatly needed.

83. The instances I was able to locate were the following: R208 (1379–1383), fols. 146r–148r (16 December 1380); C187 (1406–1408), fols. 139v–141r (20 April 1408); L269 (1377–1381), fols. 90v–91r (4 June 1380); A653 (1394–1395), fols. 11r–12r (8 February 1395); A657 (1403–1409), fols. 87r–88r (28 May 1404); G210 (1405–1407), fols. 42r–45v (10 May 1406).

84. On *retrait lignagier*, see Paolo Cammarosano, "Aspetti delle strutture familiari nelle città dell'Italia comunale (secoli xii–xiv)," 417–418; Kent, *Household and Lineage*, p. 126.

85. G676 (1300–1303), fols. 73v–74r (22 October 1301).

86. C525 (1437–1455), fols. 305r–309v (13 and 14 April 1450). See also A679 (1454–1458), fol. 93r (21 February 1455). N2 (1474–1476), fols. 69r–70r (21 April 1475), 73v (26 April 1475). Purchases by Giuliano di Giovenco de' Medici and his emancipated son Averardo, canon of the cathedral of Florence, in 1476, and by Lorenzo de' Medici in 1488 also led to emancipations of the vendors' sons to ratify the sales. Cf. C525 (1475–1488), fols. 29v, 40v–41v, 64v–65v, 74r. For Lorenzo G428 (1488–1489), fols. 70r, 72r–72v.

87. Between 1483 and 1505, I found 37 emancipations that included the ratification of a sale by the emancipatus.

88. Examples of fathers' wives: N3 (1482–1484), fol. 69r (6 January 1483); N3 (1489–1492), fol. 30v (21 April 1490); N4 (1494–1497), fols. 182v–183r (19 March 1497); A379 (1472–1475), fols. 62v–63r (12 January 1473); G425 (1473–1475), fol. 168r (20 June 1475). A case involving a brother's wife is in N4 (1492–1494), fols. 24r–24v (30 May 1492).

89. Ibid., fol. 193v (18 March 1494). Similar incidents are in N4 (1494–1497), fols. 141v–142r (5 December 1496); M666 (1481–1492), fols. 91r–91v (20 October 1485); G430 (1502–1503), fols. 143r–143v (2 December 1502).

90. G428 (1488–1489), fols. 199r (13 April 1489), 239r–240r (14 May 1489).

91. Carte cerchi 310 (Libro di ricordanze di Michele di Bindaccio di messer Consiglio de' Cerchi), fol. 18r.

92. On Vieri, see Raymond de Roover, "The Antecedents of the Medici Bank: The Banking House of Messer Vieri di Cambio de' Medici," in *Business, Banking, and Economic Thought in Late Medieval and Early Modern Europe*, ed. Julius Kirshner (Chicago: University of Chicago Press, 1974), pp. 260–266; Gene A. Brucker, "The Medici in the Fourteenth Century," *Speculum*, 32 (1957): 8–10.

93. M506 (1360–1375), fols. 73v–81r: "Quia sunt femine et mulieres et non habeant nec habent qui eadem bona et possessiones laborent, sollicitent, et gubernent, et tum propter locorum distantiam. . . . honerate sunt et ten-

entur ad plura debita persolvendum. . . . magis interest et utilius est dicte Donine vocate Nonne eam habere pecuniam quam dicta bona." We cannot be certain if the emancipation was Vieri's idea, for the same year saw the emancipation of his sister Ginevra (ibid., fol. 92r [3 August]). Cambio's emancipatory activities in 1363 seem to indicate that he was the instigator of the emancipation. Ibid., fols. 120v–121v, 166r–167r (28 June 1367).

94. L39 (1334–1338), fols. 177v–178r (10 April 1336): "Quod dictus ser Angio Dini emancipet et emancipare debeat hodie . . . dictos Franciscum et Donatum filios suos."

95. Baldus, 2 cons. 452, Consilia, fol. 121ra.

96. S639 (1444–1445), fols. 98v, 116r–120v. The heart of the arbitration lay in the following passage: "Et più sono d'achordo che da oggi inanzi ogni uno de' sopradecti faccia per sé et ciò che ogni uno guadagna sia suo, et chosì ogni utile da oggi inanzi ogni uno n'abia a fare a suo modo, et chosì di perdita, di che et dove gli guardi o altra disigratia che quello tale che la facessi l'abia a sodisfare di suo proprio."

97. When Angelo d'Amato da Corte emancipated his son on the eve of his marriage, he gave him some land and 50 lire, payable over the next four years, "ut se et uxorem suam alat et liberos nascituros, ac etiam pro sua legitima portione et pro debito bonorum subsidio sive pro debito iure nature" (F544 [1336–1340], 18 November 1339). Angelo also gave the newlyweds a room in his house and some blankets and freely obligated himself for restitution of the dowry; for his part, the son took on all the onera matrimonii. Another emancipation at marriage, without such elaborate arrangements, is in L267 (1350–1355), fol. 76v (8 August 1354).

98. B1345 (1328–1332), fols. 107v–108v (14 January 1329). A similar occurrence is in B1343 (1348), 8 May 1348.

99. N3 (1489–1492), fols. 44v–45r (14 May 1490); G428 (1493–1494), fol. 130r (1 January 1494); note also AD 11/1, fol. 30r.

100. The figure of 85 percent comes from the correlation of the names of the husbands entered in the first volume of the Monte records with the names of emancipati from 1410–1460 and was calculated and given to me by Julius Kirshner.

101. P392 (1326–1330), 11 January 1327.

102. S687 (1434–1435), 10 February 1436. Niccolò had 20 years before resisting his eldest son's attempt to gain economic independence. This conflict with Domenico is discussed in Herlihy and Klapisch, Les toscans, pp. 608–609.

103. L260 (1440–1447), fols. 139r–139v (4 October 1443): "Superlucratus est in eius exercitio et arte sua industria multas masseritias et certas mercantias quas ipse Marcus habet in eius apoteca." Ibid., fols. 61r–61v, 63r–65r (27 March 1442): "Dictus Matteus teneatur et debeat dicto eius patri in suis indigentiis providere, subvenire, ac etiam dictas eius filias et sorores nutrire et etiam pro dotibus et seu parte ipsarum dotium providere." There is also the case of Antonio di Guasparre di Santo of Anciano who sought his wife's and mother's dowries "ut possit omnino alere se et uxorem et filios suos" (G428 [1488–1489], fols. 37r–39r [4 and 5 May 1488]). In fact, the arbitrator gave An-

tonio his father's land and animals and control of the house so that "substinet onus totius domus dicti Guasparis et vix valeat satisfacere necessariis, maxime quia dictus eius pater est ottuagenarius et ultra et in decrepita etate et habet tres neptas in potestate . . . quibus non est provisio de aliqua dote."

104. G212 (1430–1432), fol. 24v (12 January 1431): "Post dictam emancippationem se cepisse vergere ad inopiam." The emancipation is in G212 (1422–1429), fol. 348r (22 May 1428).

105. Panc. 134, fols. 1v–2r.

106. G212 (1422–1429), fols. 167v (31 October 1424), 454r (10 January 1430).

107. For example, L265 (1381–1384), fols. 12r–12v (19 May 1381).

108. S642 (1450–1451), fols. 519r–522v (14 October 1451). A similar accounting took place two years later between Giovanni di Francesco della Luna and his son Antonio. Antonio received a shop and a farm "quod dictus Antonius stetit pluribus annis in civitate Vinetiarum et ibidem trafficavit et multas quantitates dictus lucratus est, que quantitates perveniunt ad manus et in utilitatem dicti Johannis, et hoc fuit post emancippationem dicti Antonii" (S643 [1453–1454], fol. 410r [10 August 1453]). Antonio's later financial problems gave rise to an important legal opinion discussed in Chapter 5.

109. S646 (1457–1467), 27 January 1467: "Substantia patris debet esse filii iure nature"; "de consensu dicti Mattei et familie sue cum dicta sua familia manet de per se et in alia domo quadam Mattei et quod dictus Jeronimus in aliquibus auxiliari ut possit se et suam uxorem et filios alere." The Bonachetti arbitration is in S689 (1438–1440), 13 January 1440.

110. G617 (1473–1475), fols. 272r–273v (18 May 1475): "In primis cum inveniamus et nobis constet qualiter cum contigisset de proximo dictum Leonardum patrem dictorum Bernardi, Bartolomei, et Cosmi fuisse extractum sorte in capitaneum et pro capitaneo Liburni, et ipsum Leonardum voluisse acceptare dictum officium et ire ad dictam terram Liburni et exercere dictum officium capitaneatus. Quod videntes et intelligentes dicti eius filii et moti amore paterno omnino id denegarent dicto Leonardo eorum patri quoniam est notorium aer in dicto loco est letale et seu valde pericolosum, maxime tempore extivo, et plurimi huc accedentes pereunt, unde temebant ne, si accederet ibi, moriretur. Et ideo instabant et supplicabant ne modo aliquo accederet sed renuntiaret dictum officium, offerentes etiam se soluturos florenos decem qui solvi debent pro renuntiando. Sed ipse Leonardus persistebat in suo proposito de volendo acceptare et accedere, allegando se omnino oportere accedere quoniam cum non haberet unde lucraretur de presenti et esset debitor plurium personarum in et de pluribus summis et pecuniarum quantitatibus quae reciperet eis satisfacere non videbat alium faciliorem modum unde posset habere pecuniam quam istum quam sibi sors dederat. Ex quo dicti eius filii deliberaverunt potius de suo ipsorum proprio satisfacere dictis creditoribus et providere quod dictus Leonardus haberet pecuniam unde posset satisfacere quam pati quod iret ad dictam terram Liburni, ubi temendum erat ne moriretur. . . . Et hoc modo induxerunt eum ad renuntiandum, et sic ipse renuntiavit dictum officium. Cumque eorum sit providere unde dicti floreni ducenti de sigillo restituantur dictis filiis et vel qualiter eis satisfiat, et cognito quod

dictus Leonardus habet intera bona immobilia que multotiens noluit alienare et que consentit dari in solutum dictis eius filiis, ut infra. . . ." The arbitrator was named Francesco di Giovanni Pucci.

111. M562 (1460–1466), 30 November 1465: "In veritate de dictis bonis in premium emancippationis per dictum Matteum traditis dictis eius filiis multa fuerant empta de propria pecunia dictorum eius filiorum. Et ad veritates pro condictione dicti Mattei famosa est discordia inter eum et dictos eius filios et eorum familiam ⟨et⟩ quod dictus Matteus impatiencissimus est et contumeliosus et condit verbis in⟨n⟩umerosissimis ⟨et⟩ afficit dictos eius filios et eorum, et propterea nulla quies, pax, aut concordia inter eos esse potest."

112. One example is F529 (1344–1346), 15 September 1346.

113. Examples: M94 (1363–1367), fols. 10v–12r (4 January 1364); M506 (1349–1359), fols. 169v–170r (13 July 1355); M506 (1360–1375), fol. 92r (3 August 1363), involving Cambio de' Medici and his daughter Ginevra.

114. S435 (1380–1389), 4 February 1387.

115. A succinct definition of dowry can be found in Julius Kirshner, *Pursuing Honor While Avoiding Sin: The 'Monte delle doti' of Florence*, p. 4. An example of a dowry gift to a daughter is in N4 (1492–1494), fol. 57r (11 October 1492), where Giuliano di Francesco Quaratesi gave his daughter a house, adding that it was to go to his sons if she did not marry.

116. On the prevalent tendency to exclude dowered women from inheritance, see Bellomo, *Ricerche sui rapporti patrimoniali tra coniugi*, pp. 163–185.

117. D78 (1372–1377), fols. 11v–14v (27 July and 1 August 1372).

118. Examples: A807 (1408–1413), 24 August 1412; A657 (1403–1404), fols. 6r–7r (14 April 1403); G210 (1405–1407), fol. 153r (5 September 1407); N125 (1400–1413), fols. 221v–225r (2 May 1410); S688 (1436–1439), 30 November 1437.

119. B697 (1320–1324), 21 June 1324.

120. G211 (1412–1416), fols. 104r–104v (29 August 1413); G211 (1417–1421), fols. 43r–49v (8 February 1418); R208 (1374–1376), fols. 224v–225r (10 January 1375); C187 (1406–1408), fols. 95r–95v (7 December 1407); G211 (1412–1416), fols. 14v–15r (21 May 1412); N220 (1350–1361), fols. 139r–139v (12 June 1354); M493 (1362–1364), 23 April 1363; L38 (1318–1326), fol. 318r (4 June 1326).

121. Before 1400, there were L38 (1318–1326), fols. 22v (29 June 1319) and 51v (24 June 1320), and S435 (1380–1389), 26 July 1383. There is a short run of female testaments of 1400 in N125 (1400–1413), fols. 7v–8r (4 August), 20v–21v (26 August), 25v–26v (11 September). A will from after 1400 is in B775 (1449–1453), fols. 94r–95v (16 and 17 December 1450). These emancipations followed by the composition of a will bring to mind the *consilium* of Pietro d'Ancarano discussed in Chapter 1. Sixty-nine of 211 emancipati in 1400 were women.

122. Examples: A657 (1403–1404), fols. 41v–42v (14 November 1403); A659 (1408–1411), fols. 80v–81r (21 November 1409); M94 (1367–1373), fols. 179r–181r (17 January 1373); G210 (1405–1407), fols. 202v–203v (5 February 1408).

123. Examples of females for the period 1355–1421: G326 (1392–1393),

fol. 380v (16 November 1393); G325 (1384–1388), 4 March 1386; M95 (1387–1391), fols. 21r–22v (14 January 1387).

124. G430 (1502–1503), fols. 128r–128v (16 November 1502).

125. L39 (1334–1338), fol. 89r (22 September 1334); A995 (1347–1349), 3 May 1349; M95 (1383–1387), fols. 139r–139v (7 June 1387); G211 (1412–1416), fols. 220r–220v (13 January 1415).

126. N221 (1365–1367), fols. 92v–93v, 116v–121r (29 October and 16 December 1366). In more detail, the *finis* between Piera and Loysio reads: "Affirmans dicta Piera qualiter prefatus Loysius pater fuit et est quampluribus, variis, et diversis debitis et usurari⟨i⟩s et quantitatibus pecunie obligatus quibusdam creditoribus vegentibus ipsum Loysium ad sibi solvendum quantitates predictas sibi debitas . . . intanto quod nisi ipsa talia debita sine more dissendio persolvantur tota ipsius Loysii substantia usurarum ipsarum voragine consumatur, et quod etiam ipsorum debitorum occaxione ipse Loysius capitenens et personaliter in comunis Florentie carceribus . . . quod nisi predictis opportuno remedio oc⟨c⟩urratur se neque dictam filiam nec aliam suam familiam alere posset. Et considerans . . . qualiter prefatus Loysius pecunias vel bona mobilia non habet nec habere sperat ex quibus satisfacere possit debita supradicta, set expedit sibi de suis bonis immobilia ali⟨e⟩nare, et quod ipse Loysius tum alimentis prestandis et pro ipsa Piera citius et commodius dotanda et ad matrimonium producenda infrascripta vult vendere et alienare Dino vocato Chavalchante condam Lapi de Chavalcantibus infrascripta bona dicti Loysii. . . ." On financial arrangements of this type between members of a lineage, see Kent, *Household and Lineage*, p. 127.

127. C525 (1475–1488), fols. 203r–203v (7 and 11 May 1485): "Dicens et asserens se esse etatis annorum decem otto completorum et ultra et . . . se habere plenissimam informationem de omnibus et singulis infrascriptis, videlicet: qualiter dictus Franciscus eius pater iam diu posuit super montem puellarum comunis Florentie certam quantitatem denariorum pro dote ipsius Alessandre adeo quod tempore nuptiis dicte Alessandre dicta dos est quantitas florenorum mille. Et qualiter dicta dos est lucrata. Et qualiter dicta dos non potest solvi nisi postquam dicta Alessandra nupserit et iverit ad maritum et nisi postquam eius vir confessus fuerit habuisse ab officiali . . . dictam dotem . . . et nisi promixit restitutionem dicte dotis in omnem casum et eventum dotis restituende, et propterea obligavit se et sua bona omnia et singula. . . . Qualiter hodie dictus Franciscus eius pater habet ultra dictam Alessandram tres alias filias feminas sine dote. Et qualiter esset quasi impossibile ut dictus Franciscus eius pater posset constituere similes dotes dictis aliis suis filiabus. Caritate et misericordia mota et ad hoc ut dictus Franciscus eius pater possit constituere dotes aliis suis filiis et sororibus dicte domine Alessandre donavit et concessit dicto Francisco eius patri presenti et recipienti pro se et suis heredibus quantitatem florenorum quingentorum ex dicta quantitate florenorum mille dotis predicte dicte domine Alessandre constitute super montem predictum."

I have found 13 other examples of this practice between 1480 and 1506. These examples often refer to the father's love for the daughter in question (as evidenced by establishing her dowry) and to her concern for his finances and familial obligations, as in N4 (1504–1509), fols. 90v–91r (28 February 1506): "Considerans qualiter dictus Dardane pater suus summopere eam dilexit et diligat et illam dotare intendit et vult ipse eius pater ultra vires sui patrimonii . . . et animadvertens etiam qualiter habet quamplurimos filios . . . et quando dictam dotem maternam etiam consequi vellet ipse eius pater una cum dictis eius filiis, nimis dominus haberet patrimonium et substantias eius et deveniret eo casu ad inopiam etc., et intendens ipsa Lisabetta stare contenta dicte doti sibi a dicto suo patre ordinata pro danda eius futuro marito et manutenere et conservare ipsum eius patrem et descendentes suos. . . ."

128. C187 (1406–1408), fols. 187r–187v (5 September 1408).

129. The same may be true of many arbitrations worked out between fathers and sons immediately after emancipation. The intensity of the conflict contained in an arbitration is hard to gauge; even immediate settlements could be erected around a core of real conflict and competition. Lawyers, at least, followed a principle that settlements immediately pursuant to the entrance into arbitration were worked out in advance (and presumably fraudulent if questions were raised). Compare the opinion of Antonio Strozzi in CS, 3rd ser., 41/3, fols. 375r–375v.

130. F300 (1432–1434), 28 May 1432.

131. U43 (1376–1380), 24 April 1380.

132. N1, (1472–1474), fol. 185r (3 July 1474). Additional examples are in A669 (1425–1427), fols. 115r–116r (5 June 1426); and S648 (1464–1465), fols. 119r–120r (21 June 1464).

133. A673 (1436–1439), fols. 86v–87r (8 August 1437), 97r (4 September 1437).

134. G329 (1397), fols. 146v–149v (2 and 23 December 1397): "Considerans infirmitatem incurabilem et perpetuo duraturam in persona sive corpore dicti Matthei, ex qua sive cuius occaxione nedum ipse Mattheus posset deinceps ex eius industria superare victum sed nisi domino nostro Yhesu Christo auxiliante vix poterit pannos aliquos pro suo dosso suis viribus inducere, nec non respiciens ad etatem et modicam sanitatem dicte domine Care. Et etiam considerans quod conveniens est dictam dominam Lisabectam ipsorum filiam pre omnibus debere ipsorum honera supportare. Et adtendens ad promissionem . . . promictendum eisdem Macteo et domine Care ut ex natura et honore tenetur ipsos Macteum et dominam Caram et superviventem ex eis donec advixerint non deserere sed ut patrem et matrem semper honorare, tenere, alere, vestire, regere, et gubernare . . . considerans promissionem per ipsos Macteum et dominam Caram eidem domine Lisabecte in remuneratione dicte sue promissionis . . . de dando eidem domine Lisabecte omnia eorum bona et iura. . . . hiis quidem oneribus . . . ipsius domine Lisabecte et in sua habitatione tenere, vestire, calciare, et nutrire et alimentare ac honorare et eis servire usque ad omnem ipsorum et cuiusque eorum indigentiam."

135. N4 (1504–1509), fols. 41v–43r (3 June 1505): "A dicta domina Ginevra ipse Antonius in eius necessitatibus et infirmitatibus subvenit dicte ipsius Ginevre propriis pecuniis etc. et per eam lucratis in se exercendo serva et famula cum aliis stando, et qualiter ipse Antonius varias alias suas filias et so-

rores dicte Ginevre dotavit et maritavit et, volens ex debito suo cognoscat ipsam Ginevram prout est conveniens."

CHAPTER FIVE

1. See Guido Rossi, *Consilium sapientis iudiciale*, pp. 1–3, 294.

2. On the techniques of interpretation and the place of the *consilium* in the development of the law, see the careful and erudite studies of Mario Sbriccoli, *L'interpretazione dello statuto: Contributo allo studio della funzione dei giuristi nell'età comunale*; Luigi Lombardi, *Saggio sul diritto giurisprudenziale*, pp. 79–199, esp. pp. 139–144; Manlio Bellomo, *Società e istituzioni in Italia tra Medioevo ed età moderna*, pp. 201–210. Ibid., pp. 356–357, reports the example of the exceptionally handsome fee of 100 florins. Lauro Martines, *Lawyers and Statecraft in Renaissance Florence*, pp. 100–101, discusses the nominal statutory-fee structure in Florence and finds that most lawyers received between 1 and 4 florins for an opinion.

3. Here, I follow the closely argued views of Lombardi, *Diritto giurisprudenziale*, pp. 123–145, in contrast to Sbriccoli, *L'interpretazione dello statuto*, pp. 319–320, 388–392, whose emphasis on the political side of the lawyers' role cannot be ignored and will be discussed later.

4. According to Martines, *Lawyers*, p. 492, Bencivenni received his doctorate in 1411, so he practiced only some 12 years. Bencivenni mentions a judgment rendered on 29 December 1420—hence, the date I have provided.

5. Princ. II, iv, 435, fol. 61r (commentary on the statute "De obligatione filii familias etc."): "In § et quilibet, in ver. officiali universitatis. Sed quid si in notificatione non apparuerit quod fuerit facta notificatio officiali, sed in libro simpliciter dicitur quod notificavit, an valeat. Videtur quod non, quia non servatur forma et non probat hoc esse. Pendet in causa d⟨omini⟩ Leonis. . . . In ver. et ipsius emancippationis. Unde respondi quod faciens emancippationem die octava martii et eandem referens dicta die et notificans factam die octava iulii nil agit, quia aut verum fuit et non suffragat tempus, contra 1. accusaturus, de adul. [D. 48.5.36(35)], aut erravit volens addere aliud tempus, et habetur pro non apponente, et non servavit formam, ut si per errorem, ut no. in l. denuntiasse [D. 48.5.18(19)], in causa ser Johannis Martini. Item debet adici etiam annus, nec sufficit annus adiectus in titulo vel libro alternative, l. aut qui aliter, quod vi aut clam [D. 43.24.5], iuncta l. libellorum in prin., de accu., cum si. [D. 48.2.3], et debet poni persona notificatoris; nec sufficit enuntiare emancippationem factam non adiecta persona notificante et officiali requirente, quia hec sunt de forma. Alex." In fact, not every notification carried complete information, as anyone can see by glancing through the registries. Bencivenni's position is also contrary to that taken by his contemporaries Antonio Roselli, Nello da San Gimignano, and Bartolomeo Vulpi (see Chapter 5, Notes 25 and 31). Their opinion may not have been written when Bencivenni wrote his commentary, which may indicate that the commentary dates more precisely from 1420 to 1421.

6. As per Strozzi, CS, 3rd ser., 41/18, fol. 397v: "Statutum curie mercantie civitatis Florentie sub rubrica de obligatione filiifamilias et qualiter pater

pro debito filii teneatur debet intelligi quod pater teneatur pro debito filii quando filius contraxit et se obligavit pro causa mercantie quam exercebat et non pro alio debito contracto extra causam dicte mercantie, ut decidunt Bal. et Saly. in l fi. per illum tex. C. ad mace. [C. 4.28.7]."

7. Princ. II, iv, 435, fols. 60r–60v: "In ver. in aliqua mercantia vel arte tamquam socius vel magister. Ut intellexit supra cum affirmative fuit loqutus, et sic ita demum possit cogi filius familias si steterit in mercantia vel arte ut socius vel magister sicut alius. Et videtur quod possit conveniri quomodocumque steterit in arte vel mercantia, quia de iure comuni potest conveniri filius familias; unde, cum non reperiatur prohibitum ipsum conveniri cum steterit in arte vel mercantia, intelligatur quomodocumque steterit posse, ut sic quam minus potest conrigari ius comune." Ibid., fol. 60v: "Sed solum dubitatur de patre quia supradixit patrem teneri demum si tanquam socius vel magister steterit, nec autem providet patrem teneri etiam si ut discipulus, sed in certis tantum casibus, videlicet si male se gesserit etc. In aliis ergo casibus pater non tenebitur, nisi ut socius vel magister steterit. Sed ipse filius sic, ut primo loco dixi."

8. CS, 3rd ser., 41/18, fol. 397v.

9. Princ. II, iv, 435, fol. 60v.

10. CS, 3rd ser., 41/18, fol. 369r.

11. CS, 3rd ser., 41/17, fol. 132r: "Contractus simulatus est ipso iure nullus . . . et in simulatione probanda sufficit probatio per coniecturas."

12. Princ. II, iv, 435, fols. 16v–17r: "Numquid stans in bonis iure familiaritatis possit conveniri ut heres, dic quod non, si ille pro quo stat in bonis possidet talia bona civiliter et naturaliter. Ergo sic videtur iure familiaritatis stans in bonis non potest possidere aliquo iure. . . . Restat videre an videat tenere, et videtur quod sic, quia omnis insistens rei videtur tenere, nam hoc verbum tenere largum est. . . . His non obstantibus, dicendum est contrarium. Ratio est quia quidam vero sunt detentores simpliciter, non possessores, sed ipsi presentant se possidere vel se dominos esse, sed nec possident quia alius possidet. . . . Quidam vero sunt qui nec possident neque tenent, usum tamen iure habentes sed non firmiter, ut puta habitatores et familiares, et iste est casus noster, nam filius, licet emancippatus, cum patre in domo paterna habitans nec possidet nec tenet, nam tenere est saltem custodiam rei here⟨ditatis⟩ . . . nam statutum istud debet intelligi quando tenet ratione sui iuris, non quando nullum ius habet in re." Salvetti's similar statements are in Princ. II, iv, 434, fols. 61v–62r.

13. This principle appears later in several of the *consilia* discussed. For the present, we note the statement of Strozzi, a lawyer much involved in cases dealing with this statute, that "statutum loquens de cessantibus et quod filii teneantur pro debito patris cessantis est odiosum et debet stricte interpretari. Ita consuluit Decius in con. 38 col. pen. et fi. vol. primo, ubi dicit quod ad hoc ut filius obligatur pro patre cessante requiritur quod pater vere sit convictus et condemnatus et non per contumaciam, et ibi etiam dicit quod si statutum loquitur de patre non habet locum in avo, et subiungit quod quando quis ex facto alterius convenitur mitius punitur et fortiores requiruntur probationes quam si ex facto proprio conveniatur" (CS, 3rd ser., 41/18, fol. 399v).

14. Princ. II, iv, 435, fol. 103r.

15. Ibid., fol. 17v: "Si enim essent bona aliena, puta filiorum emancip-patorum devoluta ad eos ex latere matris, licet tenta per patrem, posset licite per filios post obitum possidere absque timore immissionis, ut l. pro herede in prin. et § si quid tamen, de acquir. her. [D. 29.2.20], alioquin indebite damnum pateretur contra tex. l. iulianus § fi., eo t⟨itulo⟩ [D. 29.2.42]."

16. Princ. II, iv, 434, fol. 64r: "Ego autem sepissime consilia dedi et praticari feci a pluribus testatoribus qui instituant feminam heredem, vel nepotem parvum, vel alium atinentem, qui non possit capi. Et filium iusserint contentum esse eo quod habuit in vita, ut in premio emancipationis, vel pro studio, vel pro nuptiis, et similibus. Et tunc quia hereditas non defertur ei filio, non debet sibi obstare statutum, cum velit illum affici cui hereditas deferetur ex testamento vel ab intestato. Et similiter si nil relinqueret, si aprobaret testamentum vel quia presens et consentiens, vel cursu temporis, per l. filio de preterito, de inoffi. testa. [D. 5.2.16], et quod no. in auth. ex ea [*C. 3.28.6], et tutius remedium est hoc ut possit tenere bona absque preiudicio dicti statuti."

17. Martines provides a useful account of the sources in *Lawyers*, pp. 450–455, and profiles of Florentine lawyers, pp. 481–509.

18. Mag., xxix, 187, fols. 52r–53r.

19. Mag., xxix, 193, fols. 137r–152v. The manuscript preserves the originals with seals.

20. Roselli signed his *consilium* as "legens ordinarie iura civilia in civitate Florentie," which he did, according to Martines (*Lawyers*, p. 500), from 1422 to 1423. Again, according to Martines (pp. 499–501), Nello taught in Florence from 1421 to 1423 and Paolo di Castro was there from 1413 to 1424 and Vulpi began teaching in Pavia in 1421. 1421 to 1422 would have been about the time that the four could have been available as a group.

21. Roselli also later explicitly connected the authority of notaries in Bologna with that in Florence (see Chapter 5, Note 24). Of the other three, only Paolo di Castro mentions Bologna and that in a passage where he denies that the authority of a Bolognese notary in *iurisdictio ordinaria* is limited to Bolognese territory.

22. The introductory comments made by Paolo di Castro, Nello, and Bartolomeo Vulpi reveal that the order of the *consilia* in the manuscript is the order in which they were given. It is also the order of discussion followed here.

23. Mag., xxix, 193, fol. 137r: "Iudices qui vocantur cartularii nullam habent iurisdictionem ex solo tabelionatus officio, nisi quatenus eis esset in eorum privilegiis expressum."

24. In fact, Florentine law as codified by Vulpi and di Castro in 1415 did expressly give notaries *auctoritas* in emancipations: Statuta 1415, lib. 2, rub. 112, p. 204. However, the wording of the pertinent Bolognese statute provided in the *punctus* does not carry the crucial passage from the Florentine version, which stated clearly that a matriculated notary "possit authoritatem interponere emancipationibus." The Bolognese version did state that "quulibet [sic] iudex legista . . . habeat autoritatem et ordinariam iurisdictionem in emancipatione" (fol. 145r), but of notaries, it said only "quilibet notarius . . .

possit . . . dare mundualdos cuilibet mulieri petenti et tutores et curatores pupillis et adultis si privilegium habuerit eos dandi" (fol. 145v). Ibid., fol. 138r: "Sed notorium est, ut audio, Bononie sicut in civitate Florentie, quod tabeliones emancipationibus decreta interponunt, ergo valet eorum interpositio quia ex consuetudine potest dari talis facultas." The argument is based on direct reference to the Corpus, especially D. 5.1.1 and C. 2.46.3, and Bartolus' commentary on the latter.

25. Mag., xxix, 193, fol. 140v.

26. Ibid., fol. 141v: "Sola causa coniuntionis non est suficiens presumtio fraudis."

27. Ibid., fol. 142r: "Nam non dicuntur bona in quibus recipiuntur detinere vel possidere, sed potius in eis ipsi ospites et familiares detineri et possideri, si enim detinent, detinent sicut asinus sellam detinet." And ibid.: "Filippus potest tueri se ipsum quia emancipatus erat et bona sibi elargita."

28. Ibid., fol. 143r: "Interponere autoritatem emancipationibus est de mixto imperio minimo et competit civilibus magistratui municipali." Ibid., fol. 144r: "Esset enim per quas ridiculum si ipse conficeret instrumentum de emancipatione coram se facta et alius de autoritate ab eo prescita, et frustra fit per plura etc."

29. Ibid.: "Id est, quod emancipatio deducatur in publicum et in notitiam volentium cum eo contrahere."

30. Ibid., fol. 149r: "A comuni stilo qui cotidie observatur in locis enim in quibus notarii ius reddunt, conficiunt et publicant actus suos quos faciunt ut iudices."

31. Ibid., fol. 149v: "Notificatio requiritur ut sciatur emancipatio et fraus creditoribus fieri non possit, sed iste effectus resultavit ex his que facta appareat, ut de se patet, igitur satisfactum est statuto."

32. Ibid., fol. 150r: "Quod maxime verum est, quia propter longam distantiam temporis emancipationis a ruptura cessare videtur omnis fraudis prescriptio."

33. Ibid., fol. 152r: "Apparet ergo emancipatio defensata potest probabiliter dici in casu nostro cessare statutum, non nititur enim ex emancipatione tantum de qua loquitur statutum sed de emancipatione cum cursu temporis iuncta et coroborata. . . . Cum ergo in casu nostro intervenerit plusquam decennio, emancipatio erat roborata et sic cessabit statutum loquens de simplici emancipatione." Ibid., fol. 152v.

34. CS, 3rd ser., 41/5, fols. 208r–211r. The document is a *consilium*, but it lacks any signature or indication of authorship. It is in Antonio Strozzi's hand, but I do not believe it is his. Ibid., fol. 210r.

35. One such example is mentioned in the *punctus* to an interesting case, which I intend to discuss more fully elsewhere, contained in Landau-Finaly 98, fol. 410r. The invalidity of the emancipation and *praemium* from failure to register in this case was overcome by a second emancipation that was properly registered with the Signoria.

36. CS, 3rd ser., 41/7, fols. 1r–6r. I have been unable to locate any information about this jurist. Ibid., fol. 6r: "Cum ergo Jacobus fateatur se iurasse in emancipatione, ergo fatetur se fuisse emancipatum. Et si modo negat eman-

cipationem, est sibi ipsi contrarius et varius et non debet admitti ad negandum quod sua voce prius confessus est."

37. The *consilium* is found in a copy in Biblioteca Apostolica Vaticana, Urb. Lat. 1132, fols. 375r–380r.

38. The full names are omitted in the *consilium*, making identification uncertain. However, a search of the emancipation records in the 1440s and 1450s turned up only one possible candidate as the party in question. Notificazioni 5, fol. 39r, records the emancipation on 14 February 1446 of Francesco di Jacopo di Tedaldo [the emancipator] di Bartolo Tedaldi. Both of Francesco's brothers were emancipated in subsequent years: Leonardo on 18 December 1450 (Notificazioni 5, fol. 172r) and Bernardo on 5 October 1454 (Notificazioni 6, fol. 111v).

39. Niccolini had concluded (fol. 377v): "Stamus ergo regule dicenti ut donatio facta per patrem vel avum filio vel nepoti emancipato revocari non possit nisi in casibus expressis. . . . Tenuit enim emancipatio ut supra plene discussum est, et illius emancipationis notificationem valuit facta infra tempora sua post ipsam emancipationem et reddit talem emancipationem vallidam ut ex tempore emancipationis."

According to Accolti, "dico talem donationem valuisse quoniam emancipatio ab initio fuit vallida. Sed statutum anullat illam si postea non sequatur notifficatio, et talis dispositio statuti est resolutiva. Unde sicut condictio resolutiva posita in contractu non suspendit eius effectum . . . eodem modo talis dispositio statuti non suspenditur virtute emancipationis quia emancipatio tenuit a principio" (fol. 379v). Ibid., fol. 380r.

40. Mag., xxix, 193, fols. 30r–32v. The manuscript preserves the original. Baldassare d'Antonio di Santo was emancipated 28 February 1407. The emancipation was recorded in the Mercanzia registry (Mercanzia 10820, fol. 138r) the same day. In the notification the father is designated *civis et mercator.* I was unable to locate the protocol for this emancipation.

Giovanni Mantese, "Il testamento di Raffaele Raimondi da Como (1380c.– 1427)," *Archivio veneto,* 5th ser., 103 (1961): 24–31, offers no indication of when he and Fulgosio (with whom he worked closely and is often confused) were in Florence to give their opinion on the case. The two were in Padua from 1422 to 1426 and in Venice from 1426 to 1427, where both were stricken by the plague. Since Antonio died in 1417, we must assume that the *consilium* was written between that year and 1422.

41. Mag., xxix, 193, fol. 30r: "Post emancippationem de pecunia et bonis ipsius testatoris variis modis et formis habuit et extraxit et in suam baliam pervertire fecit florenos setemmilia auri et ultra." Ibid., fol. 31v: "Quia vigor iuris temperari solet et a comuni iure recedere ut equalitas servetur inter fratres, ne ex inequalitate crescat invidia."

42. Decio, 1 *cons.* 13, *Consilia,* fols. 16vb–18rb. Ibid., fols. 16vb–17ra.

43. CS, 3rd ser., 41/17, fol. 363r.

44. I have not been able to locate the other two opinions. Decio's is found in his *Consilia,* 1 *cons.* 60, fols. 69rb–70rb. The *consilia* must have been written in the period from 1484 to 1501, when all three were alive and in Florentine territory.

45. Ibid., fol. 69vb: "Sed quando non conferendo filii ad aequalitatem potius reducerentur, non debet conferri. . . . Sic etiam in donatione simplici non debet conferri, nisi quando inequalitas resultaret."

46. The opinions, in the sealed original, survive in Princ. II, ii, 376, fols. 183r–189r, 195r–206v, 210r–222r. Registration of Vincenzo's emancipation appears in Notificazioni 16, fol. 38v (13 May 1513).

47. Ibid., fol. 184v: "Quia facta a patre nec iuramento confirmata nec bene meritis precedentibus." Ibid., fol. 189v: "Quia cum eo tanquam filio conversabat, ut dicunt testes. . . . Ex quibus omnibus concludendum videtur Vincentium est admittendum equaliter cum aliis filiis prout de iure vocantur."

48. Ibid., fols. 205v–206r: "Testator fuit motus ad privandum Vincentium bonis suis ex illa ratione quia dictus Vincentius transactis temporibus fecerat multas expensas et extraxerat quedam bona et consumpserat in vita testatoris."

49. Ibid., fol. 222r.

50. Princ. II, ii, 374, fols. 20r–23r.

51. Mag., xxix, 186, fols. 131v–134v.

52. Interestingly, the city's statutes are not mentioned in assembling these arguments. The fact that emancipati were not liable for paternal debts was derived not from Florentine legislation but directly from C. 7.71.3. The Florentine statutes were in accord with the Roman law on this point.

53. Mag., xxix, 186, fol. 132v: "Ceterum non obstantibus predictis contrarium est verius de iure, cuius veritate est premictendum quod confessio vel alienatio facta in utilitatem incapacis per patrem presumitur fieri in fraudem."

54. The gift may have accompanied the emancipation of his son Lorenzo and Lorenzo's son, also named Lorenzo. See Notificazioni 13, fol. 34v (29 March 1496).

55. The sealed copy is found in CS, 3rd ser., 41/12, fols. 147r–152r; another copy in 41/3, fols. 329r–333v.

56. CS, 3rd ser., 41/12, fol. 150r.

57. Ibid., fol. 150v: "Quod talis donatio potest operari alium effectum ad quem effectum verisimiliter creditur facta fuisse donationem predictam."

58. Princ. II, ii, 374, fols. 31r–32r. The text is in his hand, without seal.

59. CS, 3rd ser., 41/14, fols. 98r and 101r–109r. This *consilium* was not used in court, although it is properly signed and sealed, according to Strozzi's appended note: "Libro A, a carta 757, scilicet idem consilium cum subscriptione, sed sunt ibi diversi articuli, licet pro eadem persona" (fol. 109v), and: "Huic consilio se plures doctores subscripserunt, ut patet libro A, a carta 757, et secundum illud fuit iudacatum" (fol. 109v). I was unable to locate this other opinion.

60. Actually, one son (Simone) had been emancipated 19 February 1482, and the others (Galeotto and Francesco) had been emancipated 25 February; see Notificazioni 11, fols. 3r and 6r.

61. CS, 3rd ser., 41/4, fols. 395r–402r. At the top of fol. 396r, Strozzi confesses that he never completed or attached his seal to this document. The substantial arguments are worth exploring, however, as an indication of how he would have handled the case. He may not have completed it because the

emancipations proved fictitious. At least a search of the registries from 1445 to 1487 turns up no emancipations by Bartolomeo d'Antonio Fei.

62. Ibid., fols. 396v–397r: "Et sicut pro filia tenetur dare dotem, ita et pro filio masculo tenetur a pari dare donationem propter nuptias. . . . Donatio enim propter nuptias fuit inventa pro securitate uxoris ut ipsa esset cauta et secura, unde posset dotem recuperare quando veniret casus restituende dotis. . . . Ita tenetur nunc pater facere illam cautam per obligationem suam et bonorum suorum in illis locis in quibus donatio ⟨non⟩ est in usu vel, si est in usu, non sit pro concurrenti quantitate dotis, et sic non potest per talem donationem esse cautam doti."

63. CS, 3rd ser., 41/9, fols. 283r–284v. Again, there is no seal or formal signature. The document may not have been published as a full-fledged *consilium*. Ibid., fol. 283v: "Sed fraudarentur creditores non habentes notitiam de emancipatione, cum putarent habere obligatum patrem et sub illa fiducia confiderent de filio eius."

64. Strozzi here cites a *consilium* by Salvetti in a case involving Giovanni Baroncelli concerning a registration with *minima solemnitas*. The surviving fragment of Salvetti's commentary in Princ. II, iv, 434, does not contain a commentary on rubric 110 of Book 2 of the Florentine statutes; nor does that fragment mention an opinion for Giovanni Baroncelli. I have not found a copy of this *consilium*.

65. Mag., xxix, 186, fols. 179r–179v: "Filium a familia sua per emancipationem separavit."

66. A copy of the *consilium* is contained among Bencivenni's papers in Mag., xxix, 187, fols. 113r–116v. Rondinelli was an active figure in the *reggimento* of the 1410s and 1420s, involved in debates, among other things, on the electoral purses (see Gene A. Brucker, *The Civic World of Early Renaissance Florence*, pp. 271, 314, 329, 335, 377). According to Dale Kent, *The Rise of the Medici: Faction in Florence, 1426–1434*, p. 137, the Rondinelli belonged to the faction in opposition to the Medici, while Taddeo and Filippo dall'Antella were allies of the Medici (p. 88). Ibid., fol. 114r: "Etiam divino iure roboratur dum dantur patres comederunt uvas acerbas et filiorum dentes stupefacti sunt," which is Jeremiah 31:29.

67. Ibid., fols. 114r–114v: "Pro qua conclusione premicto quod de iure divino filius non debet portare iniquitatem patris, non obstante eo quod superius dictum est, quia illud casualiter non dispositive refertur, iure etiam humano et civili dispositum est quod filii pro debitis patris non teneantur, C. ne filius pro patre pro toto [C. 4.13]. Grave enim et iure naturali contrarium est ut unus pro aliorum debitis erigatur. . . . Ex quibus clare infertur quod dicta ordinamenta ut suadeantur rei publice favorabilia, tamen tamquam iure divino, naturali et civili adversantia, quatenus quam contra filios et alios a personis cessantium supra disponunt odiosa, restringenda sunt, non amplianda, ymmo strictissime intelligenda, maxime cum odium irrationabile contineant."

68. In fact, only Bencivenni was on the fringes of the elite (see Brucker, *Civic World*, p. 269, n. 113); the other two were not native Florentines. It must

be allowed, however, that they may have expected or received some work as a result of this or other decisions favorable to the rich and powerful.

69. CS, 3rd ser., 41/11, fols. 216r–219r.

70. Statuta 1415, lib. 3, rub. 2, p. 520.

71. CS, 3rd ser., 41/11, fols. 216r: "Ex sola illa descriptione absque alia declaratione non poterat ab eo exigere." Ibid., fols. 216v–217r: "Volumus trahere declarationem ad tempus debiti in preiudicium filii, et hoc fieri non potest. Ratio est juris apertissima, videlicet ut non coniungantur ista duo tempora, quia talis retrotractio in casu nostro non est aliud quam inductio obligationis de persona patris in personam filii, seu prorogatio de una persona in aliam. . . . Et hoc fieri non potest in casu nostro quia extrema non sunt habilia in modo sicut mutata, et sunt contraria, et fictionem et eius effectum excludunt, nam tempore descripti debiti filius erat in potestate. Sed tamen debitum non erat debitum de quo statutum loquitur; tempore iste declarationis, et sic quando debitum vere causari potuit quo ad eum obligandum, reperiebatur talis qui non efficiebatur debitum ex persona patris, quia emancipatus, et consequenter cum tempore debiti contracti vere esse emancipatus non comprehenditur."

72. Ibid., fol. 217v: "Ideo non debemus coniungere ista tempora ad inducendas tales qualitates odiosas, ut filius portet iniquitatem patris contra ius divinum et contra ius commune . . . maxime cum stricta ratio iuris non patiatur."

73. CS, 3rd ser., 41/12, fols. 199r–202v. The section fols. 201v–202v is in one handwriting and can probably be ascribed to Corsini, whose name appears on the last page. It is not, however, in a normal *consilium* format. The first section, fols. 199r–201r, is in a very poor handwriting and was obviously a working draft. It deals very factually with one case, and my suspicion is that it was never completed. It may be the handwriting of Domenico Bonsi. Substantially the same opinion, in the same handwriting, and again a working draft, is found after Corsini's opinion, fols. 203r–205r.

74. CS, 3rd ser., 41/12, fols. 207r–208v. The *consilium* seems to belong to Bonsi, although it is a copy, and the signature is none too clear. Ibid., fol. 208r: "Sit principale factum ad corrigendum (ius civile), debet indistincte et generaliter et indefinite de omnibus intelligi." "Nec verum est quod ideo filii teneantur pro patre, quia presumantur eos esse in dolo et fraude simul cum patre, quia hec ratio non apparet scripta in statuto, nec esse potest, quia ex hoc sequitur quod similiter debeant teneri ut emancipati maiores, quia non magis constituti in patris potestate debeant dicere fraudem participare, quam emancipati, que limitatur quo ad filios qui non essent presentes."

75. Ibid., fols. 208r–208v: "Insuper verior ratio assignari posset, quia ideo voluit statutum filios affici pro patre, quoniam tam est pernitiosum in parte florentina quod mercatores decoquant et simulante summum contrahentes, quod considerant statuentes verisimiliter patres retrahi a tam pernitioso actu, magis propter hanc penam que filiis infligitur quam pro pena que sibi imponuntur. Forte enim volens fallere creditores, si cognosceret se tantum teneri, consideret aufugiendo vel aliter sibi consulere, qui quando vi-

debit suos filios innocentes teneri, retrahetur ab actu tam pernitioso in parte florentina, cuius potissima utilitas est in habundanti trafficatione seu negociatione suorum civium."

76. CS, 3rd ser., 41/14, fols. 77r–95r; this is the original. Other copies are found in 41/2, fols. 267r–274v (that of Strozzi and Sozzini only); 41/8, fols. 237r–242v (Strozzi and Sozzini only); 41/10, fols. 70r–85r. Strozzi also wrote two summaries of some of the arguments advanced in the final draft: 41/13, fols. 381r–385v, and 41/10, fols. 1r–6v. The latter is designated "pro Francisco della Luna" as is the sealed original. None of the copies give particulars of the case. The very existence of so many copies indicates how important and carefully constructed this opinion was.

77. Decree to appear is in PR 158, fols. 82v–83v, and the law, fols. 83v–84r. Francesco was indeed an *infans* legally at the time of the bankruptcy, his birthdate being listed with the Conservatori delle Leggi as 21 July 1460. Francesco was eventually emancipated on 31 July 1490 (Notificazioni 12, fol. 93v).

78. CS, 3rd ser., 41/14, fol. 83v: "Confirmantur omnia predicta quia statutum est odiosum et exorbitans, igitur in quantum fieri potest restringi debet ut minus corrigat ius commune."

79. Ibid., fol. 86v: "Pro certo omnis interpetratio est admictenda ne filii sine eorum culpa obligentur et puniantur."

80. Baldo Bartolini and Pierfilippo da Corneo were both Perugian lawyers brought to Pisa by Lorenzo de' Medici to teach law from 1473 to 1474. Both later quarreled with Bartolomeo Sozzini and returned to Perugia in 1476 (see *Dizionario biografico degli italiani*, s.v. "Bartolini, Baldo," by Roberto Abbondanza, 6:592–600). These facts would seem to indicate that the *consilia* date from 1474 to 1476; however, Strozzi was only 20 to 21 years of age then. A more likely date may be the early 1490s, after Francesco della Luna's emancipation.

81. CS, 3rd ser., 41/14, fol. 88v: "Ideo non videtur absurdum nec reprehensibile si aliqua iuris subtili ratione restringatur tale statutum et penale et hodiosum hodio inrationabili."

82. A valuable discussion of the role of law in society can be found in Jane Fishburne Collier, *Law and Social Change in Zinacantan*, and in Sally Falk Moore, *Law as Process: An Anthropological Approach*.

83. Among those who have contributed valuable research on lawyers and their activities from the point of view of social structure are Martines, *Lawyers*, esp. pp. 394–395, 410–411, and Sbriccoli, both in *L'interpretazione dello statuto*, pp. 5–10, 73–75, and in his more recent "Politique et interprétation juridique dans les villes italiennes du Moyen Âge," 99–113. For a somewhat contrary viewpoint, see Lombardi, *Diritto giurisprudenziale*, pp. 79–199; Julius Kirshner, "Some Problems in the Interpretation of Legal Texts *re* the Italian City-States"; and the thoughtful comments of E. P. Thompson, *Whigs and Hunters: The Origin of the Black Act* (New York: Pantheon, 1975), pp. 259–267.

84. Lombardi, *Diritto giurisprudenziale*, p. 373, provides a brief definition of jurisprudential creativity.

85. This fact may have been nowhere better appreciated than by the jurists themselves. Note the following statement of Francesco Guicciardini in

his *Ricordi*, p. 122: "E vulgari riprendono e iurisconsulti per la varietà delle opinione che sono tra loro: e non considerano che la non procede da difetto degli uomini, ma dalla natura della cosa in sè, la quale non sendo possibile che abbia compreso con regole generali tutti e casi particulari, spesso e casi non si truovano decisi a punto dalla legge, ma bisogna conietturarli con le opinioni degli uomini, le quali non sono tutte a uno modo. Vediamo et medesimo ne' medici, ne' filosofi, ne' giudicî mercantili, ne' discorsi di quelli che governano lo stato, tra' quali non è manco varietà di giudicio che sia tra' legisti."

86. See, for example, Sbriccoli's discussion of the interpretive principle of *ratio*, *Interpretazione dello statuto*, pp. 280–298. Samuel Kline Cohn, Jr., *The Laboring Classes in Renaissance Florence*, has recently offered a challenging study of class relations. Included in his study is a discussion of criminal prosecutions, in the course of which (p. 182) Cohn observes that Florentine lawyers concentrated their efforts on a shifting civil law rather than the more stable criminal law. I would suggest that the lawyers' concentration on civil law also had an important social dimension—that is, their efforts were in response to the role of civil law institutions in maintaining relations of social reproduction. It is a suggestion in need of further substantiation, and I hope to be able to pursue this issue in subsequent research.

87. A listing of all emancipations involving lawyers would serve little purpose; however, a single example may suffice to demonstrate the involvement of lawyers in the process. Of the four lawyers involved in the landmark decision of 1421—Roselli, di Castro, Nello da San Gimignano, and Vulpi—Nello da San Gimignano was himself emancipated (see Chapter 4, Note 6), and Roselli later emancipated a son (Notificazioni 6, fol. 9r [19 May 1451]).

CONCLUSION

1. According to the notarial language of the emancipation of Giovanni di Testa di Ruffinaccio, C480 (1324–1329), fol. 125r (1 November 1327).

2. On fraternal households and relations, see Francis William Kent, *Household and Lineage in Renaissance Florence: The Family Life of the Capponi, Ginori, and Rucellai*, pp. 29–33, 48–52; David Herlihy and Christiane Klapisch, *Les toscans et leurs familles*, pp. 497–522.

3. On the *fideicommissum* and the patriciate in later Florence, see the pioneering works of R. Burr Litchfield, "Demographic Characteristics of Florentine Patrician Families, Sixteenth to Nineteenth Centuries," 191–205; Samuel Berner, "The Florentine Patriciate in Transition from Republic to *Principato*, 1530–1609," 1–15.

4. Kent, *Household and Lineage*, pp. 136–141, discusses the use of the *fideicommissum* in fifteenth-century Florence. On dating the appearance of the *fideicommissum* in Italy and for a discussion of its legal parameters, see *Enciclopedia del diritto*, s.v. "Fedecommesso (diritto intermedio)," 17:109–114, by Mario Caravale.

5. On the *fideicommissum* and other forms of entail, see J. P. Cooper, "Patterns of Inheritance and Settlement by Great Landowners from the Fifteenth

to the Eighteenth Centuries," pp. 192–327. Cooper notes that the *fideicommissum* was detrimental to creditors (pp. 233, 265), a fact also stressed in the eighteenth century by Alfonso Longo, "Osservazioni su i fedecommessi," in *Riformatori lombardi, piemontesi, e toscani*, ed. Franco Venturi (Milan: Ricciardi, 1958), p. 228, *Illuministi italiani*, vol. 3.

6. On thirteenth-century England, see George C. Homans, *English Villagers of the Thirteenth Century* (Cambridge, Mass.: Harvard University Press, 1941), pp. 129–130, 147–154; Cicely Howell, "Peasant-Inheritance Customs in the Midlands, 1280–1700" in *Family and Inheritance: Rural Society in Western Europe, 1200–1800*, ed. Jack Goody, Joan Thirsk, and E. P. Thompson (Cambridge: Cambridge University Press, 1976), pp. 128–129. On Germany and Provence, see the contributions in *Family and Inheritance* by Lutz K. Berkner, Jack Goody, and David Sabean.

7. A study of these and other strategies used by a single Venetian family has been presented by James C. Davis, *A Venetian Family and Its Fortune, 1500–1900: The Donà and the Conservation of Their Wealth* (Philadelphia: American Philosophical Society, 1975), but see also the review of this book by Julius Kirshner, *Journal of Modern History*, 49 (1977): 505–507.

8. Kent, *Household and Lineage*, p. 300: "Families were living organisms which had a life of their own." In contrast, note the legal definition of the household given in the *catasto* law of 1427 and discussed by Herlihy and Klapisch, *Les toscans*, pp. 60–62.

9. On this theme, see Kent, *Household and Lineage*, pp. 41–61.

10. Cf. Christiane Klapisch, "'Parenti, amici e vicini': Il territorio urbano d'una famiglia mercantile nel xv secolo," pp. 959–960.

11. Cf. Herlihy and Klapisch, *Les toscans*, p. 571.

12. On the political aspect of controlling symbols and meanings, see Pierre Bourdieu, "Sur le pouvoir symbolique," *Annales*, 32 (1977): 405–411; A. P. Cohen and J. L. Comaroff, "The Management of Meaning: On the Phenomenology of Political Transactions," in *Transaction and Meaning: Directions in the Anthropology of Exchange and Symbolic Behavior*, ed. Bruce Kapferer (Philadelphia: Institute for the Study of Human Issues, 1976), pp. 87–107.

13. The role of debt in the dominance of the urban rich over the rural poor is discussed by Herlihy and Klapisch, *Les toscans*, pp. 258–261. Samuel Kline Cohn, Jr., *The Laboring Classes in Renaissance Florence*, pp. 191–192, notes an important shift in the locus of criminal prosecution of debts in Florence in the fifteenth century.

14. Herlihy and Klapisch, *Les toscans*, pp. 245–251.

15. Cf. Paolo Cammarosano, "Aspetti delle strutture familiari nelle città dell'Italia comunale (secoli xii–xiv)," 428.

Bibliography

Alberti, Leon Battista. *The Family in Renaissance Florence.* Translated by Renee Neu Watkins. Columbia: University of South Carolina Press, 1969.

———. *I libri della famiglia.* Edited by Ruggiero Romano and Alberto Tenenti. Turin, Italy: Einaudi, 1969.

———. *Opere volgari.* 2 vols. Edited by Cecil Grayson. Bari, Italy: Laterza, 1960.

Anagni, Giovanni da. *Consilia.* 1534.

Ancarano, Pietro da. *Consilia.* Venice, 1568.

Arena, Jacopo da. *Super iure civili.* 1541.

Azo. *Lectura ad singulas leges duodecim librorum codicis.* Paris, 1581.

Bartolus da Sassoferrato. *Opera omnia.* 10 vols. Venice, 1570.

———. *Opera omnia.* 10 vols. Venice, 1615.

Bec, Christian. *Les marchands écrivains: Affaires et humanisme à Florence, 1375–1434.* Paris: Mouton, 1967.

Becker, Marvin. "Changing Patterns of Violence and Justice in Fourteenth- and Fifteenth-Century Florence." *Comparative Studies in Society and History,* 18 (1976):281–296.

———. "Individualism in the Early Italian Renaissance: Burden and Blessing." *Studies in the Renaissance,* 19 (1972):273–297.

Bell, Rudolph M. *Fate and Honor, Family and Village: Demographic and Cultural Change in Rural Italy since 1800.* Chicago: University of Chicago Press, 1979.

Bellapertica, Petrus de [Jacques de Revigny]. *Lectura codicis.* Paris, n.d.

Bellomo, Manlio. "Comunità e comune in Italia negli statuti medievali 'super emancipationibus.'" *Annali di storia del diritto,* 8 (1964):81–106.

———. "Emancipazione (diritto intermedio)." In *Enciclopedia del diritto,* 14: 809–819. Milan: Giuffrè, 1965.

———. "Erede e eredità (diritto intermedio)." In *Enciclopedia del diritto,* 15: 184–195. Milan: Giuffrè, 1966.

———. "Famiglia (diritto intermedio)." In *Enciclopedia del diritto,* 16:744–779. Milan: Giuffrè, 1967.

———. *Problemi di diritto familiare nell'età dei comuni: Beni paterni e 'pars filii'.* Milan: Giuffrè, 1968.

———. *Ricerche sui rapporti patrimoniali tra coniugi: Contributo alla storia della famiglia medievale.* Milan: Giuffrè, 1961.

————. *Società e istituzioni in Italia tra Medioevo ed età moderna*. Catania, Italy: Giannotta, 1977.

Berlinguer, Luigi. "Considerazioni su storiografia e diritto." *Studi storici*, 15 (1974):3–56.

Berner, Samuel. "The Florentine Patriciate in Transition from Republic to *Principato*, 1530–1609." *Studies in Medieval and Renaissance History*, 9 (1972): 1–15.

Besta, Enrico. *La famiglia nella storia del diritto italiano*. Padua, Italy: 1933. Reprint. Milan: Giuffrè, 1962.

————. *Le successioni nella storia del diritto italiano*. Milan: Giuffrè, 1936.

Boissevain, Jeremy. "Patronage in Sicily." *Man*, n.s., 1 (1966):18–33.

Bonolis, Guido. *La giurisdizione della Mercanzia in Firenze nel secolo xiv*. Florence: Seeber, 1901.

Bourdieu, Pierre. *Esquisse d'une théorie de la pratique*. Geneva: Droz, 1972.

————. "Les stratégies matrimoniales dans le système de reproduction." *Annales*, 27 (1972):1105–1127.

Brucker, Gene A. *The Civic World of Early Renaissance Florence*. Princeton: Princeton University Press, 1977.

————. *Florentine Politics and Society, 1343–1378*. Princeton: Princeton University Press, 1962.

————. *Renaissance Florence*. New York: Wiley, 1969.

Budrio, Antonio da. *Decretalium commentaria*. Venice, 1578. Facsimile. Turin: Bottega d'Erasmo, 1967.

Bullard, Melissa Meriam. "Marriage Politics and the Family in Florence: The Strozzi-Medici Alliance of 1508." *American Historical Review*, 84 (1979): 668–687.

Calasso, Francesco. *Medioevo del diritto*. Vol. 1, *Le fonti*. Milan: Giuffrè, 1954.

Calleri, Santi. *L'arte dei giudici e notai di Firenze nell'età comunale e nel suo statuto del 1344*. Milan: Giuffrè, 1966.

Cammarosano, Paolo. "Aspetti delle strutture familiari nelle città dell'Italia comunale (secoli xii–xiv)." *Studi medievali*, 3d ser., 16 (1975):417–435.

Campbell, J. K. *Honour, Family, and Patronage*. Oxford: Clarendon Press, 1964.

Castiglionchio, Lapo da. *Epistola*. Edited by L. Mehus. Bologna, 1753.

Castro, Paolo di. *Commentaria in digesti novi partem secundam*. Lyons, 1553.

————. *Consilia*. Venice, 1580–1581.

————. *In primam digesti partem commentaria*. Lyons, 1548.

————. *In primam infortiati partem commentaria*. Lyons, 1548.

————. *In secundam codicis partem commentaria*. Lyons, 1548.

Cavalca, Desiderio. *Il bando nella prassi e nella dottrina giuridica medievale*. Milan: Giuffrè, 1978.

Cavalcanti, Giovanni. *The "Trattato Politico-Morale" of Giovanni Cavalcanti (1381– ca. 1451)*. Edited by Marcella T. Grendler. Geneva: Droz, 1973.

Certaldo, Paolo da. *Il libro di buoni costumi*. Edited by S. Morpurgo. Florence: Le Monnier, 1921.

Chapman, Charlotte Gower. *Milocca: A Sicilian Village*. Cambridge, Mass.: Schenkman, 1970.

Cherubini, Giovanni. *Signori, contadini, borghesi: Ricerche sulla società italiana del basso medioevo.* Florence: La Nuova Italia, 1974.

Cino da Pistoia. *In codicem et aliquot titulos primi pandectorum commentaria.* 2 vols. Frankfurt, 1578. Facsimile. Turin: Bottega d'Erasmo, 1964.

Cohn, Samuel Kline, Jr. *The Laboring Classes in Renaissance Florence.* New York: Academic Press, 1980.

Collier, Jane Fishburne. *Law and Social Change in Zinacantan.* Stanford: Stanford University Press, 1973.

Cooper, J. P. "Patterns of Inheritance and Settlement by Great Landowners from the Fifteenth to the Eighteenth Centuries." In *Family and Inheritance: Rural Society in Western Europe, 1200–1800,* pp. 192–327. Edited by Jack Goody, Joan Thirsk, and E. P. Thompson. Cambridge: Cambridge University Press, 1976.

Corpus iuris civilis cum glossis (Glossa ordinaria). 5 vols. Venice, 1598.

Cortese, Ennio. *La norma giuridica.* 2 vols. Milan: Giuffrè, 1962.

—————. "Per la storia del mundio in Italia." *Rivista italiana per le scienze giuridiche,* 3d ser., 8 (1955–1956): 323–474.

Corti, Gino, ed. "Consigli sulla mercatura d'un anonimo trecentista." *Archivio storico italiano,* 110 (1952): 114–119.

Cronin, Constance. *The Sting of Change: Sicilians in Sicily and Australia.* Chicago: University of Chicago Press, 1970.

Cunh, Guillaume de. *Lectura super codice.* N.d. Facsimile. Turin: Bottega d'Erasmo, 1969.

Dati, Goro di Stagio. *Il libro segreto.* Edited by Carlo Gargiolli. Bologna: Romagnoli, 1905.

Davidsohn, Robert. *Storia di Firenze.* Vol. 4, *I primordi della civiltà fiorentina.* Part 3, *Il mondo della chiesa, spiritualità e arte, vita pubblica e privata.* Translated from German by Eugenio Dupre-Theseider. Florence: Sansoni, 1973.

Davis, J. *Land and Family in Pisticci.* London: University of London, Athlone Press, 1973.

—————. *People of the Mediterranean: An Essay in Comparative Social Anthropology.* London: Routledge & Kegan Paul, 1977.

Decio, Filippo. *Consilia.* Venice, 1581.

—————. *In tit. ff. de regulis iuris.* Lyons, 1588.

Dino del Mugello. *Consilia.* Lyons, 1551.

Donahue, Charles, Jr. "The Case of the Man Who Fell into the Tiber: The Roman Law of Marriage at the Time of the Glossators." *American Journal of Legal History,* 22 (1978): 1–53.

Du Boulay, Juliet. *Portrait of a Greek Mountain Village.* Oxford: Clarendon Press, 1974.

Durantis, Gulielmus. *Speculum iuris.* Venice, 1566.

Falsini, Aliberto Benigno. "Firenze dopo il 1348: Le conseguenze della peste nera." *Archivio storico italiano,* 129 (1971): 425–503.

Fasoli, Gina. "La vita quotidiana nel medioevo." In *Nuove questioni di storia medievale,* pp. 474–483. Milan: Marzorati, 1969.

Ficino, Marsilio. *Supplementum ficinianum.* Edited by Paul Oskar Kristeller. Florence: Olschki, 1945.

Fiumi, Enrico. "Fioritura e decadenza dell'economia fiorentina." *Archivio storico italiano,* 115 (1957):385–439; 116 (1958):443–510; 117 (1959):427–502.

———. *Storia economica e sociale di San Gimignano.* Florence: Olschki, 1961.

Freemantle, Richard. "Some New Masolino Documents." *The Burlington Magazine,* 117 (1975):658–659.

Friedl, Ernestine. *Vasilika: A Village in Modern Greece.* New York: Holt, Rinehart, & Winston, 1962.

Fuller, Lon L. *Legal Fictions.* Stanford: Stanford University Press, 1967.

Gandinus, Albertus. *Quaestiones statutorum.* Edited by A. Solmi. In *Biblioteca iuridica medii aevi,* vol. 3. Bologna, 1901.

Goldthwaite, Richard A. "The Florentine Palace as Domestic Architecture." *American Historical Review,* 77 (1972):977–1012.

———. *Private Wealth in Renaissance Florence.* Princeton: Princeton University Press, 1968.

Guicciardini, Francesco. *Ricordi.* Edited by Raffaele Spongano. Florence: Sansoni, 1951.

Herlihy, David. "Deaths, Marriages, Births, and the Tuscan Economy (ca. 1300–1550)." In *Population Patterns in the Past.* Edited by Ronald Demos Lee. New York: Academic Press, 1977.

———. "Family and Property in Renaissance Florence." In *The Medieval City.* Edited by Harry A. Miskimin, David Herlihy, and A. L. Udovitch. New Haven: Yale University Press, 1977.

———. *The Family in Renaissance Italy.* St. Charles, Mo.: Forum Press, 1974.

———. "Family Solidarity in Medieval Italian History." *Explorations in Economic History,* 7 (1969–1970):173–184.

———. "The Generation in Medieval History." *Viator,* 5 (1974):347–364.

———. "Mapping Households in Medieval Italy." *Catholic Historical Review,* 58 (1972):1–24.

———. "Some Psychological and Social Roots of Violence in the Tuscan Cities." In *Violence and Civil Disorder in Italian Cities, 1200–1500.* Edited by Lauro Martines. Berkeley and Los Angeles: University of California Press, 1972.

———. "Vieillir à Florence au Quattrocento." *Annales,* 24 (1969):1338–1352.

Herlihy, David, and Klapisch, Christiane. *Les toscans et leurs familles.* Paris: Fondation Nationale des Sciences Politiques, 1978.

Horn, Norbert. *'Aequitas' in den Lehren des Baldus.* Cologne: Böhlau, 1968.

Hughes, Diane Owen. "Domestic Ideals and Social Behavior: Evidence from Medieval Genoa." In *The Family in History.* Edited by Charles E. Rosenberg. Philadelphia: University of Pennsylvania Press, 1975.

———. "Urban Growth and Family Structure in Medieval Genoa." *Past and Present,* 66 (February 1975):1–28.

Jolowicz, H. F. *Roman Foundations of Modern Law.* Oxford: Clarendon Press, 1957.

Jones, P. J. "Florentine Families and Florentine Diaries in the Fourteenth Century." *Papers of the British School at Rome,* 24 (1956):183–205.

Kaser, Max. *Das Römische Privatrecht*. 2 vols. Munich: C. H. Beck'sche, 1971.

Kent, Dale. "The Florentine *Reggimento* in the Fifteenth Century." *Renaissance Quarterly*, 28 (1975):575–638.

———. *The Rise of the Medici: Faction in Florence, 1426–1434*. Oxford: Oxford University Press, 1978.

Kent, Francis William. "A la Recherche du Clan Perdu: Jacques Heers and 'Family Clans' in the Middle Ages." *Journal of Family History*, 2 (1977): 77–86.

———. *Household and Lineage in Renaissance Florence: The Family Life of the Capponi, Ginori, and Rucellai*. Princeton: Princeton University Press, 1977.

———. " 'Più superba de quella de Lorenzo': Courtly and Family Interest in the Building of Filippo Strozzi's Palace." *Renaissance Quarterly*, 30 (1977): 311–323.

Kirshner, Julius. "*Ars imitatur naturam*: A Consilium of Baldus on Naturalization in Florence." *Viator*, 5 (1974):289–331.

———. "Paolo di Castro on *Cives ex Privilegio*: A Controversy over the Legal Qualifications for Public Office in Early Fifteenth-Century Florence." In *Renaissance Studies in Honor of Hans Baron*. Edited by Anthony Molho and John A. Tedeschi. Dekalb: Northern Illinois University Press, 1971.

———. *Pursuing Honor While Avoiding Sin: The 'Monte delle doti' of Florence*. Milan: Giuffrè, 1978.

———. "Some Problems in the Interpretation of Legal Texts *re* the Italian City-States." *Archiv für Begriffsgeschichte*, 19 (1975):16–27.

Kirshner, Julius, and Molho, Anthony. "The Dowry Fund and the Marriage Market in Early *Quattrocento* Florence." *Journal of Modern History*, 50 (1978):403–438.

Klapisch, Christiane. "L'enfance en Toscane au début du xve siècle." *Annales de démographie historique*, 9 (1973):99–122.

———. "Household and Family in Tuscany in 1427." In *Household and Family in Past Time*. Edited by Peter Laslett and Richard Wall. Cambridge: Cambridge University Press, 1972.

———. " 'Parenti, amici, e vicini': Il territorio urbano d'una famiglia mercantile nel xv secolo." *Quaderni storici*, 33 (1976):953–982.

Klapisch, Christiane, and Demonet, Michel. " 'A uno pane e uno vino': La famille rurale toscane au début de xve siècle." *Annales*, 27 (1972): 873–901.

Kuehn, Thomas. "Honor and Conflict in a Fifteenth-Century Florentine Family." *Ricerche storiche*, 10 (1980):287–310.

Leicht, Pier Silverio. *Il diritto privato preirneriano*. Bologna: Zanichelli, 1933.

———. *Storia del diritto italiano: Il diritto privato*. Vol. 1, *Diritto delle persone e di famiglia*. Milan, 1943. Reprint. Milan: Giuffrè, 1960. Vol. 3, *Le obbligazioni*. Milan: Giuffrè, 1948.

Il libro di ricordanze dei Corsini. Edited by Armando Petrucci. Rome: Istituto Storico Italiano per il Medio Evo, 1965.

Litchfield, R. Burr. "Demographic Characteristics of Florentine Patrician Families, Sixteenth to Nineteenth Centuries." *Journal of Economic History*, 29 (1969):191–205.

Lombardi, Luigi. *Saggio sul diritto giurisprudenziale*. Milan: Giuffrè, 1967.

Maino, Jason del. *Consilia*. Frankfurt, 1609.

Marongiu, Antonio. "Patria podestà ed emancipazione per scapigliatura in alcuni documenti medievali." In *Studi in memoria di Giovan Battista Funaioli*. Milan: Giuffrè, 1961.

Martines, Lauro. *Lawyers and Statecraft in Renaissance Florence*. Princeton: Princeton University Press, 1968.

———. *The Social World of the Florentine Humanists, 1390–1460*. Princeton: Princeton University Press, 1963.

Marzi, Demetrio. *La cancelleria della repubblica fiorentina*. Rocca San Casciano, Italy: 1910.

Masi, Bartolomeo. *Ricordanze di Bartolomeo Masi calderaio fiorentino, 1478–1526*. Edited by Giuseppe Odoardo Corazzini. Florence: Sansoni, 1906.

McArdle, Frank. *Altopascio: A Study in Tuscan Rural Society, 1587–1784*. Cambridge: Cambridge University Press, 1978.

Molho, Anthony. *Florentine Public Finances in the Early Renaissance, 1400–1433*. Cambridge, Mass.: Harvard University Press, 1971.

———. "Visions of the Florentine Family in the Renaissance." *Journal of Modern History*, 50 (1978):304–311.

Moore, Sally Falk. *Law As Process: An Anthropological Approach*. London: Routledge & Kegan Paul, 1978.

Morelli, Giovanni. *Ricordi*. Edited by Vittore Branca. Florence: Le Monnier, 1956.

Morrison, Alan, Kirshner, Julius, and Molho, Anthony. "Life-Cycle Events in Fifteenth-Century Florence: Records of the *Monte delle doti*." *American Journal of Epidemiology*, 106 (1977):487–492.

Mortari, Vincenzo Piano. "Il problema dell'*interpretatio iuris* nei commentatori." *Annali di storia del diritto*, 2 (1958):29–109.

Niccolini, Lapo di Giovanni. *Il libro degli affari proprii di casa di Lapo di Giovanni Niccolini de' Sirigatti*. Paris: SEVPEN, 1969.

Niccolini di Camugliano, Ginevra. *The Chronicles of a Florentine Family, 1200–1470*. London: Jonathan Cape, 1933.

Nicholas, Barry. *An Introduction to Roman Law*. Oxford: Clarendon Press, 1962.

Nicolai, Franco. *La formazione del diritto successorio negli statuti comunali del territorio lombardo-tosco*. Milan: Giuffrè, 1940.

Odofredus. *Lectura super codice*. 2 vols. 1552. Facsimile. Bologna: Forni Editore, 1969.

———. *Lectura super digesto novo*. 1552. Facsimile. Bologna: Forni Editore, 1969.

Oldradus da Ponte. *Consilia*. Venice, 1585.

Onory, Sergio Mochi. "*Manumittere et emancipare idem est*: Studio sulle origini e sulla struttura della 'persona' nell'età del rinascimento." In *Studi di storia e diritto in onore di Carlo Calisse*, 3:497–510. Milan: Giuffrè, 1939.

Otte, Gerhard. *Dialektik und Jurisprudenz: Untersuchungen zur Methode der Glossatoren*. Frankfurt: Klosterman, 1971.

Palmieri, Matteo. *Della vita civile*. Edited by Felice Battaglia. Bologna: Zanichelli, 1944.

Pandimiglio, Leonida. "Giovanni di Pagolo Morelli e le strutture familiari." *Archivio storico italiano*, 136 (1978):3–88.

Passaggieri, Rolandino. *Summa totius artis notariae*. Venice, 1574.

Pennington, Kenneth. "'Pro Peccatis Patrum Puniri': A Moral and Legal Problem of the Inquisition." *Church History*, 47 (1978):137–154.

Peristiany, J. G., ed. *Honour and Shame: The Values of Mediterranean Society*. Chicago: University of Chicago Press, 1966.

Pertile, Antonio. *Storia del diritto italiano dalla caduta dell'impero romano alla codificazione*. 2d ed., 4 vols. Turin: Unione Tipografico, 1894.

Pinto, Giuliano. "Firenze e la carestia del 1346–1347." *Archivio storico italiano*, 130 (1972):3–84.

Pitti, Buonaccorso. *Cronica*. Bologna: Romagnoli-Dall'Acqua, 1905.

Placentinus. *Summa codicis*. Mainz, 1536.

Renzo, Gigliola Villata di. *La tutela: Indagini sulla scuola dei glossatori*. Milan: Giuffrè, 1975.

Rogerius. *Summa codicis*. Edited by G. B. Palmieri. In *Biblioteca iuridica medii aevi*, vol. 1. Bologna, 1914.

Romano, Andrea, ed. *Le sostituzioni ereditarie nell'inedita 'Repetitio de substitutionibus' di Raniero Arsendi*. Catania, Italy: Giannotta, 1977.

Romano, Ruggiero. *Tra due crisi: L'Italia del rinascimento*. Turin: Einaudi, 1971.

Roncière, Charles M. de la. "Une famille florentine au xive siècle: Les Velluti." In *Famille et parenté dans l'Occident médiéval*. Edited by Georges Duby and Jacques Le Goff. Rome: École Française de Rome, 1977.

Roover, Raymond de. *The Rise and Decline of the Medici Bank, 1397–1494*. Cambridge, Mass.: Harvard University Press, 1963.

Rosciate, Alberico da. *In primam ff. vet. partem commentaria*. Venice, 1585. Facsimile. Bologna: Forni Editore, 1974.

Rossi, Guido. *Consilium sapientis iudiciale*. Milan: Giuffrè, 1958.

Rucellai, Giovanni. *Zibaldone quaresimale*. Edited by Alessandro Perosa. London: Warburg Institute, 1960.

Sacchetti, Franco. *Le novelle*. 2 vols. Florence: Salani, 1925.

———. *Il trecentonovelle*. Edited by Vincenzio Pernicono. Florence: Sansoni, 1946.

Sahlins, Marshall. *Culture and Practical Reason*. Chicago: University of Chicago Press, 1976.

Salatiele. *Ars notarie*. Edited by Gianfranco Orlandelli. 2 vols. Milan: Giuffrè, 1961.

Saliceto, Bartolomeo da. *In secundam digesti veteris partem commentaria*. Venice, 1574.

———. *In vii, viii, et ix codicis libros commentaria*. Venice, 1574.

———. *In tertium et quartum codicis libros commentaria*. Venice, 1574.

Sapori, Armando. *Studi di storia economica (secoli xiii-xiv-xv)*. 3d ed., 3 vols. Florence: Sansoni, 1955.

Sbriccoli, Mario. *L'interpretazione dello statuto: Contributo allo studio della funzione dei giuristi nell'età comunale*. Milan: Giuffrè, 1969.

———. "Politique et interprétation juridique dans les villes italiennes du Moyen Age." *Archives de philosophie du droit*, 17 (1972):99–113.

Schneider, Jane. "Of Vigilance and Virgins: Honor, Shame, and Access to Resources in Mediterranean Societies." *Ethnology*, 10 (1971):1–24.

Schneider, Jane, and Schneider, Peter. *Culture and Political Economy in Western Sicily.* New York: Academic Press, 1976.

Schneider, Peter. "Honor and Conflict in a Sicilian Town." *Anthropological Quarterly*, 42 (1969):130–154.

Sercambi, Giovanni. *Novelle.* Edited by Giovanni Sinicropi. 2 vols. Bari, Italy: Laterza, 1972.

Silverman, Sydel. *Three Bells of Civilization: The Life of an Italian Hill Town.* New York: Columbia University Press, 1975.

Sozzini, Bartolomeo. *Commentaria ad digestum vetus.* Venice, 1579.

Statuta populi et communis Florentiae, anno salutis mcccxv. 3 vols. Freiburg [Florence], 1778–1783.

Statuti della repubblica fiorentina. Edited by Romolo Caggese. Vol. 1, *Statuto del capitano del popolo degli anni 1322–25.* Florence: Galileiana, 1910. Vol. 2, *Statuto del podestà dell'anno 1325.* Florence: E. Ariani, 1921.

Summa institutionum vindobinensis. Edited by G. B. Palmieri. In *Biblioteca iuridica medii aevi*, vol. 3. Bologna, 1914.

Tamassia, Nino. *La famiglia italiana nei secoli decimoquinto e decimosesto.* Milan: Sandron, 1910.

Tartagni, Alessandro. *Consilia.* Venice, 1570.

———. *In primam et secundam codicis partem commentaria.* Venice, 1586.

———. *Super primam infortiati partem commentaria.* Venice, 1570.

Torelli, Pietro. *Lezioni di storia del diritto italiano: Diritto privato: La famiglia.* Milan: Giuffrè, 1947.

Trexler, Richard. "In Search of Father: The Experience of Abandonment in the Recollections of Giovanni di Pagolo Morelli." *History of Childhood Quarterly*, 4 (1976):225–252.

———. "Ritual in Florence: Adolescence and Salvation in the Renaissance." In *The Pursuit of Holiness in Late Medieval and Renaissance Religion.* Edited by Charles Trinkaus and Heiko A. Oberman. Leiden, Netherlands: Brill, 1974.

Ubaldis, Angelus de. *Consilia.* 1539.

———. *Super codice.* N.d.

Ubaldis, Baldus de. *Consilia.* Venice, 1575. Facsimile. Turin: Bottega d'Erasmo, 1970.

———. *In primam digesti veteris partem commentaria.* Venice, 1577.

———. *In primam et secundam infortiati partem commentaria.* Venice, 1577.

———. *In primum, secundum, et tertium codicis libros commentaria.* Venice, 1577.

———. *In quartum et quintum codicis libros commentaria.* Venice, 1577.

———. *In quatuor institutionum libros.* Venice, 1615.

———. *In vii, viii, ix, x, et xi codicis libros commentaria.* Venice, 1577.

———. *In sextum codicis librum commentaria.* Venice, 1577.

———. *Super institutionibus commentum.* 1507.

Ullmann, Walter. "Baldus's Conception of Law." *Law Quarterly Review*, 58 (1942):386–399.

Vidari, Gian Savino Pene. *Ricerche sul diritto agli alimenti: L'obbligo 'ex lege' dei familiari nel periodo della Glossa e del commento.* Turin: Giappichelli, 1970.

Violante, Cinzio. "Quelques caractéristiques des structures familiales en Lombardie, Émilie, et Toscane aux xiᵉ et xiiᵉ siècles." In *Famille et parenté dans l'Occident médiéval.* Edited by Georges Duby and Jacques Le Goff. Rome: École Française de Rome, 1977.

Vismara, Giulio. *Famiglia e successioni nella storia del diritto.* Rome: Editrice Studium, 1970.

———. "I patti successori nella dottrina di Paolo di Castro." *Studia et documenta historiae et iuris*, 36 (1970):265–303.

Index